# IBM® AS/400®
## A BUSINESS PERSPECTIVE

*FOURTH EDITION*

# Related titles of interest from Wiley . . .

*IBM Personal Systems: A Business Perspective,* Sixth Edition (G325-0400), Hoskins
*IBM RISC System/6000: A Business Perspective,* Third Edition (GA23-2674), Hoskins
*IBM ES/9000: A Business Perspective* (GB35-4289), Hoskins
*Managing Software Development Projects: Formula for Success,* Whitten

# IBM® AS/400®
## A BUSINESS PERSPECTIVE

### FOURTH EDITION

## JIM HOSKINS

**JOHN WILEY & SONS, INC.**
*New York • Chichester • Brisbane • Toronto • Singapore*

**Library of Congress Cataloging-in-Publication Data**

Hoskins, Jim.
    IBM AS/400 : a business perspective / Jim Hoskins. — 4th ed.
      p.  cm.
    Includes index.
    ISBN 0-471-58063-5 (alk. paper)
    1.IBM AS/400 (Computer)  2.Business — Data processing.
    I.Title
  QA76.8.I25919H671993
  004.1'45 — dc20                                92-32803
                                                       CIP

Printed in the United States of America

93 94 10 9 8 7 6 5 4 3 2 1

*To my loving wife Monica,*
*who gave me a son, Nikolas,*
*and to my parents, for everything*

## TRADEMARKS

## ACKNOWLEDGMENTS

Many "IBMers" assisted me in preparing the fourth edition of the book despite their demanding schedules. Some provided me with information concerning their products. Others read the manuscript and provided helpful comments. To all those who assisted, I thank you. I would like to give special thanks to JoAnn Miller for once again helping to coordinate this edition, and to Susan Whitney for her all-important support.

I would also like to thank Daniel P. Anderson, Mike Anderson, Jim Bainbridge, Terry J. Bird, Kent Bruinsma, Bill Burmesch, Al Calvano, Nat Calvert, Earl Emerick, Kathy Evans, Steve Finnes, Joseph Friedrich, Linc Harker, Jessie Kempter, Les

Knutson, Deb Landon, Steve Lund, Linda Miller, Jake Muldrow, Ron Peterson, Rick Rud, Tim Schuetz, Marshall Sheppard, Debbie Strand, Bob Swift, and Hank Van Wier for their assistance.

Finally, hats off to the entire AS/400 development team and management.

## READER COMMENTS

Any comments you would like to make are welcome and are important in guiding future revisions of this book. Send comments Attn: Katherine Schowalter, John Wiley & Sons, 605 Third Ave, New York, NY 10158. Alternately, you can send your comments directly to the author through IBM's PROFS electronic mail system at IBMMAIL(USBRCN7C), or through IBMLink's electronic mail system at HONE84(DEV3338). Finally, a Reader Feedback sheet is provided at the end of this book and can be used to fax or mail in your comments.

## DISCLAIMER

This book is not intended to replace IBM product documentation or personnel in determining the specifications and capabilities of the included products. IBM product documentation should always be consulted, as the specifications and capabilities of products are subject to frequent modification. The reader is solely responsible for the choice of all configurations and applications of computer hardware and software. All configurations and applications of computer hardware and software should be reviewed with proper IBM representatives prior to making any commitments or using the configuration. While the author of this book has made reasonable efforts to ensure the accuracy and timeliness of the information contained herein, the author assumes no liability with respect to loss or damage caused or alleged to be caused by reliance on any information contained herein and disclaims any and all warranties, express or implied, as to the accuracy of said information. This book is not sponsored in any part or in any manner by IBM. IBM does not endorse or represent the accuracy or appropriateness of any information contained herein.

*Note:* Appendix B has been reprinted with permission from the *Application System/400 Publications Guide* © 1991, International Business Machines Corporation.

# Foreword

The IBM AS/400 may be the most successful product of any kind introduced in the past 10 years.During the four years it has been on the market IBM has sold almost 200,000 systems. It has generated over $25 billion in revenue to IBM and another 10 billion in other revenue was the indirect result of AS/400 sales.

The AS/400 has become IBM's first real "cult" computer. Buyers and users of the AS/400 seem to form a strong emotional attachment to their computers. Customer satisfaction among AS/400 owners is very high.

The AS/400 has been a great success largely because it has created a whole new category of computer. Even though IBM calls it a "midrange" system, size or capacity is not it most important characteristic. The AS/400 combines tightly integrated system software, exceptional ease of use, a very large application portfolio, with hardware that can be field upgraded to newer more cost effective models each year. No other computer offers this particular combination of characteristics. As a result the AS/400 has come to dominate an important segment of the computer market.

Typial AS/400 buyers need a general purpose computer to solve commercial or business problems. AS/400 systems are used to schedule factories, manage hospitals, prepare payrolls, and make reservations for cruise ships. They are most effective handling interactive applications that can take advantage of the AS/400's built in database.

The AS/400 offers sophisticated features matched only by very expensive mainframe computers without the associated need for an army of technical support personnel. As a result AS/400 computers are growing rapidly in popularity as an alternative for mainframe processing.

AS/400 computers are very different from anything else on the market. They come with their own vocabulary and a new set of concepts which can be very confusing to newcomers to the AS/400 world. We at ADM Consulting are thus very pleased that Jim Hoskins has created *IBM AS/400: A Business Perspective*. This book fills the need for a readable and complete introduction to the world of the AS/400. It is also a handy reference guide for working AS/400 professionals. The new fourth edition brings this important book up to date with all the latest improvements to the AS/400.

It is appropriate for IS executives, consultants, industry watchers, and computer professionals to understand the unique nature of the AS/400. This book offers a great way to get started.

*David Andrews*
President
ADM Consulting, Inc.

# Contents

# IBM® AS/400®
## A BUSINESS PERSPECTIVE

### FOURTH EDITION

# Introduction

## WHAT THIS BOOK IS

This book is dedicated to IBM's mid-size business computers, namely, the **Application System/400®** (**AS/400**) family and the **AS/Entry 5363**. Together, these computers make up IBM's strategic direction in mid-sized business computing. For convenience, the AS/400 family and the AS/Entry 5363 are collectively referred to as IBM's **Application Systems**. First, the Application Systems are introduced. The features of these new computers are compared with those of the earlier System/36 and System/38 family in a way understandable to the business user.

Second, you are guided through a "hands-on" session with an AS/400 computer and the programs that come with each system. To help you with software buying decisions, the different types of software necessary to do "real work" are also described.

Finally, we discuss ways to apply Application Systems to improve business operations. Proper selection and usage of Application Systems products is impossible unless you understand how you can use these components to fill business needs. Specific Application Systems hardware and software configurations for typical environments are offered. Many important computer automation planning issues are also discussed.

## WHAT THIS BOOK IS NOT

Many computer books try to be all things to all people, covering everything from checkbook balancing to the Space Shuttle's redundant flight computer complex. This book is not a general overview of computers. It is specific to IBM's Application Systems (a broad enough subject for any single book). This book is neither a technical reference manual (IBM will sell you that) nor a guide to computer programming. It does, however, provide a good understanding of IBM's Application Systems and how to use them in the business environment.

Finally, this book does not expect you to be an engineer. Business people are typically short on time and patience as far as technical matters are concerned. Although some technical discussions are necessary, I have tried to keep these as simple and concise as possible while still conveying necessary and useful information.

## HOW TO USE THIS BOOK

Chapter 1 introduces the entire AS/400 family and the AS/Entry 5363. The latter part of the chapter examines the elements (built-in database, multi-processor architecture, etc.) that make up AS/400 computers. These elements of the AS/400 family are contrasted to those of the System/3X computers.

Chapter 2 surveys the many hardware options available for Application Systems, including terminals, printers, disk expansion, and communications. It is provided primarily as a reference to help you identify and select the proper options for your Application System.

Chapter 3 guides you through a "hands-on" session with an AS/400 computer system. You learn how to sign on and use the on-line education provided with every AS/400 computer. The latter part of the chapter describes the role of the three types of programs necessary to do productive work with AS/400 computers: application programs, operating systems, and Licensed Internal Code.

Chapter 4 continues the discussion of application programs. Some Application Systems application programs useful to most businesses are discussed. Further, industry-specific application programs are introduced with an example. Finally, the question of "prewritten" vs. "custom" application programs is addressed.

Chapter 5 continues the discussion on operating systems. First, basic operating system concepts such as "multi-user" and "interactive processing" are defined in terms of their usefulness in the business environment. Then the Application System's operating system products are described.

Chapter 6 shows how specific AS/400 options and software products are used to participate in the computer communications environments commonly found in businesses.

Chapter 7 discusses issues related to the selection of Application Systems hardware and software for small, medium, and large businesses. Hypothetical businesses are outfitted with the appropriate Application Systems. Important topics such as user training, ergonomics, security, maintenance, leasing versus buying, and cost justification are then discussed.

Appendix A lists older peripheral equipment supported (and not supported) by AS/400 systems.

Appendix B is a guide to other AS/400 publications.

Appendix C is a listing of some AS/400 educational offerings.

To help you better understand the topics covered in this book, key terms and phrases are defined and **highlighted.** These key terms are also listed in the index at the back of this book. If while reading you forget the definition of a key term or phrase, the index will quickly provide the page(s) on which the term was originally discussed.

## A GLANCE BACKWARD AT THE SYSTEM/3X FAMILY

On July 30, 1969, IBM executives from the entire company joined 1200 IBMers at their plant site in Rochester, Minnesota, to announce the System/3 computer shown in Figure I.1. This system was the first computer totally developed in Rochester. Although only of historical interest today, the System/3 represented some significant advances in the technology of its time. For example, it introduced Monolithic Systems Technology, which allowed engineers to package more circuitry in a smaller space, as well as a punch card one third of normal size that held 20 percent more

**Figure I.1.** IBM System/3.

information. This was the first advancement in punch-card technology in over 40 years. To celebrate the announcement of the System/3, Rochester IBMers held a dance featuring Ralph Marterie and his orchestra in a newly constructed building. The Rochester plant, which became a full IBM Division in November of that year, was tasked at developing a "low-end" computer family. One System/3, fondly named "Old Reliable," ran faithfully until it was shut down in September 1973. When it was finally retired, its meter showed that it had run for 15,377.97 hours, representing more run time than any other system in existence.

The System/32, shown in Figure I.2, was the next member of the family. It was announced in January 1975 and featured direct keyboard data entry and a display that could present up to 6 rows of text 40 characters long. The System/32 had up to 32K of memory and up to 13 MB of fixed disk storage.

The System/34 computer, announced in April 1977, was the first system truly designed to manage multiple (local and remote) workstations (i.e., terminals and printers), each being up to 5000 feet away from the computer. This allowed it to perform tasks for up to eight local users simultaneously. The System/34, shown in Figure I.3, provided up to 256K of memory and 13 MB of fixed disk.

Next came the System/38, announced in October 1978. This represented a divergence from its S/3X predecessors, offering a new architecture optimized for application development productivity. The System/38, shown in Figure I.4, could support up to 32 MB of memory, 14 GB of disk storage, and 256 local workstations.

Once again, building on the architectural base of the System/34, the first Sys-

**Figure I.2.** IBM System/32.

**Figure I.3.** IEM System/34.

**Figure I.4** IBM System/38.

**Figure I.5.** IBM System/36 Model 5360.

tem/36 was announced in May 1983 (Figure I.5). It grew to support up to 7 MB of main memory, 1.4 GB of disk storage, and 72 local workstations. Other models of the System/36 varying in processing power and capacity were announced over time. Collectively the System/3, System/32, System/34, System/36, and System/38 are known as the **System/3X** family of computers.

The last S/36 model (the 5363) was enhanced and renamed the **IBM AS/Entry** system. IBM has announced its intentions to provide future enhancements to the AS/Entry products. This means that they are vital to IBM's mid-range product strategy, as we will see later in the book.

On June 20, 1988, IBM unveiled the AS/400 family of products. The AS/400 has close architectural ties with System/38, while in most cases providing application program compatibility with both the System/36 and the System/38. Since the original announcement of the AS/400 family, IBM has regularly announced new AS/400 hardware and software products — a trend that shows no sign of slowing.

# 1

# IBM AS/400— A New Beginning

This chapter provides an overview of the IBM AS/400 family of computers, covering the highlights of these new systems and then moving in for a closer look at the details. The characteristics of the AS/400 computers are compared with those of the IBM System/3X family.

## MEET THE FAMILY

The IBM Application System/400 (AS/400) family of products represents IBM's next generation of mid-size business computing systems. As with their predecessors, the System/3X family, they are **multi-user** computer systems, meaning a single computer can interact with more than one user at a time. In developing the AS/400 systems, designers drew from the ease-of-use features of the System/36 and combined these with the advanced architecture and productivity of the System/38 and new functions. Many application programs developed for the System/36 and System/38 computers can be migrated to and used on AS/400 systems by applying the migration tools available.

Many users have no conception of what equipment makes up the computer system they use daily. Fortunately, it is not necessary for them to, just as it is not necessary to understand the inner workings of a carburetor to drive a car. However, it is helpful to have a fundamental view of what general elements make up an AS/400. Figure 1.1 shows the components of a very simple AS/400 system configuration. The heart of the system is the System Unit, which contains the "brain" that runs the computer programs and controls all activities. People interact with the computer system through terminals (or PS/2s acting as terminals) that display computer informa-

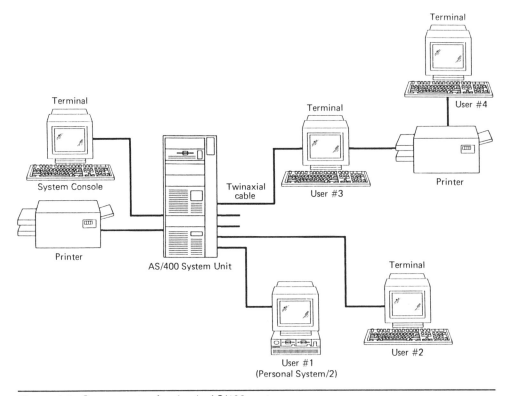

**Figure 1.1.** Components of a simple AS/400 system.

tion and allow for keyboard entry. The terminal shown on the left side of the figure is the **System Console**. The System Console is a specially designated terminal used by the system operator to manage the day-to-day operations of the computer system. The other terminals are for general-purpose use. The printers shown in the figure are used to generate reports, documents, graphs, and the like. A printer can be a work-station used to fill the needs of specific user(s) or it can be shared by all users. Both terminals and printers are attached to the System Unit via twinaxial cable typically laid in the building's walls or ceiling.

Three basic computers form the core of the IBM AS/400 family: the 9402, 9404, and 9406 systems. Let us briefly look at each of these. The three 9402 models (F02, F04, and F06) are currently the smallest AS/400 systems in the family (see Figure 1.2). They replace the less powerful AS/400 9402 Models E02, E04, and E06 offered earlier in the evolution of the AS/400 family; however, "E" Models can be upgraded to "F" models. Like their predecessors, the Models F02, F04, and F06 are packaged into a small deskside unit, which is then cabled to the necessary AS/400

**Figure 1.2.** The IBM AS/400 9402 (shown near the back of the office beside a desk) is the smallest AS/400 system in the family.

workstations and printers. These models use the same OS/400 operating system as the rest of the AS/400 family. This means that application programs and data on a 9402 system can be used unchanged on larger AS/400 systems as a business grows.

In addition to the three 9402 models just discussed (F02, F04, and F06), there is a fourth 9402 model (Y10) that is a little different from the others. It is called the Application System/Entry 9402 Model Y10. The 9402 Model Y10 is an entry-level system based on the same architecture as the IBM System/36 family that preceded the AS/400 family. In fact, the 9402 Model Y10 replaced the System/36 Model 5363 (later called the AS/Entry 5363). Because the 9402 Model Y10 is based on the System/36 architecture and operating system (SSP), it can run programs and use data originally designed for the popular System/36 family. While the 9402 Model Y10 does not have the same operating system or architecture as the AS/400 family members, it is usually straightforward to migrate AS/Entry (or System/36 family) programs and data to the AS/400 family. Further, by replacing elements in its chassis, the AS/Entry 9402 Y10 can be converted into an AS/400 9402 F model.

Figure 1.3 shows an IBM AS/400 9404 system in a typical office setting. The 9404 systems are packaged in a self-contained chassis slightly larger than that of the AS/400 9402. Like the 9402, the 9404 can utilize the normal 110-V electrical power found in every office, eliminating the need for specially installed high-voltage outlets.

When the original AS/400 family was introduced, the 9404 offerings consisted of the models B10 and B20. These 9404 models were later replaced by "C" models, which were later replaced by "D" and then "E" models. The current 9404 Models are the more powerful F10, F20, and F25.

The AS/400 Model 9406 systems make up the larger end of the AS/400 family, as is shown in Figure 1.4. The 9406 systems include the most powerful AS/400 computers, thereby providing for higher performance, more users, more communica-

**Figure 1.3.** IBM AS/400 9404 computer system in an office setting.

**Figure 1.4.**  IBM AS/400 9406 computer system in a typical business environment.

tions, more storage, and greater expendability than either 9402 or 9404 systems. Originally, there were four 9406 AS/400 systems: Models B30, B40, B50, and B60. Now, all 9406 systems have been replaced with eight 9406 "F" models, each offering increased performance and capacity over the last. All 9406 computers are mounted in one or more industry-standard racks. This rack-mounted approach provides for modular growth and configuration flexibility while minimizing space requirements.

For clarity, we will refer to all AS/400 and AS/Entry systems as **Application Systems**. When we discuss a specific product, the specific name will be used.


## How AS/400 Computers Differ from System/3X

What characteristics make IBM AS/400 computers different from the System/3X family of computers? The answer lies in the areas of compatibility, performance, expansion capability, and usability.

The AS/400 computers offer more **compatibility** across the product line than did the S/3X computers. One operating system and architecture is used consistently across the entire AS/400 family. This means that programs and data can be freely exchanged among any AS/400 systems and used without any changes. This was not possible in the S/3X family, in which different architectures and operating systems prevented the S/36 from running S/38 programs without change (and vice versa). Further, the AS/400 operating system was the first "mid-size computer" operating system to participate in IBM's **Systems Application Architecture (SAA)**, which promises to allow programs to be exchanged among PS/2s, AS/400s, and System/390.

AS/400 computers can also run programs written for the S/3X family. Many of those written for the System/38 will need little or no change, and many of those written for the System/36 can be migrated to AS/400 systems using available tools. This means that S/3X users can move their custom-written S/3X application programs to AS/400 computers. Also, many of the System/3X software companies have migrated their application program offerings to the AS/400 systems, allowing users to choose from a vast array of software to solve business problems. Chapter 3 looks more closely at AS/400 compatibility.

The **performance** of a computer is the speed at which it can work. The higher the performance the better. For example, the largest AS/400 computers offer performance many times that of the largest System/38. The performance advantage of the AS/400 family is afforded primarily by a combination of faster processors, more efficient architectures, more storage, and improved disk units. We look more closely at performance later in the chapter.

The AS/400 computers offer more **expansion capability** to support growing needs. First, since the AS/400 computers are fully compatible from the smallest system to the largest, users can grow without the disruption of conversion that used to accompany moving from a System/36 to the larger System/38 family. With the AS/400 family, there is a much wider range of growth between the largest and smallest systems. The rack-mounted approach used in the larger AS/400 systems better lends itself to configuration flexibility and modular expansion than did the "box" approach of the System/38. The largest AS/400 systems can span several of these racks and accommodate up to 165.2 GB (billion bytes) of disk storage in a single system, compared with the 14-GB maximum of the largest System/38. Further, the AS/400 system can support up to 64 communications lines, surpassing the maximum of 12 lines with the System/38.

Each AS/400 computer also offers expansion slots that can accept various controllers and adapters to add function and performance. For example, main storage can be expanded from 128 MB to 512 MB in the largest AS/400 computer through the addition of storage expansion adapters. This is 16 times the storage of the largest System/38. As necessary, additional expansion slots can be added to the 9406 systems by installing additional I/O card units in an AS/400 rack. Chapter 2 describes many optional controllers and adapters that can be installed to add capability to AS/400 computers.

Although AS/400 computers offer more advanced capabilities, they are also *easier to use* than comparable S/3X systems. The operating system required for normal operation comes preloaded on all systems, eliminating the tedious installation process. The user interface of this operating system conforms to IBM's Systems Application Architecture, providing on-line help and consistency with other SAA environments (e.g., Operating System/2 on the Personal System/2). Those used to System/3X computers will also see many similarities when interacting with the operating system for AS/400 computers. Also, most of the familiar S/3X devices (terminals, printers, etc.) can be used with the new family of computers. The electronic customer support offered for all AS/400 systems is another way to get help when you have a question. Every AS/400 system also comes with computer-based education programs that teach new users about many aspects of the new AS/400 computers. Some authoring tools are also available on AS/400 computers that allow you to design your own courses to meet specialized training needs. Chapter 3 guides you, step by step, through some of the training programs provided with AS/400 systems.

## 9402 System Specifics

The 9402 systems are the smallest of all Application Systems and are housed in a box designed to sit beside a desk. To allow the built-in fan to cool internal components, air vents are provided on the front and sides. The control panel on the front of the System Unit is used by the system operator and service personnel to control the 9402 system. From this panel, power can be turned on or off, the system can be initialized, and system problems can be analyzed. Many of these functions, including turning on the system power, can also be performed remotely through communications lines. The key-lock on the control panel can be used to secure the system from unauthorized operation. The standard tape unit and optional diskette unit can also be seen. The 9402 can be plugged into a standard electrical outlet (90–140 VAC) or a high-voltage outlet (180–260 VAC) and meets "quiet office" guidelines (fewer than 5.5 dB) for operational noise. This along with its attractive appearance allows it to easily fit in an office environment by a desk or in a corner.

Three AS/400 models and one AS/Entry model use the 9402-style mechanical package. The three AS/400 9402 system models (F02, F04, and F06) come standard with 8 MB of main storage (see Figure 1.5). Also provided with these AS/400 systems is one 3.5-inch, 988-MB disk unit. The 8 MB of main storage can be expanded to 24 MB (Models F02 and F04) or 40 MB (Model F06) by installing the appropriate

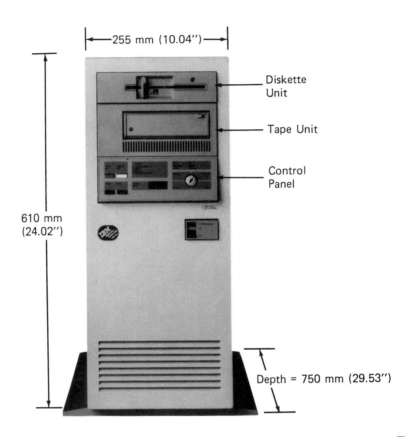

255 mm (10.04")

Diskette Unit

Tape Unit

Control Panel

610 mm (24.02")

Depth = 750 mm (29.53")

*Standard Equipment*

F02, F04, or F06 Processor
Main Storage
    F02 = 8 MB (24 MB max)
    F04 = 8 MB (24 MB max)
    F06 = 8 MB (40 MB max)
Fixed Disk—988 MB Disk Unit
    F02 = 988 MB (1976 MB max)
    F04 = 988 MB (3952 MB max)
    F06 = 988 MB (7904 MB max)
1.2 GB Tape Unit (with compression)
Multi-Function I/O Processor
Communications
    F02 = None
    F04 = (1) EIA 232/V.22 Adapter
    F06 = (1) EIA 232/V.22 Adapter
Key-lock security
System Control Panel
Battery powered clock/calendar
UPS Interface
Workstation Controller (Twinax or ASCII)

*Expansion*

8 or 16 MB Storage Expansion Options
Card Expansion: (1) I/O expansion slot
    F02 = 1 max
    F04 = not supported
    F06 = not supported
*Expansion Gate: (3) I/O expansion slots
    F02 = not supported
    F04 = 1 max
    F06 = 1 max
1.2 MB Diskette Drive (5.25")
Battery Power Unit
Communications lines:
    F02 = 8 max
    F04 = 8 max
    F06 = 14 max
Maximum Twinax Workstation Controllers
    F02 = 2 (28 workstations)
    F04 = 2 (68 workstations)
    F06 = 3 (108 workstations)
Maximum ASCII Workstation Controllers
    F02 = 2 (18 workstations)
    F04 = 4 (66 workstations)
    F06 = 6 (102 workstations)

*See chapter 2 for features that can be installed in these slots.

**Figure 1.5.** IBM AS/400 9402 System Unit.

main storage options. Since the main storage expansion options used on these models attach directly to the processor card, no expansion slots are consumed. The disk units exploit **thin-film** technology, which allows for high-density recording. Additional 988-MB disk units can be added, to achieve the System Unit maximum 1976-MB (Model F02) and 3952-MB (Models F04 and F06) configurations. The standard 1.2 GB 1/4-Inch Cartridge Tape Unit can be used to load programs, to exchange data between systems, or as a disk backup device. The Model F06 can be further expanded to accommodate up to 7904 MB of disk storage by adding the optional expansion unit (#7115).

Also provided with all three AS/400 9402 models is a multi-function input/output (I/O) processor. This is a small microprocessor-based computer packaged on a card that manages the disk units, 1/4-inch tape unit, workstation traffic, and up to two communications lines. By delegating these tasks to the multi-function I/O processor, the System Processor is freed up to more effectively run users' programs. To make a complete communications line, a communications adapter is also needed to work in conjunction with the multi-function I/O processor. One communications adapter (EIA 232/V.24) is provided as standard equipment on Models F04 and F06. This communications line is intended for use with Electronic Customer Support (described in Chapter 7). The Model F02 does not come standard with a communications adapter, so it must be ordered separately if the F02 is to utilize Electronic Customer Support. The multi-function I/O processor provided with all 9402 systems can support up to three communications adapters (i.e., three independent communications lines). With the addition of multi-function I/O processors and communications adapters, a single AS/400 9402 can have up to 3 (Model F02), 8 (Model F04) or 14 (Model F06) communications lines of varying types.

The user must also choose either a Twinaxial Workstation Controller or an ASCII Workstation Controller to become part of the standard configuration. The Twinaxial Workstation Controller is used to attach terminals and printers (i.e., workstations) specially designed and optimized to work with AS/400 systems and earlier IBM S/3X computer systems. The ASCII Workstation Controller is used to attach terminals and printers designed to be used with many different computer systems (both IBM and non-IBM). The first Twinaxial Workstation Controller can support up to 14 (Model F02) or 34 (Models F04 and F06) workstations in any combination of printers and terminals. The first ASCII Workstation Controller can support up to 9 displays and 9 printers, but AS/400-based graphics is not supported on ASCII devices attached in this way. That is, application programs that use only alphanumeric characters should work well, but those that draw bar charts, pie charts, and so on, won't be able to draw these images on ASCII devices attached in this manner.

We saw earlier in the chapter that each AS/400 system must have a System Console (i.e., a specially designated terminal) used by the system operator to manage the day-to-day operations of the computer system. The System Console can be a standard terminal attached through a workstation controller. However, when the first workstation attachment feature (Models F04 and F06 only) is ordered, a System Console is built into the AS/400 System Unit. That is, the electronics that make up a simple terminal are built into the System Unit and a keyboard is provided. The user simply attaches a monitor (e.g., an 8504 monochrome display) and the System Console is ready to use. A printer port is also provided to allow for the attachment of a simple printer (e.g., IBM Personal Printer Series II) to support basic printing needs. This approach is designed to lower the overall cost of the system by providing a low-cost System Console.

In order to install additional multi-function I/O processors, or other optional adapters in 9402 systems, the optional Expansion Gate is needed. The Expansion Gate provides three expansion slots in the AS/400 9402 Model F04 and F06 systems. The Expansion Gate is not supported in Model F02 systems. However, one slot is provided in 9402 F02 systems when the Card Expansion option is installed.

The Main Storage of all 9402 systems can be expanded beyond that provided as standard by installing 8- or 16-MB Main Storage expansion options. The Main Storage expansion options used on 9402 "F" Models attach directly to the Processor Card so the Expansion Gate is not required and its slots are not consumed.

A Battery Power Unit is available as an option that keeps the computer system operating for at least five minutes in the event of a power failure. If power is not restored within five minutes, the system will perform an orderly shutdown, making the restart of the system easier. Alternately, an external **uninterruptible power supply (UPS)** can be attached to a 9402 system via the provided UPS interface.

You can upgrade a Model F02 to a Model F04 or a Model F04 to a Model F06 at any time. Although you can use all the same workstations, modems, and so on, you must replace the 9402 System Unit with a 9404 or 9406 System Unit to grow beyond the Model F06.

It is interesting to note that the standard 1.2 GB tape drive has replaced the standard diskette drives provided on System/3X computers. In fact, diskette drives are not provided as standard equipment on any AS/400 system, because programs written for the AS/400 are distributed via tape and not on diskettes as with System/3X. Tapes hold more information than diskettes, which makes them better program distribution vehicles. The standard tape drive is also better suited for disk storage backup than are diskettes.

The 9402 Model Y10 (shown in Figure 1.6) comes standard with 1 MB of main storage, 160 MB of disk storage, a 5.25-inch diskette drive, and a workstation controller. The 1 MB of main storage can be expanded to 2 MB, which is the system maximum. The 160 MB of disk storage is provided by a 5.25-inch disk unit. By adding additional 160-MB disk units or 200-MB disk units, the disk storage can be expanded up to a maximum of 760 MB. The 1.2-MB 5.25-inch Diskette Drive can

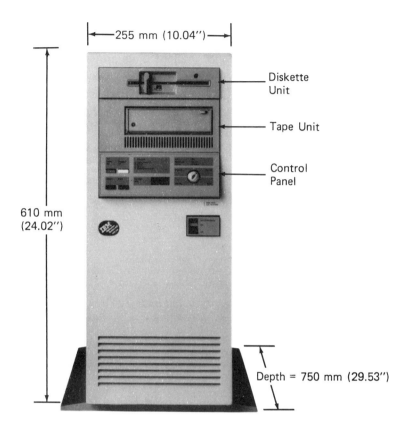

| Standard Equipment | Expansion |
|---|---|
| Y10 Processor | *(3) I/O expansion slots |
| 1 MB Main storage (2 MB max) | Processor Expansion |
| 160 MB fixed disk (760 MB max) | Main Storage Expansion |
| 1.2 MB Diskette Drive (5.25″) | 160 or 200 MB Disk Units |
| Key-lock security | 1.2 MB Diskette Drive (5.25″) |
| System Control Panel | 120 MB 1/4-inch Tape Unit |
| Battery powered clock/calendar | Workstation Expansion to 28 workstations |
| Twinax Workstation Controller | Battery Power Unit |
| (14) devices spread over 4 ports | Up to 3 communications lines |

*See Chapter 2 for features that can be installed in these slots.
To use these slots, system must be equipped with the Processor Expansion option.

**Figure 1.6.** IBM AS/Entry 9402 System Unit.

be used to load programs, exchange data between systems, and back up disk storage. Alternately, a 120-MB 1/4-Inch Cartridge Tape Unit can be installed and used for disk storage backup. Also, since the tape units provided as standard on AS/400 9402 "F" models can read and write these same tape cartridges, data can be exchanged between these systems and Y10 systems as necessary.

The Twinaxial Workstation Controller provided as standard can support up to 14 terminals and printers in any combination. The workstation expansion option allows up to 28 terminals and printers to attach to a single Y10 system. The three I/O slots along with the optional processor expansion allow the Y10 system to be expanded in the area of communications with adapters like the Expanded Communications Adapter and the 16/4 Mbps Token-Ring Adapter. You can upgrade a Model Y10 to a Model F04 or F06 at any time.

## 9404 System Specifics

The 9404 System Unit is shown in Figure 1.7. The boxlike mechanical packaging of this system resembles that of the smaller System/36 computers. Like all AS/400 systems, the 9404 relies on fans to force air through the mechanical frame to cool internal components. The control panel on the front of the System Unit is used by the system operator and service personnel to control the 9404 system. From this panel, power can be turned on or off, the system can be initialized, and system problems can be analyzed. As with the Model 9402, many of these functions can also be performed remotely through communications lines. The key-lock on the control panel can be used to secure the system from unauthorized operation. The standard tape unit and optional diskette unit can also be seen. The 9404 can be plugged into a standard electrical outlet (90–140 VAC) or a high-voltage outlet (180–260 VAC) and meets "quiet office" guidelines (fewer than 5.5 dB) for operational noise.

There are three current 9404 models: the F10, F20, and F25 — each more powerful than the last. These more powerful 9404 models replace the earlier 9404 "B," "C," "D," and "E" models. For this reason, we will only focus on the "F" models. The Model F10 comes standard with 8 MB of main storage and 988 MB of disk storage. The Models F20 and F25 come standard with 16 MB of main storage and 988 MB of disk storage. By installing the appropriate main storage expansion options, main storage can reach 72 MB, 80 MB, and 80 MB on the Models F10, F20, and F25 respectively. The 988 MB of standard disk storage is made up of one 3.5-inch disk unit. This is the same disk unit used in the AS/400 Model 9402 F02, F04, and F06 systems described earlier. The disk storage in all 9404 "F" models can be expanded beyond the 988 MB provided as standard. First, a second 988-MB disk unit can be added to the standard disk unit, resulting in a **dual disk unit** that offers

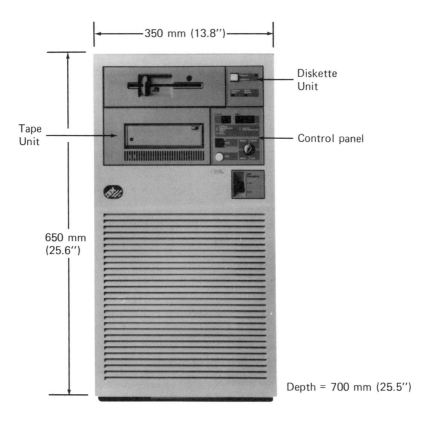

350 mm (13.8")

Diskette Unit

Tape Unit

Control panel

650 mm (25.6")

Depth = 700 mm (25.5")

*Standard Equipment*

F10, F20, or F25 Processor
Main Storage
   F10 = 8 MB (72 MB max)
   F20 = 16 MB (80 MB max)
   F25 = 16 MB (80 MB max)
Fixed disk
   F10 = 988 MB (11,856 MB max)
   F20 = 988 MB (11,856 MB max)
   F25 = 988 MB (15,808 MB max)
1.2 GB tape unit (with compression)
Multi-Function I/O Processor
EIA 232/V.22 Adapter
Battery Power Unit
Key-lock security
UPS Interface
System Control Panel
Battery powered clock/calendar
Workstation Controller
   Twinax (40 devices spread over 8 ports)
   ASCII (12 devices spread over 6 ports)

*Expansion*

(2) System busses
   (7) I/O expansion slots
   (2) I/O or Main Storage
      expansion slots
988 or 1,976 MB Disk Units
1.2 MB Diskette Drives
   (5.25" or 8")
1.2 GB tape unit
Communications lines:
   F10 = 14 max
   F20 = 20 max
   F25 = 26 max
Maximum Twinax Workstation
   Controllers:
   F10 = 4 (160 workstations)
   F20 = 6 (240 workstations)
   F25 = 6 (240 workstations)

Maximum ASCII Workstation Controllers:
   F10 = 9 (162 workstations)
   F20 = 9 (162 workstations)
   F25 = 9 (162 workstations)
Expansion Unit (1 max per system)
   *(5) additional I/O only slots
   Space for (3) more Disk Units
   Space for (1) more 1/4-inch Tape Unit
   Space for (1) more Diskette Drive
**Storage Expansion Unit (Model F25 only)
   Space for (2) additional Single or Dual
      Disk Units
   Space for (1) more Diskette Drive

*See Chapter 2 for features that can be installed in these slots.
**Only supported by 9404 Model F25 systems that include an Expansion Unit.

**Figure 1.7.** IBM AS/400 9404 System Unit.

1976 MB of disk storage. Next, two more disk units (either single 988-MB disk units or 1976-MB dual disk units) can be installed in the system unit, providing up to 5928 MB. Further expansion to 11,856 MB is possible on all models by adding the 9404 Expansion Unit (discussed in Chapter 2), which can house an additional three dual disk units. Finally, the Model F25 can be expanded still further to 3,952 MB by adding the Storage Expansion Unit (supported only on the F25), which can house two additional dual disk units. The standard 1.2 GB 1/4-Inch Cartridge Tape Unit can be used to load programs, exchange data between systems, or as a disk storage backup device. Circuitry is provided to compress data such that the capacity of a single tape cartridge can be as much as doubled.

Also provided with all AS/400 9404 models is a multi-function input/output (I/O) processor. This is a small microprocessor-based computer that manages the disk units, 1/4-inch tape unit, workstation traffic, and up to two communications lines. Delegating these tasks to the multi-function I/O processor frees the System Processor to spend its efforts running users' programs. To make a complete communications line, a communications adapter is also needed to work in conjunction with the multi-function I/O processor. One communications adapter (EIA 232/V.24) is provided and intended for use with Electronic Customer Support (described in Chapter 7). A second optional communications adapter can be supported by the multi-function I/O processor, providing a total of two communications lines. By adding additional multi-function I/O processors and communications adapters, a single AS/400 9404 can have more communications lines of varying types.

The user must also choose either a Twinaxial Workstation Controller or an ASCII Workstation Controller to become part of the standard configuration. The Twinaxial Workstation Controller is used to attach terminals and printers specially designed and optimized to work with AS/400 systems and earlier IBM S/3X computer systems. The ASCII Workstation Controller is used to attach terminals and printers designed to be used with many different computer systems (both IBM and non-IBM). The Twinaxial Workstation Controller can support up to 40 devices (printers or terminals in any combination). The ASCII Workstation Controller can support up to 6 displays and 6 printers, but AS/400-based graphics is not supported on ASCII devices attached in this way. That is, application programs that use only alphanumeric characters should work well, but those that draw bar charts, pie charts, and so on, won't be able to draw these images on ASCII devices attached in this manner.

All 9404 Model "F" System Units have two independent input/output (I/O) busses, providing a total of nine expansion slots. Having two independent busses is a performance advantage in that two information transfers can occur simultaneously, making for an improvement in overall system performance. Seven of these expansion slots are exclusively used to add I/O devices to the system (e.g., additional multi-function I/O controllers and removable media device attachments). The remaining two expansion slots can support I/O devices or main storage expansion options (e.g., the 8-MB Main Storage Expansion). The 9404 Expansion Unit is used to add more disk storage, tape units, and diskette units to a 9404 system while also adding five additional I/O expansion slots.

A Battery Power Unit is provided as standard equipment to help keep the computer system operating through short power outages. In the event of a long power outage, the system detects when the Battery Power Unit is getting low on energy and automatically performs an orderly system shutdown. This orderly shutdown significantly reduces the time it takes to restart the system after power is finally restored. Alternately, an external **uninterruptible power supply (UPS)** can be attached to a 9404 system via the provided UPS interface.

You can upgrade a Model F10 to an F20 or to an F25 at any time by swapping components within the System Unit. You can also upgrade a Model F20 to Model F25 at any time. Although you can use all the same workstations, modems, and so on, you must replace the 9404 System Unit with a 9406 System Unit to grow beyond the F25.

## 9406 System Specifics

The AS/400 9406 systems represent a departure in mechanical packaging from that of the System/3X family. The components that make up 9406 systems are mounted in one or more **rack enclosures**. The rack is a structure, similar to an empty stereo cabinet, that conforms to industry standard dimensions. It provides the power for the installed components. The components needed to build a given 9406 system are mounted in these racks to provide a complete computer system. A 9406 system may consist of a single rack or multiple racks, depending on the user's requirements. This rack-mounted approach allows for flexible 9406 system configurations and modular growth as the business grows.

Seven different predefined racks can be combined in a building-block fashion to yield 9406 systems of many different configurations (see Figure 1.8). These consist of a System Unit rack, a System Unit Expansion rack, a Bus Extension Unit rack, a General Purpose I/O rack, a 9332 Disk Unit rack, a 9335 Disk Unit rack, and an I/O Card Unit Expansion rack. Figure 1.8 shows the items that can be installed in each type of rack. Every 9406 system must have one System Unit rack, which contains the processor that is the heart of any 9406 system. In fact, the smaller 9406 models can be contained in a single System Unit rack. However, the larger 9406 models can span many racks.

A multi-function I/O processor and associated EIA 232/V.22 Adapter is pro-

| AS/400 9406 Predefined Rack Types | Devices Housed | Comments |
|---|---|---|
| System Unit Rack | Main Processor(s), 9331 Diskette Units, 9332/9336/9337 DASD Units, 9347/9348 Tape Units, and I/O Card Units | One System Unit Rack is required with every AS/400 9406 system |
| System Unit Expansion Rack | Two additional system busses with 6 I/O card slots each, 9331 Diskette Unit, 9332/9336/9337 DASD Units, 9347/9348/3490 Tape Units, and I/O Card Units | Battery Power Unit and UPS interface are supplied as part of rack |
| Bus Extension Unit Rack | 11 I/O card slots, 9331 Diskette Units, 9332/9336/9337 DASD Units, 9347/9348/3490 Tape Units, and I/O Card Units | Battery Power Unit and UPS interface are supplied as part of rack |

**Figure 1.8.** AS/400 9406 systems are built by selecting the appropriate predefined 9406 racks. This figure lists the different rack types and shows the devices that can be housed in each.

vided as standard and is intended for use in Electronic Customer Support. A Battery Power Unit is also provided as standard equipment. This is designed to supply power to the critical system elements like the processor and I/O controllers (e.g., disk unit controller circuitry) during short power outages. It does not, however, provide power to the entire system (e.g., the disk units). Rather, by keeping power supplied to the critical system elements, the Battery Power Unit provides the power necessary to successfully ride through short outages and to log the state of the system (main storage dump) in the event of a lengthy power outage. This main storage

| AS/400 9406 Predefined Rack Types | Devices Housed | Comments |
|---|---|---|
| General Purpose I/O Rack | 9331 Diskette Units, 9336/9337 DASD Units, 9347/9348/3490 Tape Units, and I/O Card Units | Recommended secondary rack type |
| 9332 Disk Unit Rack | 9332/9336/9337 DASD Units, 9331 Diskette Units, 9347/9348 Tape Units, and I/O Card Units | Only recommended for systems that will use 9332 DASD Units |
| 9335 Disk Unit Rack | 9335/9336/9337 DASD Units | Only recommended for systems that will use 9335 DASD Units |
| I/O Card Unit Rack | I/O Card Units and 9336 DASD Units | Only recommended when the AS/400 system has three or more I/O Card Units installed |

**Figure 1.8.** *(Continued)*

dump helps reduce the time it takes to recover the system after power is restored. Alternately, the standard UPS interface allows for the attachment of a user-supplied UPS system to keep the systems running in the event of a power failure. A control panel, similar to that of the 9404 system, allows the systems operator and service personnel to interact with the system and provides a key-lock for security. Many control panel functions, such as turning on the power and initializing the system, can also be performed remotely through communications lines. There are currently eight 9406 model "F" systems from which to choose: Models F35, F45, F50, F60, F70,

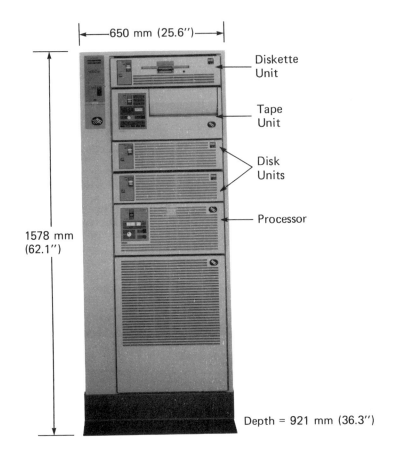

650 mm (25.6")

Diskette Unit

Tape Unit

Disk Units

Processor

1578 mm (62.1")

Depth = 921 mm (36.3")

*Standard Equipment*

F35 or F45 Processor
Main Storage:
   F35 = 16 MB (80 MB max)
   F45 = 16 MB (80 MB max)
Multi-Function I/O Processor
1.97 GB Disk Storage (39.3 GB max)
Battery Power Unit
UPS Interface
EIA 232/V.22 Adapter
Key-lock security
System Control Panel
Battery powered clock/calendar

*Expansion*

*(2) System Busses
   (2) Main Storage Expansion Slots
   (11) I/O Expansion Slots
*Various Disk Units
*Various Magnetic Tape Devices
Slot for 1/4" Cartridge Tape Unit
Up to (2) 1.2 MB Diskette Drives (5.25" or 8")
*Up to (4) Bus Extension Units each providing:
   (11) more I/O Expansion Slots
   Space for more Disk Units/Tape Units/
   I/O Card Units
Maximum Communications lines:
   F35 = 20
   F45 = 33
Maximum Twinax Workstation Controllers:
   F35 = 12 (480 workstations)
   F45 = 18 (720 workstations)
Maximum ASCII Workstation Controllers:
   F35 = 12 (216 workstations)
   F45 = 18 (324 workstations)

*See Chapter 2 for a description of features that are supported.

**Figure 1.9.** IBM AS/400 9406 Model F35/F45 specifics.

F80, F90, and F95 — each providing more performance and capacity than the last. Any 9406 model can be upgraded to any other model at any time by simply swapping out the modular processor section (or components therein).

Figure 1.9 shows a 9406 Model F35 consisting of a single System Unit rack that contains the processor, disk units, a diskette unit, and a tape unit. This, with the appropriate displays and printers, makes a complete 9406 computer system. This photo could just as easily have been a 9406 Model F45 system, which can also be contained in a single System Unit rack. Alternately, either the Model F35 or F45 can be configured as a larger multi-rack system supporting up to 39.3 GB of disk storage. Models F35 and F45 both have two I/O busses over which information flows to and from any optional Memory Expansion and I/O cards installed in the provided card slots. Eleven expansion slots are provided for I/O cards (e.g., the multi-function I/O processors discussed in Chapter 2). By adding additional Bus Extension Units, F35 and F45 systems can offer up to 55 I/O expansion slots. Two main storage card slots are also provided to allow for larger main storage configurations.

The Model F35 comes with 16 MB of storage expandable to 80 MB and can have up to 20 communications lines and 12 Twinaxial Workstation Controllers installed. Since 40 workstations can be attached to each workstation controller, up to 480 local workstations can be attached to a Model F35. The Model F45 also comes with 16 MB of main storage expandable to 80 MB. It can support up to 33 communications lines and 18 Twinaxial Workstation Controllers (up to 720 workstations).

Figure 1.10 shows an example 9406 Model F50/F60/F70 system configuration. All 9406 Model "F" systems come standard with 1.97 GB of internal disk storage. This storage is built into small rectangular boxes that are installed in the processor structure itself much like a communications adapter. The Model F50 comes with 64 MB of main storage expandable to 192 MB and supports up to 74.7 GB of disk storage. The Models F60 and F70 both come standard with 128 MB of main storage and have the ability to expand to 256 MB and 512 MB respectively. The base Model F50 System has three independent I/O busses that together provide 18 I/O expansion slots. As with the Models F35 and F45, more I/O busses operating independently typically translates into improved overall system performance. By adding the optional Bus Extension Units, a single F50 system can have up to 140 I/O expansion slots and is afforded additional space for disk units. The Models F60 and F70 also come standard with three I/O busses, but these models can be expanded to five I/O busses by installing the optional System Unit Expansion. The System Unit Expansion attaches to the 9406 System Unit via a laser-driven fiber optic cable and adds additional space for disk units and two I/O busses with six I/O expansion slots on each I/O bus (total of 12 additional I/O expansion slots). With this option and the appropriate number of Bus Extension Units, a single F60 and F70 system can have up to 140 and 195 I/O expansion slots respectively. The F60 and F70 systems also

Tape/DASD
Rack

System Unit
Rack

DASD
Rack

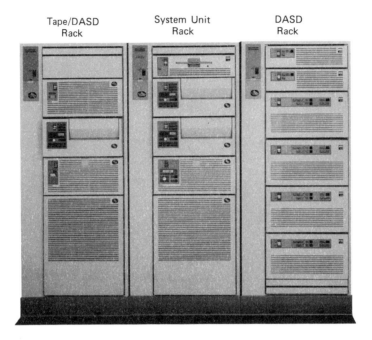

| Standard Equipment | Expansion | |
|---|---|---|
| F50, F60, or F70 Processor | *(3) System Busses | Maximum Communications lines: |
| Main Storage: | (5) Main Storage Expansion Slots | F50 = 33 |
| F50 = 64 MB (192 MB max) | (18) I/O Expansion Slots | F60 = 49 |
| F60 = 128 MB with Cache | *Various Disk Units | F70 = 64 |
| (256 MB max) | *Various Magnetic Tape Devices | Maximum Twinax Workstation Controllers: |
| F70 = 128 MB with Cache | Slot for 1/4" Cartridge Tape Unit | F50 = 25 (1000 workstations) |
| (512 MB max) | Up to (2) 1.2 MB Diskette Drives | F60 = 35 (1400 workstations) |
| Multi-Function I/O Processor | (5.25" or 8") | F70 = 60 (2400 workstations) |
| F50 = 1.97 GB (74.7 GB max) | **Up to (6) Bus Extension Units each | Maximum ASCII Workstation Controllers: |
| F60 = 1.97 GB (110.1 GB max) | providing: | F50 = 25 (450 workstations) |
| F70 = 1.97 GB (165.2 GB max) | (11) more I/O Expansion Slots | F60 = 35 (630 workstations) |
| Battery Power Unit | Space for more Disk Units/Tape | F70 = 60 (1080 workstations) |
| UPS Interface | Units/I/O Card Units | |
| EIA 232/V.22 Adapter | *Additional System Unit Expansion(s) | |
| Key-lock security | F50 = 0 | |
| System Control Panel | F60 = 2 | |
| Battery powered clock/calendar | F70 = 2 | |

*See Chapter 2 for a description of features that are supported. Model F70 has 17 available I/O Extension slots.
**Maximum number of I/O Card Units supported is reduced by one for each Bus Extension Unit installed on
  the same I/O bus.

**Figure 1.10.**  IBM AS/400 9406 Model F50/F60/F70 specifics.

have a special high-speed memory area called a **cache**. As the AS/400 executes programs, this cache automatically accumulates information likely to be needed during subsequent processing. If the accumulated information is indeed called for (as it almost always is), the cache steps in and provides it faster than could the main storage. The result is an improvement in the overall performance of the system.

The Model F80/F90/F95 systems are covered in Figure 1.11. Like the Models

| Standard Equipment | Expansion |
|---|---|
| Main Processors: | *(3) System Busses |
|   F80 = 2 |   (5) Main Storage Expansion Slots |
|   F90 = 3 |   (17) I/O Expansion Slots |
|   F95 = 4 | *Various Disk Units |
| Main Storage: | *Various Magnetic Tape Devices |
|   F80 = 128 MB (512 MB max) | Slot for 1/4" Cartridge Tape Unit |
|   F90 = 128 MB with Cache (512 MB max) | Up to (2) 1.2 MB Diskette Drives (5.25" or 8") |
|   F95 = 128 MB with Cache (512 MB max) | **Up to (14) Bus Extension Units each providing: |
| Multi-Function I/O Processor |   (11) more I/O Expansion Slots |
|   F80 = 1.97 GB (165.2 GB max) |   Space for more Disk Units/Tape Units/ |
|   F90 = 1.97 GB (165.2 GB max) |     I/O Card Units |
|   F95 = 1.97 GB (165.2 GB max) | Additional System Unit Expansion(s) |
| Battery Power Unit |   F80 = 0 |
| UPS Interface |   F90 = 2 |
| EIA 232/V.22 Adapter |   F95 = 2 |
| Key-lock security | Up to 64 Communications lines |
| System Control Panel | Up to 60 Twinax Workstation Controllers |
| Battery powered clock/calendar |   (2400 workstations) |
| | Up to 60 ASCII Workstation Controllers |
| |   (1080 workstations) |

*See Chapter 2 for a description of features that are supported.
**Maximum number of I/O Card Units supported is reduced by one for each Bus
  Expansion Unit installed on the same I/O bus.

**Figure 1.11.** IBM AS/400 Model F80/F90/F95 specifics.

F60 and F70, the Models F80, F90, and F95 have a cache memory to improve over-all system performance. However, the thing that most clearly sets the F80/F90/F95 systems apart from the other AS/400 systems is that they implement the AS/400's **N-Way Multi-Processor** architecture. That is, the AS/400 Models F80/F90/F95 employ multiple system processors to attain higher performance than any of the other AS/400 systems covered so far. In the F80's implementation of this architecture, two independent system processors — each as powerful as the system processor in a Model F70 — are working together to perform the user's tasks. As one might expect, having two coordinated system processors in one computer results in a significant boost in the performance of the F80.

The same N-Way architecture is expanded to include three system processors in Model F90 systems and four system processors in Model F95 systems to attain further gains in processing power. The N-Way architecture and its effects on performance will be discussed further later in the chapter.

All F80/F90/F95 systems come standard with 128 MB of main storage expandable to 512 MB and 1.97 GB of disk storage.

## Performance Overview

One important aspect of a computer system is the speed at which the computer can perform work, or the performance of the computer. The higher the performance, the more work the computer can do. Many things — such as the processor, main storage, disk storage, and program design — affect the performance of a computer system. It is difficult and often misleading to predict the overall performance of a computer system by looking at selected specifications of the individual components that make up the computer system. Although things such as disk unit seek times and raw processor speed (usually measured in millions of instructions per second, or MIPS) are important, they do not provide the whole picture in terms of overall system performance.

A better way to compare the overall performance of different computers is to perform **benchmark testing**. This involves loading the computer system with a number of users running various programs and measuring how the system behaves under the load. Through this benchmark testing, all elements of the computer system come into play and the overall performance of selected computer systems can be meaningfully compared.

IBM has conducted benchmark testing (based on the RAMP-C benchmark) to compare the relative performance of the various IBM AS/400 and AS/Entry models with one another and with System/36 and System/38 computers. This testing was done by loading the computers with specially written programs that exercise the AS/400 computers as they would operate in a typical business environment, running application programs like order entry, accounts payable, and accounts receivable. It should be understood that to perform benchmark testing, the test group must make assumptions about the kind of work being done and the behavior of the users at each workstation. For this reason, the performance measurements in this benchmark may vary significantly from what users will get if their business environment is different from the assumptions made in the testing. For example, word-processing users typically load a system down even more than users performing business transactions. Therefore, a system with heavy word-processing activity will usually not be able to support as many users as a system performing order entry, for example. However, because all assumptions are the same for all computers included in the benchmark testing, you can get a good feeling for the relative performance of the computer systems.

IBM reports AS/400 benchmark results at 70 percent of maximum system processor utilization. Although the AS/400 system may provide acceptable performance beyond this limit for some applications, the benchmark rating was calculated at this level.

Two measurements were then taken to evaluate the performance of the computers under the workload: **interactive throughput** and **interactive response time**. Interactive throughput measures the amount of work the computer system performs for active users in a given period of time. The amount of work is defined as the number of user requests for activity or **transactions** a computer system can perform per hour. Since businesses buy computers to perform work, this is an important indicator.

Interactive response time is a measurement of the amount of time an individual user would have to wait from the time the user hits the enter key, initiating a transaction, until the completed transaction appears on the display screen. Response time, usually measured in seconds, is important because it has a direct effect on the productivity and satisfaction of users. A slow response time makes users wait every time they hit the enter key, which can decrease concentration and cause frustration.

Not only are response time and throughput each important in their own right, they are also related to each other. As the throughput of a computer system is increased by adding more users or having each user perform more work, the response time increases (the system appears to slow down).

Another point to understand is that the benchmark testing was done with each computer system operating in its most optimum or **native** environment — with application programs designed to take advantage of that particular system. That is, the AS/400 systems ran application programs designed for the AS/400 architecture in their native environment. Similarly, the System/36 and System/38 computers shown on the graph ran application programs specifically designed for the System/36 and System/38 architectures respectively.

The AS/400's **System/36 Environment** allows a program originally written for a System/36 architecture to be migrated to and used on an AS/400 system. However, System/36 application programs that are not redesigned to take advantage of the AS/400 architecture will not run as efficiently as an application program designed specifically for the AS/400. Therefore, if you intend to migrate System/36 programs to the AS/400 and run them in AS/400's System/36 Environment, this performance graph can be misleading. Migrated S/36 application programs running in the AS/400's S/36 environment may experience performance problems when they make heavy use of features unique to System/36. However, with proper tuning (modifications), the performance level of System/36 application programs running on an AS/400 in its System/36 Environment can approach the performance of native application programs specifically designed to take advantage of the AS/400 architecture. In an effort to reduce the performance tuning needed with System/36 application programs, IBM has made improvements to the AS/400 System/36 environment itself by more efficiently implementing System/36 functions commonly used by System/36 application programs. Still, this must be considered in each case when sizing an AS/400 system that will directly replace a System/36 and operate in an S/36 environment.

Figure 1.12 shows the maximum throughput (number of transactions per hour) that the various AS/400 and System/3X computers can perform without running beyond 70 percent utilization. The smallest AS/400, Model F02, can handle up to 13,050 transactions per hour. That is well over twice as many transactions as the smallest System/38 could handle and about 28% more transactions than the F02's predecessor, the Model E02. The Model F70 can handle 141,525 transactions per hour, or about seven and one half times more than the largest System/38. The Model F80 AS/400, which employs two system processors in its N-Way multi-processor architecture, can handle 246,150 transactions per hour. This is about 74% more transactions per hour than a model F70 can handle. Since the F80 employs two F70-class System Processors, why isn't the F80 100% faster than the F70? The reason is that the two F80 System Processors must spend some of their processing power coordinating activities with one another. They must also share the same main storage, I/O bus(ses), disk storage, and so on. For these reasons, adding a second system processor does not result in doubling the performance of the system. The Models F90 and F95 show the significant performance advantage afforded by their use of three and four system processors respectively.

By making certain assumptions about the way users are interacting with the system, you can predict how many users each computer system can support without going beyond the 70 percent utilization point. For the purposes of performance estimating, assume a business user will consistently generate transactions every hour (almost four per minute, with most of the time spent by the user thinking and keying information at the display station). In actuality, this represents a fairly heavy use. Based on these assumptions, Figure 1.13 shows how many of these users can be actively working without driving the computer system beyond 70 percent utilization.

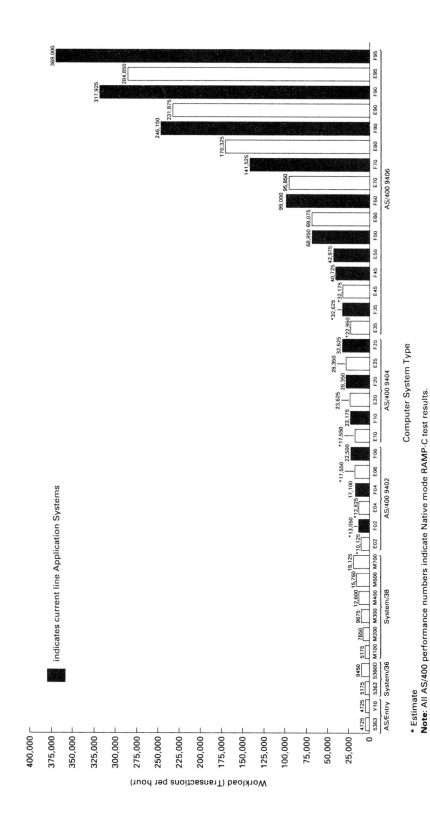

**Figure 1.12.** Amount of work that can be done by various computer systems operating at 70% capacity. Data shown are based on RAMP-C interactive commercial applications. RAMP-C is not representative of a specific customer environment. Results in other environments may vary significantly.

**32**

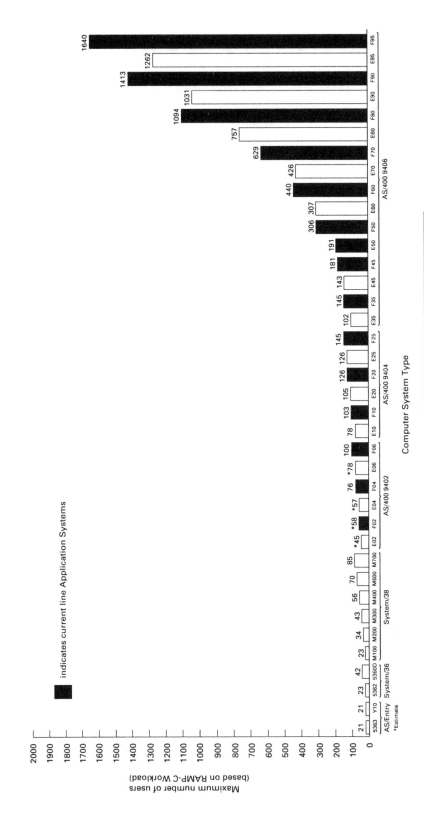

**Figure 1.13.** Maximum number of simulated computer users for various computer systems. Data shown are based on AMP-C interactive commercial applications. RAMP-C is not representative of a specific customer environment. Results in other environments may vary significantly.

When choosing a multi-user computer system, it is important to understand that the maximum number of active users is different from the maximum number of workstations that can be attached to a system. For example, an AS/400 9404 Model F35 can have up to 480 Twinaxial Workstations locally attached, but the figure shows that 145 users is a maximum before driving the system beyond 70 percent utilization. The maximum number of users is therefore not a system configuration limitation but rather a system performance limitation for the benchmark used. However, if occasional users are among the user population, it may be desirable in some cases to put more workstations on a system than can be simultaneously supported.

Response time is as important as, if not more important than, throughput. The satisfaction and productivity of users can be drastically affected by a computer's sluggish response time. As mentioned earlier, response time is related to the workload on the computer system. Figure 1.14 shows how the response times of an AS/400 family system change in relation to the throughput or workload imposed on

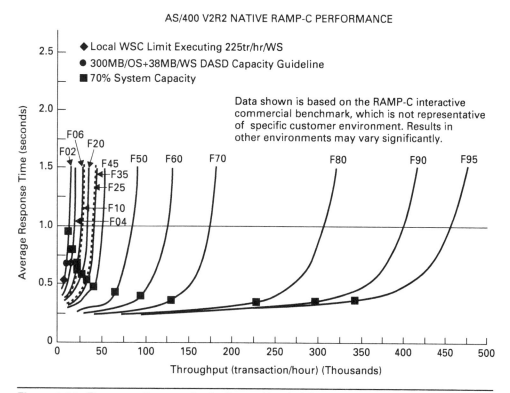

**Figure 1.14.** Response time graph. As the workload of the system is increased, the average response time for a single transaction is increased. Data shown are based on RAMP-C interactive commercial applications. RAMP-C is not representative of a specific customer environment. Results in other environments may vary significantly.

the computer (number of transactions per hour). Notice, for example, that the Model F90 provides subsecond response time at the 70 percent utilization point (indicated by a square on the response time curve). At the 400,000 transactions per hour point, response time is still not bad—about one second. As the workload continues to increase, the response time continues to lengthen. As 100% system processor utilization is approached, response time becomes infinitely long. This is why benchmark rating was calculated at a more realistic 70% of system processor utilization.

## A CLOSER LOOK

There are many things that together provide the functions and performance of IBM AS/400 computers. The remainder of this chapter provides a "closer look" at the following aspects of the IBM AS/400 systems:

- Hardware architecture
- Built-in database
- Storage management
- Auxiliary storage
- Packaging technology

Before the AS/400 systems are examined more closely, it should be mentioned that many of the concepts used in the AS/400 system were built on those of IBM's System/38 computer. This fact is a testimonial to the rich function and growth capability built into the original System/38.

### Hardware Architecture

The underlying configuration of a computer system's electrical components is called its **hardware architecture**, which is the fundamental structure on which all system functions are built and has the largest effect on the way the computer system can behave. A basic understanding of the AS/400 system architecture makes the reader better able to compare AS/400 computers with other systems and also to understand important aspects of system performance and capacity.

Figure 1.15 shows a simple block diagram of the basic AS/400 hardware architecture used in all but the largest AS/400 systems. The core of the AS/400 computer is the **system processor**, which is the circuitry that actually executes a computer program's instructions and does all the mathematical calculations. The smallest piece of information in the computer is called a **bit**. These bits are grouped into bytes (8 bits), half words (16 bits), and full words (32 bits) inside the computer to

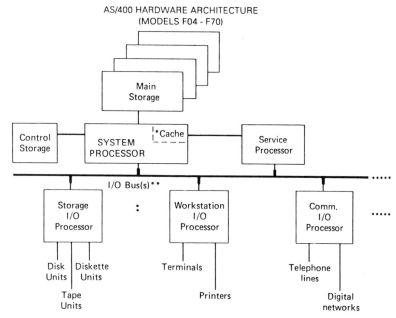

AS/400 HARDWARE ARCHITECTURE
(MODELS F04 - F70)

*Cache memory provided only on AS/400 9406 models F60 and above.
**See Table:

| Model | Number of I/O Busses |
|---|---|
| F02 | 2 |
| F04 | 1 |
| F06 | 1 |
| F10 | 2 |
| F20 | 2 |
| F25 | 2 |
| F35 | 2 |
| F35 | 2 |
| F50 | 3 |
| F60 | 3 - 5 |
| F70 | 3 - 5 |
| F80/F90/F95 | See Figure 1.16 |

**Figure 1.15.** Block diagram of AS/400 hardware architecture used in all single-processor AS/400 systems (Models F02 through F70).

form the computer's representation of numbers, letters of the alphabet, and instructions in a program. AS/400 system processors can move information one full word at a time, producing efficient information flow. Other bits inside the system processor are used to uniquely identify or **address** storage and input/output devices (e.g., a disk unit) within the computer system. AS/400 system processors group 48 bits together to form an address. This 48-bit addressing provides 281 trillion ($2^{48}$) unique addresses, which is more than any other IBM computer system from PS/2s to the largest System/390 computers. Although this is more than enough addresses for today's mid-size computer environment (and even for the foreseeable future), the architecture on which AS/400 is based allows future computers to use 64-bit addresses, providing 18,446,744 trillion ($2^{64}$) addresses. This shows the kind of growth inherent in the AS/400 architecture.

The "memory" or **main storage** is the set of electronic circuits that provides a "workspace" for the system processor. Since the system processor spends a great deal of time moving information in and out of main storage, the speed of the main storage significantly affects system performance. Why is so much time spent moving information between the system processor and the main storage? There are two major reasons. First, all programs currently being executed by the system processor reside in main storage. Therefore, the system processor must retrieve every instruction from the main storage. Second, the main storage holds the data to be acted on by the system processor. Since the information traffic between the system processor and main storage is heavy, the speed of the main storage is important. The speed of storage is measured by the time it takes to respond to a request to store or recall information, or the **cycle time**. The main storage cycle time for AS/400 computers varies depending on the model. The shorter the cycle time, the better the system performance. The largest AS/400 computers can have up to 384 MB of main storage. The main storage in all Application Systems provides **error detection** and **error correction**. As we have seen, every main storage location in AS/400 main storage consists of 32 pieces of information or bits. All information in main storage is encoded using these 32-bit groupings, called *full words*. In addition to the 32 bits of information, each word in main storage has several additional bits (called **check bits**) that are generated based on the value of that particular 32-bit word. In the event that one or two of the 32-bit words is somehow corrupted, the check bits notify the AS/400 computer that the error exists. If only one of the 32 bits is corrupted, as is usually the case, the check bits actually restore the corrupted bit and correct the error. This main storage error detection and correction works to protect the all-important integrity of user information in the computer system.

The **control storage** provides a small, high-speed memory area that contains the most commonly used **licensed internal code (LIC)**. This is a set of extremely simple instructions (never seen by the computer programmer or user) that are directly performed by the electronic circuits within the system processor. All user program instructions are automatically converted into a series of these LIC instructions, which are then executed by the system processor.

The size of the control storage in AS/400 systems is either 4096 locations (4K words) or 8192 locations (8K words), depending on the model. In either case, because there are more LIC instructions than can fit in control storage, some must reside in the slower main storage area. Most LIC instructions in control storage will execute in one control storage cycle time or the time it takes the control storage to respond to the system processor's request for the LIC instruction. Because all actions of the system processor are dictated by LIC instructions, the system processor runs in lockstep with the control storage cycles. When needed LIC instructions are in the slower main storage, the system processor is delayed, reducing the overall system performance. The larger control storage area provided in the AS/400 computers holds more of the LIC instructions, thus contributing to their higher system performance.

The input/output processors shown in Figure 1.15 are responsible for managing any devices attached to the AS/400 system. Each of these specialized processors has independent responsibilities and performs tasks in coordination with the system processor. A computer that has multiple processors working together with the system processor like this is said to have a **multi-processor architecture**. The advantage of having multiple processors performing work simultaneously is simply that more work can be done in a given period of time. For example, the workstation (I/O) processor manages the detailed processing associated with the multiple terminals and printers attached to the system, allowing the system processor to concentrate on doing more productive work for the user. The same is true of the other specialized I/O processors, such as the storage I/O processor that manages disk, diskette, and tape devices attached to the AS/400 system.

The I/O processors communicate with the system processor over an I/O **bus**, which is a group of wires that carry information very quickly from one area to another inside the computer system.

As indicated in Figure 1.15, some AS/400 systems have a single I/O bus whereas others have multiple I/O busses. Because only one information transfer can occur on any one bus at any one time, systems with multiple busses have the advantage of allowing overlapping transfers between I/O processors and the system processor or main storage. Therefore, multiple busses contribute to the overall system performance advantages of larger AS/400 systems. The various controllers and adapters, discussed in Chapter 2, plug into physical slots that provide electrical connections to the bus.

In addition to I/O processors, a service processor, built into every AS/400, is responsible for starting the system and constantly monitoring the health of the entire computer. It interacts with the system operator through the control panel and helps with things like system fault isolation, error detection, and error reporting. It is the equivalent of having a built-in service person who watches over things with relentless consistency.

Figure 1.16 shows the architecture of the AS/400 models F80, F90, and F95. Unlike the rest of the AS/400 models which use a single system processor, these

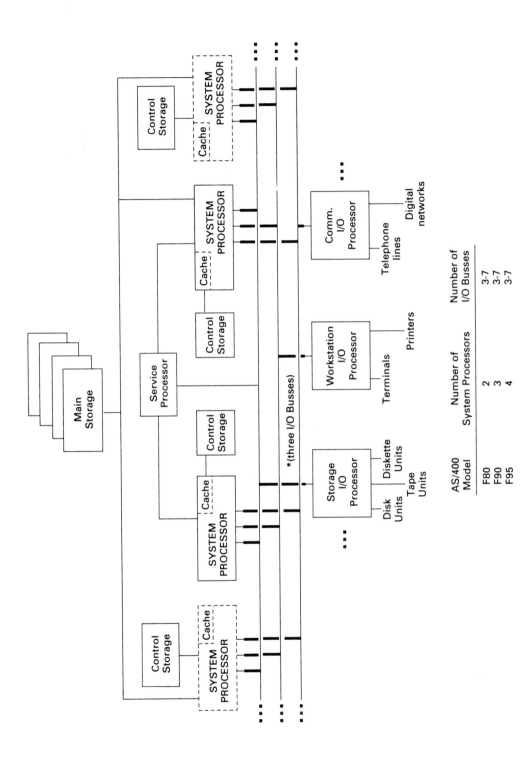

**Figure 1.16.** Block diagram of AS/400 N-Way Multi-Processor Architecture used in Models F80, F90, and F95 only.

| AS/400 Model | Number of System Processors | Number of I/O Busses |
|---|---|---|
| F80 | 2 | 3-7 |
| F90 | 3 | 3-7 |
| F95 | 4 | 3-7 |

models employ multiple independent but closely coordinated system processors. All AS/400 systems employ a multi-processor architecture in that they have a system processor and multiple specialized processors (e.g., a multi-function I/O processor) to handle specific tasks such as managing the disk transfers or communications lines. However, the Models F80, F90, and F95 employ multiple **system** processors contained in a single AS/400 System Unit and cooperatively executing a single copy of the operating system (OS/400), thus appearing to be a single large processor. This multiple system processor architecture is called the **N-Way Multi-Processor** archi-tecture. Since the F80 has two system processors, its implementation is called a **2-Way Multi-Processor**. Similarly, the Model F90 with its three system processors and the Model F95 with its four system processors are called **3-Way** and **4-Way Multi-Processors** respectively.

The F80 has two system processors, each as powerful as the system processor used in a Model F70, housed in a single AS/400 System Unit. While one might think that having two system processors would double the performance of a system, this is not the case. As we saw in Figure 1.12, the F80 enjoys a 74% performance improve-ment over the Model F70, which employs a system processor equivalent in power to either of the two system processors in a Model F80. While a 74% performance improvement is a very large improvement, it is not the 100% improvement one might expect to result from doubling the system processors.

One reason the F80 does not offer a 100% improvement is that some of the processing power of the two system processors is consumed coordinating activities between them. Another reason is that both system processors share the same main storage, I/O busses, disk storage, and so on. This sharing means that one processor will at times have to wait for the other processor to finish with one of the shared resources. The result of these factors is getting a 74% performance improvement instead of a 100% performance improvement.

The Model F90 adds a third system processor, and the Model F95 adds a fourth system processor. As shown in Figure 1.16, all system processors share the same I/O busses, I/O processors, and main storage.

## Built-In Database

To deal with large amounts of information efficiently, it is necessary to organize the information in a uniform manner. For example, the information in a telephone book is organized into an alphabetical list of names, addresses, and telephone numbers. If you have ever lifted a Manhattan telephone book, you know that phone books can contain a fair amount of information.

Computers also require that information be organized in some fashion. A collection of information stored inside a computer system is called a **database**. There are various ways to organize the information in a database and the best way depends on how you intend to use the information. Deeply embedded in the architecture and operating system of AS/400 computers (but not the AS/Entry) lies a support for the development and manipulation of a **relational** database. In a relational database, each piece of information is "related" to the others using a simple tabular structure. This provides great flexibility when defining the database and using the information it contains.

Inside the AS/400's database, information is stored as **records** and **fields**. Do not be intimidated by the words. This is exactly how the information in a phone book is structured. Figure 1.17 shows an example of a telephone book listing and the corresponding relational database structure found in an AS/400 computer. The phone book itself is analogous to a set of information or a database. The information about one person in the phone book would be analogous to a record. The records contain the information for a given entry, and all other records contain similar information about their respective entries. In this case, a record would contain the name, address, and phone number of the person. Each of these three items would be analogous to a field. For example, the address part of a phone book entry would be called the "address field."

Manually looking up information in a phone book is time-consuming and quickly becomes fatiguing. The same is true for manually manipulating any large body of information. Once the information is entered into a database, however, it can be retrieved quickly and easily by the computer. Databases can contain information about a department store's inventory, a library's books, personnel records, medical records, or virtually any other type of information. Organizations such as banks, airlines, and insurance companies commonly use extremely large databases shared by many users.

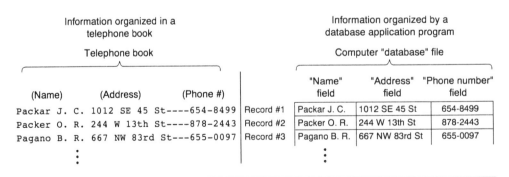

**Figure 1.17.** Information in a data base is organized much like the information in a telephone book.

Now that you understand what a database is, let us see what the built-in database capability of the AS/400 has to offer. The first thing to understand is that in AS/400 computers the database structure can be defined independently of any program on the computer. That is, the data in the database are available to all user programs for analysis, report generation, update, and so on, but the database definition does not reside in a user's programs. The data are therefore said to be **externally described** and do not live "inside" any one program. Instead, the definition "lives" inside the AS/400's built-in database system and in that respect leads an existence independent from any one program. This is a subtle but important point, because it improves the consistency and thus the maintainability of application programs. Now the programmer has one source for all information pertaining to the database structure and how application programs use the database. Externally described data contribute to improved programmer productivity.

Another important feature of AS/400 database support is the support for **logical files**. Up to now we have been dealing with real or **physical** database files, which are a grouping of information inside a computer. The concept of logical files allows a given program or user to change the appearance of the physical database to better suit individual needs. For example, we have a personnel data base on an AS/400 computer for a fictitious company named Atole Enterprises. The organization of the personnel information is shown in Figure 1.18. This is the physical database file that contains all personnel information and was described externally to any user programs. Now we wish to have a clerk (Jim) keep an up-to-date mailing list of all employees for the company magazine; however, to protect employees' privacy, Jim should not have access to the wage information that is part of the physical database file. To meet these needs, a logical database file is defined that contains no informa-

| | Name | Address | Phone | Wages | SS# | Date of hire | Marital status |
|---|---|---|---|---|---|---|---|
| Record 1 | | | | | | | |
| Record 2 | | | | | | | |
| Record 3 | | | | | | | |
| Record 4 | | | | | | | |
| Record 5 | | | | | | | |
| Record 6 | | | | | | | |
| Record 7 | | | | | | | |
| Record 8 | | | | | | | |
| ⋮ | | | | | | | |
| Record X | | | | | | | |

**Figure 1.18.** Physical data base containing personnel information.

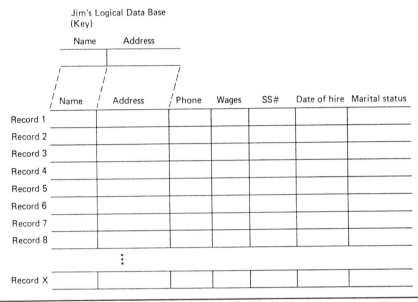

**Figure 1.19.** Jim's logical data base provides a "view" of the physical data base needed to perform his job.

tion but only a "view" of the physical database that meets Jim's needs. The logical database file restricts Jim's view of the physical database file to only the information he needs. Further, since Jim looks up employees by name, this is the **key** field defined in his logical database file. He is able to access the information by alphabetical order of employee name (his key field) rather than by the order in which the names actually appear in the physical database file. Jim's logical data base file structure is shown in Figure 1.19.

Now let us extend the example by adding another logical database file for the same physical data, this time for a different clerk (Nancy), who tracks employee service anniversaries. Her logical database file structure is shown in Figure 1.20. Nancy looks up employees by their date of hire, so this will be the key field in her logical database file. Again, only the fields needed to do her job are made available to Nancy. As the needs of Atole change, many logical database files can be defined to meet those needs without affecting any other user or the physical database file. This example illustrates how multiple users can use a single copy of a physical database to do completely different jobs. Without the logical files, multiple physical databases (one meeting the specific needs of each clerk in addition to the original database holding the wage information) would have to be kept in the computer system, wasting space (Figure 1.21). In addition to wasting space, there are other problems associated with

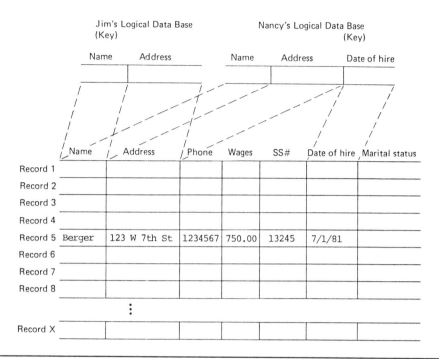

Jim's Logical Data Base (Key)

Nancy's Logical Data Base (Key)

| Name | Address |
| --- | --- |

| Name | Address | Date of hire |
| --- | --- | --- |

|  | Name | Address | Phone | Wages | SS# | Date of hire | Marital status |
| --- | --- | --- | --- | --- | --- | --- | --- |
| Record 1 |  |  |  |  |  |  |  |
| Record 2 |  |  |  |  |  |  |  |
| Record 3 |  |  |  |  |  |  |  |
| Record 4 |  |  |  |  |  |  |  |
| Record 5 | Berger | 123 W 7th St | 1234567 | 750.00 | 13245 | 7/1/81 |  |
| Record 6 |  |  |  |  |  |  |  |
| Record 7 |  |  |  |  |  |  |  |
| Record 8 |  |  |  |  |  |  |  |
| ⋮ |  |  |  |  |  |  |  |
| Record X |  |  |  |  |  |  |  |

**Figure 1.20.** Multiple logical data bases can be constructed providing different views of the same physical data base.

Jim's Data Base

| Name | Address |
| --- | --- |
|  |  |
|  |  |
|  |  |
| Berger | 333 E 27th St |
|  |  |
| ⋮ |  |
|  |  |

Physical Data Base #1

Nancy's Data Base

| Name | Address | Date of hire |
| --- | --- | --- |
|  |  |  |
|  |  |  |
|  |  |  |
| Berger | 123 W 7th St | 7/1/81 |
|  |  |  |
| ⋮ |  |  |
|  |  |  |

Physical Data Base #2

Payroll Data Base

| Name | Address | Phone | Wages | SS# | Date of hire |
| --- | --- | --- | --- | --- | --- |
|  |  |  |  |  |  |
|  |  |  |  |  |  |
|  |  |  |  |  |  |
| Berger | 123 W 7th St | 1234567 | 750.00 | 2344322 | 7/1/81 |
|  |  |  |  |  |  |
| ⋮ |  |  |  |  |  |
|  |  |  |  |  |  |

Physical Data Base #3

**Figure 1.21.** Without logical data base views, multiple physical data bases would be necessary, wasting space and compromising data integrity.

having multiple physical databases. For example, one morning Jim receives notice that an employee (Mr. Berger) has a new mailing address and Jim promptly updates the database. Later that same morning, Nancy searches for that month's service anniversaries and finds that the month is Mr. Berger's seventh anniversary with the company. She checks his address and sends him an anniversary card. Without the logical file approach, in which Jim and Nancy share one physical copy of the data, Mr. Berger's card would be sent to the old address. With the logical database of the AS/400 computers, as soon as Jim updates Mr. Berger's address, it is available to Nancy, and Mr. Berger gets his card on time.

There are ways to keep multiple copies of information up to date on computer systems without logical files. But if our example is extended to a real business environment with many different clerks, many different programs undergoing changes, and many different types of databases, managing the problem becomes time-consuming and difficult. With the logical file approach, there is no data redundancy problem to manage.

This one simple example illustrates how logical database files can be used to provide the user with the information needed in the way that it is needed. There are other logical database file structures possible with the AS/400 computer that can, for example, pull together selected information from multiple (up to 32) physical database files into a single logical file. This further expands the ability to deliver the right information to the various users without duplicating information in different databases. Through the AS/400 "built-in" database, users have access to information, the integrity of the data is protected, and programmer productivity is improved.

## Storage Management

The two primary types of storage available for user programs and data in AS/400 computer systems are main storage and disk storage. All programs and information currently being used by the computer system must be contained in the main storage. Main storage is relatively expensive and responds at very high speeds when called on to provide or store information. Because main storage loses all information when the computer system is turned off, it is called **volatile** storage.

Disk storage is less expensive but cannot provide or store information as quickly as main storage. Disk storage is said to be **nonvolatile** because it does not lose its information when the power is turned off (or lost owing to a power failure). As a result of this nonvolatility and relatively low cost, disk storage is commonly used to hold all information that must be readily available to the computer.

The way in which a computer system manages main storage and disk storage is called the computer's **storage management** and is basic to the capabilities of the

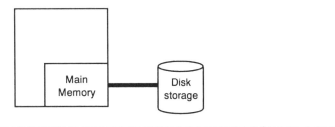

**Figure 1.22.** AS/400 main storage and fixed disk storage.

computer. Understanding the basics of this storage management provides insight into one of the unique features of AS/400 computers as compared with traditional computer systems. Figure 1.22 shows conceptually what the storage in AS/400 computers looks like. The main storage is contained inside the computer's System Unit. The disk storage may be either inside the System Unit or inside a separate box cabled to the System Unit (as shown here).

When the AS/400 computer is first turned on, information vital to an orderly startup and smooth operation is automatically copied from the disk to the main storage. Once normal system operation is established, users can begin to do their work. During the course of this work, users will start various computer programs. As each program is started, it is copied from the disk to main storage and then executed. Depending on the work being done by the user, the computer programs manipulate various sets of data that are also loaded from the disk as needed. It does not take long to realize that the main storage in a computer can quickly become filled up with programs and data as the system is called upon to do more and more work. In earlier days of computing, the main storage size limited the amount of work a computer could manage at any one time. This limitation capped the size of programs, the number of programs that could be run concurrently, the number of users that could share the system, and so on. In today's environment, a technique called **virtual storage** alleviates the need to squeeze all active programs and data into main storage. In computers that support virtual storage, the computer basically "fakes out" the computer programs and users and appears to have much more main storage than it actually has. The virtual storage supported by AS/400 systems is a whopping 281 terabytes (TB) in size (over 281 trillion unique addresses). This 281 TB of addressing capability is enough to keep track of the information contained on over 140 trillion pages of single-spaced computer output—a stack of paper over 13 million miles high that can stretch between the earth and the moon 50 times. Virtual storage therefore allows more programs, data, and users to be simultaneously active on the system than could be supported in real main storage without virtual storage.

Virtual storage works as follows. A user tells the computer to start a word-processing program. The computer first attempts to load the needed portion of the word-processing program into main storage. If there is no space left in main storage, some space is made available by overwriting an inactive portion of some program or by "swapping" out some inactive data to a temporary space on the disk. The needed portion of the word-processing program can then be loaded in the available space and the user can then begin typing the memo. If the program that was overwritten or the data that were "swapped" out are again needed, they are reloaded from a disk unit to some other available main storage area. Therefore, a virtual storage computer system is constantly swapping programs and information between main storage and disk storage, robbing Peter to pay Paul and vice versa. Virtual storage allows the maximum size program or combination of all programs and data to be limited only by the combined amount of storage and disk storage space rather than by the amount of storage alone. The advantage of virtual storage is that neither the programmer nor the user of any AS/400 system needs to be concerned with main storage size. To them, the system seems to have as much main storage as they need, and they are never made aware that information is constantly being swapped from main storage to disk storage and back again. The computer system manages this "swapping" automatically.

Although virtual storage is a powerful system feature, the "swapping" between disk and main storage is processing overhead that can reduce the overall system performance. A little swapping does not appreciably hurt performance; however, increased swapping does reduce system performance. When the swapping performed by a virtual storage system becomes excessive, the system is said to be **thrashing** or spending too much time swapping information between disk and main storage. Thrashing can be reduced by increasing the amount of main storage in the AS/400 system through the installation of main storage expansion options, described in Chapter 2. Increasing the main storage in the system provides more room for programs and data, reducing the amount of virtual storage swapping. Thrashing can also be reduced through system management means such as rescheduling work for off-peak periods.

The virtual storage concept is implemented in many of today's computer systems to one degree or another. AS/400 systems implement their virtual storage scheme through a concept called **single-level storage**. This term simply means that in AS/400 systems, no distinction is made between disk storage and main storage. All storage appears to be one homogeneous sea of main storage accessed in exactly the same way. This consistency provides for a simple and efficient virtual storage implementation that is the same for programs, data, temporary holding areas, and so forth. Other virtual storage implementations must create and manage separate address spaces and often treat programs differently from data, for example. The simplicity of single-level storage results in a consistent and more complete virtual storage system than most other implementations.

Another difference between AS/400 storage management and that of conventional computer systems is its **object-oriented access**. With this concept, all programs, databases, documents, and so on stored in AS/400 computers are stored as independent entities called **objects**. The AS/400's object-oriented access again provides the user and the programmer with a simple and consistent way of managing all programs and information in the system. Users can access an object by simply referring to its name. The AS/400 security system will check to make sure that the user has authorization to use the object and that it is being used properly. This is called **capability-based addressing**. The AS/400 system manages the complexities associated with the physical location and addressing of the information. AS/400's implementation of single-level storage and capability-based addressing spreads information through various disk units in a way that optimizes storage efficiency. Objects provide consistency in the areas of security, usage, and systems management for all items stored on AS/400 systems.

Objects can be organized into groups called **libraries**. A library (which is also an object) is analogous to a drawer in a file cabinet (or a subdirectory, for those familiar with PS/2 disk management). A library might contain all programs related to the accounting function of a business to keep things organized. Because access to libraries can be restricted by the AS/400 security system, a payroll database, for example, might be kept in a library separate from other business information for security reasons.

## Auxiliary Storage

**Auxiliary storage**, commonly used in all computers, is a relatively inexpensive way to store computer data and programs. The information kept on auxiliary storage can be easily modified or kept unchanged over long periods of time as an archive. Because all auxiliary storage is nonvolatile, the information stored remains intact whether the computer is turned on or off. The AS/400 systems use three types of auxiliary storage: **diskette**, **disk**, and **tape**.

### *Diskette Storage*

Diskettes are a portable magnetic storage medium that can be used to record and later retrieve computer information via a **diskette unit**. The diskettes consist of a flexible disk with a magnetic surface permanently enclosed in a square, protective outer jacket as shown in Figure 1.23. The diskettes are manually inserted into a diskette unit that spins the circular disk inside the jacket. The **read/write head** inside the diskette unit makes contact with the spinning disk much as a record

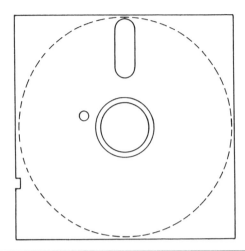

**Figure 1.23.** Diskette used with Application Systems.

player's needle contacts a record. As the disk spins, the head magnetically reads and writes information on the disk's surface.

All 9404 and 9406 AS/400 systems can be configured with diskette units that allow them to use diskettes either 5.25 inches or 8 inches in diameter (or both). Either type of diskette can hold up to 1.2 MB (million bytes) of information. While the AS/Entry and AS/400 9402 systems support a 5.25-inch diskette drive option, IBM does not offer an 8-inch diskette drive option for these systems.

One of the primary functions of diskettes is to provide portable storage, allowing for the transfer of programs and data between computers. To this end, all similarly configured AS/400 computer systems can freely exchange programs and data via diskettes. Also, information on System/3X diskettes can be freely exchanged with a properly configured AS/400 computer. Chapter 2 looks at specific diskette units that can be used with AS/400 systems.

## Disk Storage

Earlier in the chapter we introduced another kind of auxiliary storage used with AS/400 systems called **disk units** or **direct access storage devices (DASDs)**. These are high-capacity magnetic storage devices commonly used in all types of computers from PS/2s to large mainframe computer systems. The basic anatomy of a disk unit is shown in Figure 1.24. Disks consist of a drive mechanism with permanently installed metallic disks often called **platters** (because they are shaped like a dinner plate). These platters have a magnetic surface that can store information. A single disk unit usually has multiple platters to store more information. The platters con-

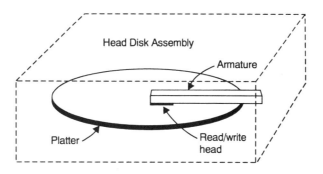

**Figure 1.24.** The anatomy of a disk unit.

stantly spin at very high speeds while the built-in read/write head(s) record or recall information on the disk's surface. The arm that positions the read/write head is called the **actuator**.

Unlike diskettes, the read/write heads in disk units never actually touch the platter's magnetic surface but are positioned extremely close to that surface. Together, the read/write heads and the platters form a **head disk assembly**. The primary function of disk storage is to hold information that must be readily available to the computer system. It contains programs and data and provides a temporary holding area used by Application Systems.

All Application Systems can accommodate many different disk unit configurations. The AS/Entry 9402 Model Y10 comes standard with 160 MB of disk storage contained in the System Unit. The largest AS/Entry can contain up to 760 MB by installing additional disk units. The AS/400 9402 and 9404 System Units come with 988 MB of disk storage, also residing within the System Unit. Additional disk storage can be added to these systems to provide from 1976 MB to 3952 MB in AS/400 9402 systems and from 11,856 to 15,808 MB for 9404 models (depending on the model).

The 9406 System Units now come standard with 1.97 GB of disk storage built into the processor. Expansion beyond the 1.97 GB of standard disk storage is done by installing internal or external disk units (e.g., the 9337 discussed in Chapter 2). Model 9406 disk storage can be as large as 165.2 GB.

Disk unit performance is important to the overall performance of a computer system in most applications. This is particularly true in virtual storage and/or multi-user environments in which there is heavy transfer of information between disk storage and main storage. The performance of a disk unit refers to the rate at which information can be located and transferred between the disk unit and the main storage. The speed at which a disk unit can position the read/write head over the proper region of the platter is the **average seek time**, usually expressed in milliseconds (1/1000 of a second). After the read/write head is properly positioned, the system must wait as the platter spins until the needed data begin to pass under the read/write head. The average time it takes for the platter to rotate to the proper position is called the **average latency** (also expressed in milliseconds). Finally, once the read/write head is positioned and the data begin to pass by on the spinning platter, the information is transferred from the disk unit to the computer system. The speed at which this is done is called the **data transfer rate** and is usually expressed in millions of bytes per second (MB/second). The shorter the average seek time and the average latency, and the higher the transfer rate, the better the performance of the disk storage subsystem and the overall computer system. Figure 1.25 shows the average seek times, average latency, and data transfer rates for the internal disk units that are provided as standard equipment on Application Systems.

In addition to the disk unit specifications, there are other performance considerations when configuring the disk storage subsystem of an AS/400 system. Some disk units have multiple actuators, whereas others only have one. Because each actuator in a disk unit can often perform independently of the other(s), the more actuators you have for a given amount of disk storage, the better the performance. In fact, choosing disk storage configurations that have more actuators for a given amount of storage can result in higher performance than selecting disk units with faster specifications but fewer actuators. This is particularly true with AS/400 systems because single-level storage tends to spread information over many areas of the disk units. This spreading of information produces more efficient operation because the actuators can all share the load, but it does emphasize the need to follow proper backup procedures as discussed in Chapter 7.

Each disk unit attaches to the computer through control circuitry contained within the System Unit. This might be the **multi-function input/output (I/O) pro-**

Standard Disk Configuration/Specifications

| Computer System | Standard Configuration | Fixed Disk Devices Used | Average Seek Time | Data Transfer Rate | Latency | Number of Actuators |
|---|---|---|---|---|---|---|
| AS/Entry Y10 | 160 MB | One 160 MB Disk Unit | 12.5 ms | 2 MB/sec | 7.0 ms | 1/drive |
| AS/400 F02–F25 | 988 MB | One 3.5-inch 988 MB Disk Unit | 11.0 ms | 3 MB/sec | 7.0 ms | 1/drive |
| AS/400 F35–F95 | 1.97 GB | Two 3.5-inch 988 MB Disk Units | 9.8 ms | 3 MB/sec | 7.0 ms | 1/drive |

**Figure 1.25.** Internal fixed disk devices provided as standard in AS/400 systems.

**cessor** provided with the systems or an **optional controller card** like the Direct Access Storage Device Controller. A multi-function I/O processor is capable of handling the standard disk storage and can also support tape units and communications lines. The optional controller cards provide the circuitry to attach disk storage beyond that provided as standard with AS/400 systems. Chapter 2 looks more closely at the specific disk storage options and optional controllers used with the various Application Systems.

## Tape Storage

The last type of auxiliary storage to be covered is **magnetic tape** or simply "tape." One primary purpose of tape is to provide a backup storage medium for information on the computer's disk storage. The low cost and high recording densities inherent in tape also make it ideal for archiving information. Tape is also very useful in distributing programs and transferring information from one computer system to another. Diskettes can be used for these same functions, but the higher storage capacity of tapes is preferred if you are dealing with a large amount of information. Tape consists of a long flexible strip coated with magnetic material and rolled on a reel or into a cartridge. A **tape unit** reads and writes information on the tape much as a cassette recorder records and plays music on audio cassette tapes. In either case, the tape unit runs the tape across the read/write head, which is in contact with the tape surface. Electrical impulses in the read/write head are used to transfer information to and from the tape surface. However, the recording quality is much higher and the format employed is very different in tape units designed for use with computers as compared to those of audio cassette recorders. Chapter 2 explores some of the tape units used with Application Systems.

## Packaging Technology

The circuitry in AS/400 systems was built using IBM's version of **very large-scale integration (VLSI)** technology called **Complementary Metal Oxide Semiconductor (CMOS)**. This is a packaging technology that builds circuits with 0.8-micrometer-sized elements that allow up to 440,000 high-speed transistors to reside in a single chip. The main storage is implemented using both IBM's 4-Mb (4-million-bit) memory chips and the new 16-Mb (16-million-bit) memory chip technology. The use of these chips allows for large main storage configurations in a small physical space while also improving the reliability of the main storage subsystem.

There are two basic mechanical designs used in AS/400 computers. The 9402/9404 systems use a box design similar to that of the smaller System/36 computers. This box, called a **tower**, contains the system processor, storage, tape, disk units, and diskette devices. All circuitry is packaged on 9×11-inch cards that are plugged into an internal card chassis (called a **cage**), allowing for electrical connections to the bus. The design is very modular, and the various elements can be easily added or replaced without the need for IBM service personnel. There is a distributed power system contained in the 9404 box that supplies 24 V to all system components, which then adjust the voltage level as necessary to accommodate their needs. This distributed power approach differs from the distribution schemes used in most computers, in which the various voltages are distributed at the voltage levels needed. The distributed power approach used in the 9402/9404 provides for better voltage regulation and flexibility in 9402/9404 component design.

The mechanical design of the AS/400 9406 computer systems has taken a somewhat different approach from that of the 9402/9404 systems. All components of an AS/400 computer are installed in one or more 1.6-meter-high rack(s). The rack itself is an integral part of the AS/400 computer system — providing power, power controls, operator controls, noise reduction, and so forth. As with the AS/400 9406 "F" models, the **System Power Control Network (SPCN)**, replaces the simple 24-volt signal and mechanical relay control system of earlier AS/400 9406 systems with an intelligent, dedicated digital communications network. A group of specially programmed microprocessors installed at various positions in the AS/400 racks forms the heart of the SPCN. These microprocessors send and receive messages that control system power on/off and battery backup operations, and that monitor selected system elements for power faults.

As computing needs grow, the rack design of 9406 systems allows for simple modular expansion by upgrading the processor, adding more components, or adding additional racks. A new **fiber optic I/O bus** design allows the larger 9406 systems to add additional I/O busses to AS/400 system, which allows the system to accommodate more I/O devices without loading down existing I/O busses. The fiber optic cable that attaches these additional I/O busses (i.e., System Unit expansion features) uses laser light rather than electrical signals to exchange information with the rest of the AS/400 system. Using light allows the additional I/O busses to operate at full speed over greater distances and eliminates the electrical interference inherent in electrical cables carrying high-speed signals. With these optical cables, the various racks of an AS/400 system can be located up to 100 meters apart rather than within the 12-foot limit imposed by earlier electrical I/O bus cables. Furthermore, optical cable configurations are available that will allow inter-rack distances of up to 2 kilometers in some situations.

In discussing mechanical design, the **cable-thru** feature of all Application Systems carried over from the System/3X products should be mentioned. Cable-thru

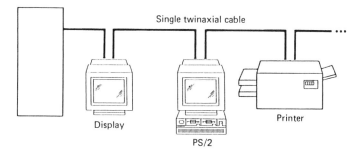

**Figure 1.26.** All Application Systems use the "cable-thru" approach to attaching local workstations.

allows multiple displays or printers to be attached together in a **daisy-chain** fashion as shown in Figure 1.26. Rather than running a separate cable from the computer to each workstation, cable-thru allows a single cable from the computer to attach up to seven workstations over a distance of up to 5000 feet.

# Options and Peripherals

Application Systems are likely to be found in many diverse environments — from fish markets to insurance companies. The activities performed by people in these environments vary widely, and so do their computing needs. Application Systems can be customized to many environments by selecting the appropriate optional equipment. This includes **feature cards** and **peripherals**. Feature cards are circuit boards containing electronics that provide some additional capacity or function(s) to Application Systems. They can be installed in one of the I/O expansion slots provided in all Application System computers. Peripherals are devices that attach to Application System computers, usually via a cable, and perform functions under the computer's control. In this chapter we cover:

- Workstations
- Main storage expansion options
- Auxiliary storage options
- Communications options
- Other options

Although this chapter does not provide comprehensive coverage of all the optional equipment that can be used with Application Systems, it does introduce the reader to many devices that are representative of those most commonly used in the business environment.

## WORKSTATIONS

The devices used to interact with Application Systems are known as **workstations**, which can be either **terminals** or **printers**. A computer terminal is the "TV-like" device that converts the computer's electrical signals into light images that convey information to the user. Terminals also come equipped with a keyboard that allows the user to send information back to the computer. Printers are electromechanical devices that print the computer's electronically encoded information onto paper. If a workstation is near the computer system — for example, in the same building — it can be **locally** attached to the computer system via a cable. If the workstation is not near the computer — for example, in another state — it can be **remotely** attached over communications lines. Either way, the function provided to the workstation user is the same. Some type of workstation is required to allow the user to interact with the Application Systems.

Many types of workstations can be used with Application Systems. In this chapter, we look at the following:

- InfoWindow II 3486/87 Display Station
- InfoWindow II 3488 Modular Display Station
- PS/2 terminal emulation
- 4230 Printer
- 4224 Printer
- 4234 Printer
- 6252 Printer
- 6262 Printer
- 4028 Laser Printer
- 3816 Page Printer
- 3825 Page Printer
- 3835 Page Printer
- 3827 Page Printer

We also take a brief look at the workstation controllers that allow the attachment of workstations to Application Systems. While there are many other terminals and printers that can be used with AS/400 systems, this list provides the reader with a representative sample. A list of some other workstations that were tested with AS/400 computers is provided in Appendix A, "Peripheral Compatibility Guide." Further, because the AS/400 workstation interfaces are compatible with those of System/3X, other workstations not covered or listed in the appendix may also work with AS/400 computers.

## InfoWindow II 3486/87 Display Station

The 3486 and 3487 Display Stations (Figure 2.1) are members of the InfoWindow II family of text-only display stations (also called *terminals*) for use with the Application Systems. The 3486 is the entry member of the InfoWindow II family of dis-

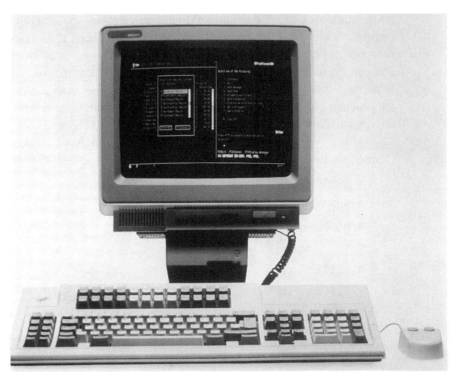

|  | Model 3486 | Model 3487 |
|---|---|---|
| Display: | 14" Monochrome | 15" Monochrome<br>14" Color |
| Features: | Tilt/swivel<br>printer port | Tilt/swivel<br>printer port |

**Figure 2.1.** InfoWindow II 3486/3487 Display Station.

plays. It is compatible with the earlier 3476 and 3196 displays while providing some additional features. First, the 3486 supports an Enhanced User Interface which employs a mouse and special graphical characters (e.g., scroll bars, radio buttons, push-buttons, check boxes, and continuous window frames) to ease the user's interaction with application programs. This enables AS/400 applications (specially written or used in conjunction with the IBM WindowTool™/400 product [5798-RYF]) to provide pop-up menus and help screens popular with Personal Computer users. Also provided by the 3486 is support for two display sessions and one printer, split screen viewing of new 32×8 and 49×8 screen formats, and a built-in calculator. Like all InfoWindow II displays, the image presented on the 3486 display screen has been improved (new character fonts, reduced flicker, etc.) to comply with emerging display-quality standards (ISO 9241 part 3). Finally, the 3486 can support a PS/2-type printer (for example, an IBM Personal Printer Series II), which can be cabled directly to a port provided on the rear of the 3486. This printer can be used as a system printer, just like other printers attached to the Application System, or it can be used to print an image of whatever is on the 3486's screen. Printers supported now include laser printers like the IBM 4019 and 4029 or the Hewlett-Packard LaserJet™ III. The 3486 displays are monochrome only and have 14-inch display screens.

The displays can be either green-on-black (BG models) or amber/gold-on-black (BA models). Which you choose is purely a matter of individual taste. Either version can display 24 lines of text 80 characters in length while still leaving a row at the bottom to display status messages. The display comes with a tilt/swivel base to allow a comfortable viewing angle. The Record/Play Mode feature of the 3486 displays includes the ability to store up to 1500 often-used keystroke sequences that are recalled by pressing a single command key. The display can be set up to go blank after a specified time of keyboard inactivity to protect the display's **phosphors**. The phosphors in a workstation, much like those used in a television, are deposited on the inside surface of the display and glow, when excited by electronic signals generated by the display station, to create an image. When a display station is left on but unattended, an image can be permanently "burned" into the phosphors. The blanking feature prevents this. A blanked image is automatically restored when any key is pressed. This feature can be adjusted through operator setup functions, as can the alarm volume, keyboard clicker volume, cursor shape, and other items. The provided key-lock disables the keyboard and display, helping to prevent unauthorized entering or viewing of information.

You also have the choice of either a 102-key keyboard (IBM Enhanced Keyboard) like those used with Personal System/2 computers or a 122-key typewriter keyboard. Either keyboard has an adjustable slope (6- or 12-degree tilt). The primary difference in keyboards is that the 122-key keyboard has more programmable function keys.

The InfoWindow II 3487 Display Stations are compatible with the older InfoWindow 3477 and 3179 display stations. They are functionally the same as the 3486 Display Stations described above but offer larger display screens on all models and a color display on one model:

- 14-inch color display (HC models)
- 15-inch green-on-black display (HG models)
- 15-inch amber/gold-on-black display (HA models)

Color can be used to effectively highlight and associate information on a display, making the information more clear. While some highlighting capability is provided on most monochrome displays, color provides additional flexibility in this area while providing a more pleasing image. The 15-inch display offers larger characters, which is especially helpful when operating the 3487 in its "27 lines of 132 characters" mode. The image presented on the display screen of all InfoWindow II displays has been improved (new character fonts, reduced flicker, etc.) to comply with emerging display-quality standards (ISO 9241 part 3).

Finally, an optional bar code/magnetic badge reader (i.e., the 7695 Model 250)

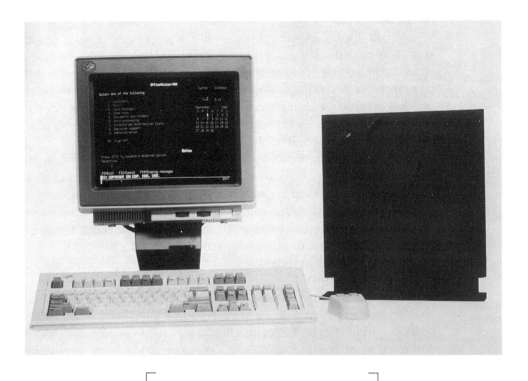

Display type:     Personal computer display
                  (user selected)

Features:         Separate Display Logic Module

**Figure 2.2.** InfoWindow II 3488 Modular Display Station. Separate Display Logic Module can be seen on the right.

can be attached to the 3487 to allow data entry through bar codes or magnetic badges in addition to normal keyboard entry.

## InfoWindow II 3488 Modular Display Station

The InfoWindow II 3488 Modular Display Station (Figure 2.2) embodies a new modular design which allows the user to attach a Personal System/2 display (any VGA or VGA-compatible display) to the 3488 Display Logic Module. That is, the user has the flexibility to customize the display station to suit his or her needs by selecting from any PS/2-type monitor. As user needs change, the monitor can be upgraded. Conversely, if the user moves up to a Personal Computer workstation, he or she can retain the monitor and use it with the Personal Computer. Functionally, the 3488 provides the same functions as the 3486/3487 Display Stations discussed above.

## PS/2 Terminal Emulation

With the proper feature card and software (e.g., PC Support), a Personal System/2 (PS/2) (Figure 2.3) or a Personal Computer can also be used as a terminal for Application Systems. In this case, the PS/2 is said to be "acting like" or **emulating** a terminal. In the simplest case, the PS/2 appears to the Application Systems as any other terminal with no special capabilities. The user can then interact with the Application Systems just as with any other terminal discussed so far. Further, a printer attached to the PS/2 can be used both as a printer for PS/2 application programs and as a system printer for the AS/400 application programs. Hitting a simple keystroke combination temporarily suspends terminal emulation and the PS/2 is changed back into a normal PS/2 able to run the many PS/2 programs available today.

Since the PS/2 is a computer, not just a terminal, it has its own **intelligence**. It is therefore called an **intelligent workstation**. This intelligence can be used to run PS/2 programs independent of the Application Systems or it can be used to work with the Application Systems. This "intelligence" provides for the direct interaction between PS/2 programs and those running on Application Systems. This type of interaction can be done without user intervention to perform functions ranging from simply transferring a file between the PS/2 and the Application Systems to more complex program-to-program communications (i.e., cooperative processing). You can also concurrently interact with multiple Application Systems with a single PS/2 or sign on to a single system as more than one terminal. Chapter 6 further discusses interaction between PS/2s and Application Systems. For more information about PS/2, refer to *IBM Personal Systems: A Business Perspective* (IBM document #G325-0400) (John Wiley & Sons).

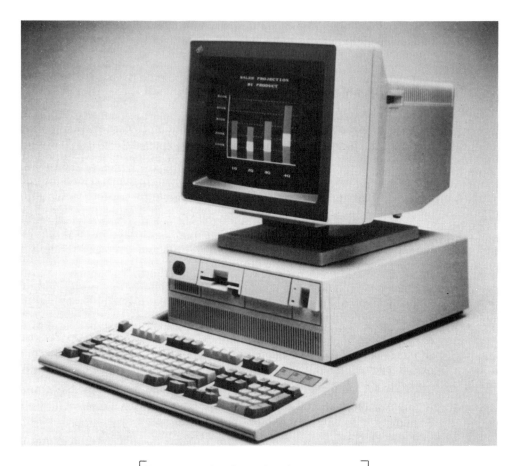

| Type: | Color/text and graphics |
| --- | --- |
| Features: | Local intelligence, advanced graphics |
| Options: | Various models, connection type |

**Figure 2.3.** Properly configured PS/2s can be used as workstations for Application Systems.

## 4230 Printer

The 4230 Printer is shown in Figure 2.4. This tabletop printer can produce data-processing-quality documents (in Fast Draft mode) at a speed of 375 to 480 characters per second (cps) depending on the model. In Data-Processing (DP mode), Data-Processing text (DP text) or near-letter-quality modes, the clarity of the documents produced is improved at the cost of reduced printing speed.

| | |
|---|---|
| Type: | Near-letter-quality |
| Technology: | Dot-matrix (9-wire head) |
| Printing Speed:<br>(pitch of 10) | 375/480 cps (Fast Draft mode)<br>300/400 cps (DP mode)<br>150/200 cps (DP text mode)<br>  75/100 cps (Near-letter quality mode) |
| APA resolution: | 1.44 x 1.44 |
| Print line: | 335 mm (13.2") |

**Figure 2.4.** 4230 Printer.

There are four different 4230 versions, all of which are highly compatible with IBM's 4214, 3268, 3287, and 4224 printers. The 4230 prints more quietly (58 dBA) than these other printers, making for less noise in the office. Model 101 has a maximum speed of 375 cps (Fast Draft mode) and provides a print buffer 32 KB in size. The print buffer acts as a temporary storage area, improving the efficiency of information flow between the printer and the computer system. The 4230 Model 1I1 also prints up to 375 cps in Fast Draft mode. However, the Model 1I1 supports the **Intelligent Printer Data Stream (IPDS)** allowing it to print more advanced images like bar codes and graphics. It also comes with 128 KB of memory, expandable by adding the 512 KB Extended Memory Feature. The 4230 Model 1S2 is a faster version of the 4230 Model 101. The Model 1S2 can print up to 480 cps, comes with 32 KB of memory, and does not support IPDS. Similarly, the Model 102 is a faster version of the Model 1I1, printing at up to 480 cps and supporting IPDS printing. The Model 102 comes with a 128 KB print buffer which can be expanded by installing the 512 KB Extended Memory Feature. All 4230 printers can be upgraded to the next more powerful 4230 Model.

The 4230 printers are based on the dot-matrix printing technique. With this technique, the image is created by causing a series of small pins (nine on the 4230) contained in the print head to strike a ribbon which in turn strikes the paper. By selecting the proper pins, a fine dot pattern is generated. As with the dot pattern illuminated on a TV set or computer's display, the human eye naturally blends these printed dots to form the desired image. The 4230 can operate in alphanumeric mode or **all-points-addressable (APA)** mode. These two modes refer to the method used to generate the image. In alphanumeric mode, the printer can generate any alphanumeric (letter or number) character and some special symbols from a predefined library called the *character set*. In APA mode, virtually any combination of dots can be generated, allowing complex images to be generated.

A Dual Purpose paper module provides a tractor feed that will move continuous forms through the printer. These continuous forms can be blank paper, preprinted forms, or multi-part forms (with up to six parts). Due to variations in multi-part forms, however, your specific forms should be tested before you purchase the printer.

This is especially true for five- and six-part forms. The Dual Purpose paper module also supports the **Document on Demand** function, allowing you to tear off a form just printed without having to wait for the next form to be printed or having to eject a blank form, creating waste. With Document on Demand, the user can temporarily eject some blank forms, tear off the one needed, and then roll the remaining forms back into printing position with a few keystrokes. Another option automatically feeds individual sheets of paper from a stack (cut sheets) into the printer.

## 4224 Printer

The 4224 printer is shown in Figure 2.5. This tabletop printer can produce data-processing-quality (DP mode) documents at a speed of 200 to 600 characters per second (cps), depending on the model. When the printer is operating in "Data-Processing text (DP text)" or "near-letter-quality" modes, the clarity of the documents produced is improved at the cost of reduced printing speed. Model 101 has a maximum speed of 200 cps (DP mode) and provides a print buffer 64 KB in size.

The print buffer acts as a temporary storage area, improving the efficiency of information flow between the printer and the computer system. Models 102, 1E2, and 1C2 all produce DP mode documents at a rate of up to 400 cps. Models 1E2 and

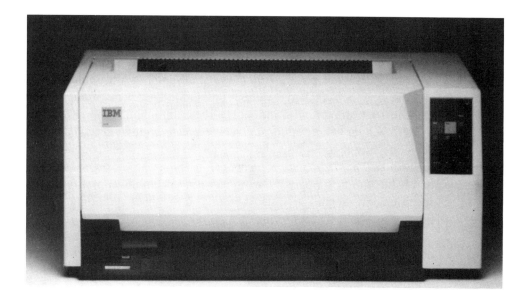

| Type: | Near-letter-quality |
|---|---|
| Technology: | Dot-matrix (9- or 18-wire head) |
| Printing Speed: (pitch of 10) | 200/600 cps (Data-processing mode) 100/300 cps (Data-processing text mode) 50/150 cps (Near-letter-quality mode) |
| APA Resolution: | 144 x 144 PELS per square inch |
| Print Line: | 335 mm (13.2'') |

**Figure 2.5.** 4224 Printer.

1C2 increase the print buffer size to 512 KB, which is recommended if you will be using the Business Graphics Utility (BGU) or GDDM graphics programs (discussed in Chapter 4). Model 1C2 also has the capability of printing four to eight different colors, depending on the ribbon used. Model 102 can be upgraded to a Model 1E2 at any time, but for BGU and GDDM, IBM recommends initially purchasing Model 1E2. Finally, the Model 1E3 is the fastest 4224, printing at up to 600 cps.

The 4224 supports IBM's intelligent printer data stream (IPDS) protocol, which provides for advanced printing functions such as the generation of bar code labels and optical character recognition (OCR)–type characters. The 4224 can also be configured as an **Advanced Function Printer (AFP)**. AFP is a printer "language" that allows application programs to control the merging of form templates, image, graphics, and text onto a single page (more on AFP in Chapter 5).

Like the Model 4230, the 4224 is based on the dot-matrix printing technique and can operate in alphanumeric mode or all-points-addressable (APA) mode. There are several options (called *features*) for handling paper in different ways, and at least one must be ordered with the 4224. These options can be easily changed by the printer operator to accommodate the immediate printing need. The continuous forms device feature (#4001) provides a tractor feed that moves continuous forms through the printer. These continuous forms can be blank paper, preprinted forms, or multi-part forms (up to six parts). Owing to variations in multi-part forms, however, your specific forms should be tested before you purchase the printer. This is especially true for five- and six-part forms.

The document on demand feature (#4002) allows you to tear off a form just printed without having to wait for the next form to be printed or having to eject a blank form, creating waste. With this feature, the user can temporarily eject some blank forms, tear off the one needed, and then roll the remaining forms back into printing position with a few keystrokes. The document on demand feature is not available for the 4224 Model 1C2.

The document insertion device feature (#4003) allows the user to insert individual sheets of paper or forms. It is not available for the 4224 Model 1C2.

## 4234 Printer

Figure 2.6 shows the 4234 printer. This printer is called a **line printer** because it prints an entire line of text at one time rather than one character at a time as does the 4224 printer just discussed. This line-at-a-time printing makes the 4234 faster than the fastest 4224. The 4234 is designed to stand on the floor. There are two models designed to attach to the twinaxial cable typically used with AS/400 systems: Model 8 and Model 12. The 4234 Model 8 can print draft-quality documents at a speed of up to 475 lines per minute (lpm), while the Model 12 can print up to 800 lpm (not to be confused with characters per second). In either near-letter-quality or data-processing-quality modes, the clarity of the document produced is improved at the cost of reduced printing speed.

The 4234 uses a **band-matrix** printing technique. This is similar to the dot-matrix printing technique in that the image is created by causing a series of small dots to impact a ribbon, which in turn strikes the paper. With the band-matrix technique, however, images can be printed more quickly because multiple characters (i.e., a line) are being printed simultaneously.

As with the 4230 and 4224, the 4234 can operate in alphanumeric or APA

| Type: | Near–letter–quality |
|---|---|
| Technology: | Dot-band matrix |
| Printing Speed:<br>(pitch of 10) | 800 lpm (Draft mode)<br>600 lpm (DP mode)<br>200 lpm (Near-letter-quality mode) |
| APA Resolution: | Variable depending on band |
| Print Line: | 335 mm (13.2″) |

**Figure 2.6.** 4234 Printer.

mode. In alphanumeric mode, the printer can generate any alphanumeric character and a number of special symbols from a predefined character set. In APA mode, complex images can be generated by allowing virtually any combination of dots to be generated. The user can install various print bands that provide different dot sizes, thus different print resolution. The 4234 can also be configured as a Advanced Function Printer (AFP). AFP is a printer "language" that allows application programs to control the merging of form templates, images, graphics, and text onto a single page.

## 6252 Impactwriter

The 6252 can produce 800 to 1200 lines per minute using the **print-band** printing technique. With this technique, a metal band engraved with the character set spins at high speeds within the printer. As the needed character on the spinning print band aligns with the correct spot on the paper, an impression is made. The 6252 Model T08 attaches to Application Systems twinaxial workstation controller while the

Type:
Tec

| Type: | Letter quality |
| --- | --- |
| Technology: | Print Band |
| Printing Speed: | 1,200, 1,400, or 2,200 lpm |
| APA Resolution: | Not supported |

**Figure 2.7.** 6262 Printer.

Model A08 can be attached to an ASCII Workstation Controller. Both of these 6252 models can print up to 800 lines per minute. The 6252 Models T12 and A12 are faster versions, printing up to 1200 lines per minute.

## 6262 Printer

The 6262 printer is shown in Figure 2.7. The 6262 is a floor-standing, letter-quality printer based on the same print-band technique used by the 6252. There are three models of the 6262 available for Application Systems: Models T12, T14, and T22. They are the same except that the Model T12 prints up to 1200 lpm, the Model T14 can print up to 1400 lpm, and the Model T22 can print up to 2200 lpm. Model T12 can be field upgraded to a Model T14 at any time, but you cannot upgrade from either a T12 or T14 to a T22. All of these models attach via twinaxial cable and use the standard 120-V electrical power readily available. There are corresponding "A" models of the 6262 which can be attached to an ASCII Workstation Controller in an AS/400 system.

Enhancements in the 6262 as compared to the older IBM 4545 print-band printer include easier-to-use forms setup procedures, improved reliability, and quieter operation (58 dB). An 80-character display presents messages to the operator. Up to 6-part forms can be printed using the 6262. Option features of the 6262 allow the printer to generate industry-standard bar codes.

## 4028 Laser Printer

The IBM 4028 Laser Printer is a tabletop letter-quality printer (Figure 2.8). The printers discussed in this chapter so far print documents one character or one line at a time. The 4028 Laser Printer produces a whole page at a time. It prints on individual sheets of paper called **cut sheets**, not continuous forms as do the other printers discussed so far. The 4029 Laser Printer Model 001 can produce up to ten pages per minute and is designed to handle a load of up to 1,000 pages per day or 20,000 pages per month.

The 4028 Laser Printer uses the **laser/electrophotographic (EP)** process to print an entire page at a time. This technique uses the laser to produce a charged image on a drum inside the printer. Ink (toner) is attracted to the charged portions of the drum and then transferred to the paper as with a copy machine. The print cartridges containing the toner can typically print about 10,000 to 15,000 pages before they need to be replaced. This EP printing technique makes for the highest quality of printing of any printer covered so far.

The 4028 comes standard with a 200-sheet autofeeder as well as a 250-sheet

| | |
|---|---|
| Type: | Letter-quality |
| Technology: | Laser/EP |
| Printing Speed: (any pitch) | 10 impressions/minute (max) |
| APA resolution: | 300 x 300 PELs |
| Recommended usage: | 1000 pages/day or 20,000 pages/month |

**Figure 2.8.** 4028 Laser Printer.

output tray with a sensor to automatically stop the printing when the output tray is full. A 500-sheet input tray and optional envelope feeder (75-envelope capacity) are offered as options.

There are 32 internal fonts provided with the 4028 Laser Printer and more can be downloaded from the AS/400 with the appropriate 4028 memory and AS/400 software. The 4028 Laser Printer supports IBM's intelligent printer data stream (IPDS) protocol, which provides for advanced printing functions such as the generation of bar code labels and optical character recognition (OCR)–type characters.

## 3816 Page Printer

The IBM 3816 Page Printer, shown in Figure 2.9, is a member of IBM's 3820 series of printers. The 3816 Page Printer, as the name implies, produces a whole page at a time. It prints on individual sheets of paper or cut sheets (not continuous forms) and can handle a workload of up to 40,000 impressions/month. This tabletop printer uses the laser/electrophotographic (EP) process to print a page.

However, since Laser/EP is a nonimpact technique, it cannot be used to print on multi-part forms that depend on the impact to produce carbon copies.

The 3816 can produce up to 24 letter-quality impressions (i.e., pages) per minute. The High Capacity Paper Input option allows you to load 1200 sheets of paper for high-volume printing environments. As with all the 3820 family of printers, the 3816 is also a computer in its own right, with 3.5 MB of memory, and is therefore called an **intelligent printer**. This intelligence allows the 3816 to support advanced functions such as font selection, rotation, vector graphics, and duplex printing through IBM's **Intelligent Printer Data Stream (IPDS)** and **Advanced Function Printing (AFP)** protocols. There are two 3816 models: Model 01S (prints only on one side of a page) and Model 01D (capable of printing on both sides of a page).

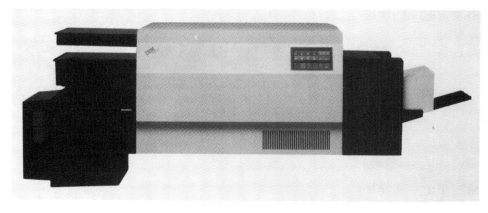

| Type: | Letter-quality |
|---|---|
| Technology: | Laser/EP |
| Printing speed: (any pitch) | 24 impressions/minute (max) |
| APA resolution: | 240 × 240 PELs |
| Recommended usage: | Up to 40,000 impressions/month |

**Figure 2.9.** The IBM 3816 Page Printer produces high-quality text and graphics.

## 3825 Page Printer

The 3825 Page Printer is a member of the 3820 family of printers. This printer also uses the high-quality Laser/EP technique to produce up to 58 impressions (pages) per minute on cut sheets. In terms of usage, the 3825 is built to handle up to one million impressions/month. Like the 3816, the 3825 has the intelligence necessary to support the AFP and IPDS printing protocols. Up to 63 downloaded fonts can be stored per page and orientations of 0°, 90°, 180°, and 270° are supported.

The 3825 has a built-in display with a touch-sensitive screen that allows the operator to manipulate the printer by touching the screen with his finger. On-line help is provided to assist the operator in performing various printer tasks. Paper is loaded into two input trays—a primary tray containing up to 2600 sheets and a secondary tray containing up to 500 sheets. These two input trays can be used to hold two different kinds of paper or they can be loaded with the same paper to facilitate continuous operation during paper reloads. The single-output stacker can hold up to 3150 sheets. The 3825 is floor-standing and requires about 12 square feet of floor space. It can be attached to an AS/400 system via a Token-Ring Network.

## 3835 Page Printer

Like the 3825, the 3835 prints using the Laser/EP process and supports both AFP and IPDS protocols. However, the 3835 prints on fan-fold paper rather than cut sheets. It is designed to print up to 1,300,000 feet of paper/month at a speed of 88 to 91 pages/minute. The 3835 can hold about 4000 fan-fold sheets, which are fed as input paper, and about 3000 fan-fold sheets at the output stacker. It can be attached to an AS/400 system via a Token-Ring Network.

## 3827 Page Printer

The 3827 Page Printer can be thought of as the big brother of the 3825. Like the 3825, the 3827 prints on cut sheets, supports AFP and IPDS protocols, can have up to 63 downloaded fonts per page, and so on. However, the 3827 can produce up to 92 impressions/minute and can handle up to two million impressions/month. To support this higher volume, the two paper input trays can together hold up to 3500 sheets. The single-output stacker can hold about 2500 sheets. The visual display unit and keyboard provided on the printer allow the operator to manipulate the printer as needed. It can be attached to an AS/400 system via a Token-Ring Network.

## Workstation Controllers

To attach any local workstation to an Application System computer system, the proper **workstation controller** must be installed in the computer's System Unit. (Note: remote workstations are attached through communications lines, not through a workstation controller.) The workstation controller acts as an intermediary between the workstation and the Application System processor. By managing the workstation traffic (e.g., keystrokes), the system processor in the Application System computer is free to run user application programs. The result of this multi-processor architecture, as discussed in Chapter 1, is that the AS/400 system is able to do more work in a given amount of time. There are two types of workstation controllers that can be used with AS/400 computers: Twinaxial Workstation Controllers and ASCII Workstation Controllers.

### *Twinaxial Workstation Controllers*

Twinaxial Workstation Controllers are the most commonly used controller. They allow the attachment of the most popular workstations (including all terminals and printers discussed in this book). The controller itself is cabled to a box that provides twinaxial connectors. One end of a twinaxial cable is attached to one of the connectors, called a **port**, on the box. The other end of the cable can be attached to from one to seven local workstations in a daisy-chain fashion over a distance of up to 5000 feet (see Figure 1.26). This daisy-chain feature is called **cable-thru** and greatly simplifies the wiring needed to connect workstations to an AS/400 system. Information moves through the twinaxial cable at over a million bits/second, allowing for fast information flow.

The AS/Entry comes standard with a Twinaxial Workstation Controller that provides 4 ports and can support up to a total of 14 local workstations. Notice that even though each port can support up to 7 workstations and there are 4 ports, a maximum of 14 local workstations cannot be exceeded in the standard configuration. If more than 14 local workstations are needed, the **workstation expansion feature (#2551)** can be installed, upping the total number of local workstations to 28. (Note: The AS/Entry must have the processor expansion [#2602] to support the workstation expansion feature.)

The 9402 Model F02 systems come standard with either Base Twinaxial Support (#9148) or Base ASCII Workstation Support (#9147) — specified at the time the system is ordered. Base Twinaxial Support provides for up to 14 local workstations (any mix of terminals and printers) daisy chained over 2 ports (up to 7 workstations per port). By adding a Twinaxial Workstation Controller (#6050), you can have up to 28 workstations attached to a 9402 F02 — the system maximum.

The 9402 Models F04 and F06 also come standard with either Base Twinaxial Support (#9148) or Base ASCII Support (#9147). However, the Base Twinaxial Support on F04 and F06 systems provides 4 ports and supports a maximum of 28 workstations. By adding another Twinaxial Workstation Controller (#6050), 9402 F04 systems can support up to 68 local workstations. Similarly, three more Twinaxial Workstation Controllers (#6050) can be added to a 9402 F06 providing for up to 108 workstations. One other twinaxial workstation attachment option for 9402 is called the First Workstation Attachment Feature (#6143 for F02 and #6145 for F04/F06 systems). This option provides a System Console (including the keyboard), and a printer port is built right into the AS/400 9402 System Unit. That is, the electronics that make up a simple terminal are built into the System Unit and a keyboard is provided. The user simply attaches a monitor (e.g., an 8504 monochrome display) and the System Console is ready to use. Also, a simple printer (e.g., the IBM Personal Printer Series II) can be attached to support simple printing needs. This approach is designed to lower the overall cost of the system by providing a low-cost System Console.

The AS/400 9404 F10, F20, and F25 systems also come standard with either a Base Twinaxial Support (#9140) or a Base ASCII Support (#9141). The Base Twinaxial Support for the 9404 provides 8 ports that can support a total of 40 workstations (no more than 7 on any one port). By adding four optional Twinaxial Workstation Controllers (#6050), Model F10 systems can support up to 160 twinaxial attached workstations over 32 ports. 9404 Model F20 and F25 systems can have up to 6 Twinaxial Workstation Controllers providing for up to 240 workstations over 48 ports.

In the 9406 system, the Twinaxial Workstation Controller (#6050) is an option. As can that of the 9404 system, this controller can support up to 40 workstations distributed over 8 ports. A 20-foot cable is attached between the controller and an external box that provides the 8 port connectors. This external box is designed to be mounted on the floor, wall, or tabletop. From 9 to 2400 Twinaxial Workstation Controllers can be attached to a single AS/400 9406 system.

## ASCII Workstation Controllers

Although twinaxial workstations are preferred with AS/400 systems, the systems can also support low-cost **American Standard Code for Information Interchange (ASCII)** terminals and printers. ASCII workstations transfer information at a slower rate (maximum of 38,400 bits per second [bps]) than twinaxial workstations (1,000,000 bps). However, the ASCII workstation controller is useful if you already have a significant investment in ASCII terminals and printers, because it allows you to use them with an AS/400 system. There is no ASCII workstation controller for the AS/Entry systems. However, ASCII terminals can be attached to the AS/Entry or any of the Application Systems via the 5208 protocol converter covered later in this chapter.

Base ASCII Workstation Support (#9147) can be selected for inclusion in the standard configuration of any AS/400 9402 system. It is able to support up to 12 workstations (6 terminals and 6 printers) over 6 ASCII ports. Actually, one terminal or one printer is cabled directly to each of the 6 ports — making for 6 devices. To get to the Base ASCII Support's configuration maximum of 12 ASCII devices, you must directly cable 6 ASCII terminals to the 6 ASCII ports and then attach one printer to each terminal, totaling 12 devices. Adding the ASCII Workstation Expansion (#6144) adds 6 more ASCII ports for a total of 12. This allows 12 ASCII devices (any combination of terminals and printers) to be directly attached to the F02 System Unit. While this also allows up to 24 ASCII devices to be attached (12 terminals and 12 printers cabled to the terminals), 18 simultaneously active ASCII devices are the maximum number supported on an F02.

To attach more ASCII workstations to F04 or F06 systems, you can install one or more optional ASCII Workstation Controllers (#6141), each of which will add 6 ASCII ports to the system. For further expansion and more flexibility, you can add an ASCII 12-Port Workstation Attachment (#6142) to each ASCII Workstation Controller. By adding an ASCII 12-Port Workstation Attachment to an ASCII Workstation Controller, you go from 6 ports capable of supporting 6 ASCII terminals and 6 ASCII printers to 18 ports capable of supporting 18 ASCII workstations (any combination of terminals and printers). The Model F04 can have up to 2 ASCII Workstation Controllers, each equipped with an ASCII 12-Port Workstation Attachment, which provides for up to 48 ASCII Workstations. The Model F06 can have up to three ASCII Workstation Controllers, each equipped with an ASCII 12-Port Workstation Attachment, which provides for up to 66 ASCII Workstations.

As with the AS/400 9402 systems, AS/400 9404 systems must include support for either twinaxial or ASCII workstations in their standard configuration. For those who choose ASCII support, an ASCII Workstation Controller (#9141) is included in the standard configuration of an AS/400 9404 system. In this standard ASCII workstation configuration, you can have up to 12 workstations attached to a system (6 terminals and 6 printers) over 6 ports. Again, one terminal or one printer is cabled directly to each of the 6 ports — making for 6 devices. To get to the standard configuration's maximum of 12 ASCII devices, you must directly cable 6 ASCII terminals to the 6 ports and then attach one printer to each terminal, totalling 12 devices. For more ASCII workstation support, additional ASCII Workstation Controllers (#6141) can be installed. Each additional ASCII Workstation Controller provides 6 ports (support for 6 terminals and 6 printers). By adding the ASCII 12-Port Workstation Attachment(s) (#6142) to an ASCII Workstation Controller, you can get 18 ports on a single ASCII Workstation Controller. Since 18 is also the maximum number of workstations that an ASCII Workstation Controller can handle, you get one port for each device and thus the flexibility to attach any combination of terminals and printers.

All 9404 Models support up to 9 ASCII Workstation Controllers (one standard and 8 optional). If each ASCII Workstation Controller is equipped with an ASCII 12-Port Workstation Attachment, you can have 162 ASCII workstations attached to an AS/400 9404 system.

The AS/400 9406 systems also provide a choice between ASCII or twinaxial support in the standard configuration. The ASCII support in 9406 systems is provided by the same ASCII Workstation Controller (#9141/6141) and ASCII 12-Port Workstation Attachment (#6142) used with 9404 systems. Since from 12 to 60 ASCII Workstation Controllers can be installed in a single AS/400 9406, depending on the model, from 216 to 1080 ASCII devices may be attached to a single 9406 system, depending on the model.

## PROTOCOL CONVERTERS

Whether a workstation is attached locally or remotely, it must speak the same "language" or **workstation protocol** as the computer system and its programs. There are three workstation protocols that you should know of (but not necessarily understand): **5250 protocol, 3270 protocol**, and **ASCII protocol**.

The 5250 protocol is the set of rules used by workstations designed specifically for use with Application System computers as well as earlier System/36 and System/38 computers. The 5250 protocol and twinaxial cable can be considered the "native tongue" of IBM's Application Systems. The protocol gets its name from the 5250 family of workstations designed for the System/3X family.

The 3270 protocol is the set of rules used by workstations designed specifically for use with IBM's larger System/390 family of mainframe computers. This protocol gets its name from the 3270 family of workstations designed for the System/390 computers.

Finally, the ASCII protocol is the set of rules used by a wide variety of devices (including terminals and printers) made for the computers of many different computer manufacturers.

If the user wishes to attach a workstation using a workstation protocol different from that being used by the AS/400 computer system, a **protocol converter** is required. This is a standalone device that accepts the information from a workstation using the workstation protocol and converts the information to the desired workstation protocol being used by the computer system. The protocol converter can be thought of as a "translator" that sits between the workstation and the computer. There are many situations in which a user might need a protocol converter (for example, the user has a workstation that uses the 3270 protocol attached to a System/390). With a protocol converter and some other equipment, the user could use these same workstations to access Application Systems. Or a user is switching from a computer that primarily uses an ASCII Workstation to Application Systems. With a protocol converter, the investment in ASCII terminals could be preserved by using them with the Application Systems. However, the ASCII Workstation controller is the preferred way of attaching ASCII devices to AS/400 systems. Let us now look at some protocol converters that can be used with Application Systems.

## 5208 Link Protocol Converter

The 5208 Link Protocol Converter attaches on one side to up to 7 workstations that use the ASCII workstation protocol. The other side of this device is then attached via twinaxial cable to either a local (e.g., Twinaxial Workstation Controller) or remote workstation controller (e.g., 5394, covered later in the chapter) that uses the 5250 workstation protocol. With this configuration, a workstation actually using the ASCII protocol appears to the computer to be a workstation using the 5250 protocol. There are some limitations, however, for workstations attached in this fashion in the areas of BGU and PC support programs. Further, since ASCII devices typically cannot move information as fast as twinaxial workstations, response time may suffer.

## 5209 Link Protocol Converter

The 5209 Link Protocol Converter is shown in Figure 2.10. This device attaches up to 7 workstations that use the 3270 workstation, using coaxial cable, to Application Systems. The other side of this device is then attached to either a local (e.g., Twinaxial Workstation Controller) or remote workstation controller (e.g., 5394) that uses the 5250 workstation protocol via twinaxial cable. With this configuration, a workstation actually using the 3270 protocol appears to the computer to be a workstation using the 5250 protocol. Up to seven 3270 workstations can be attached to the 5209.

## MAIN STORAGE EXPANSION OPTIONS

Nothing seems to grow faster than the computer user's appetite for main storage. Several different options allow the user to expand the main storage in AS/400 computers. However, because of technical differences inside the systems, main storage expansion options are not necessarily interchangeable between the different Application System models.

**Figure 2.10.** 5209 Protocol Converter.

## AS/Entry Main Storage Expansion

All AS/Entry systems come standard with 1 MB of main storage. The 2-MB main storage feature (#2585) can replace the standard 1 MB main storage, yielding 2 MB of total main storage. This is the maximum amount of main storage supported by an AS/Entry. When this option is installed, the original 1-MB card provided with the system must be returned to IBM.

## 9402 Main Storage Expansion

All AS/400 9402 systems come standard with 8 MB of main storage. To expand them beyond 8 MB you can install either the 8-MB main storage feature (#3117) or the 16-MB main storage feature (#3118). Since these main storage features attach directly to the System Processor circuit board, no expansion slots are consumed to expand main storage.

The Model F02 can accommodate either one 8-MB main storage feature, providing 16 MB of total main storage, or one 16-MB main storage feature, providing 24 MB of total main storage (the maximum in F02 systems).

To bring a 9404 F04 system to its maximum main storage size of 24 MB, you can install either two 8-MB main storage features or one 16-MB main storage feature.

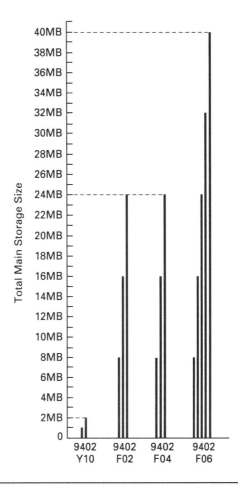

**Figure 2.11.** The possible main storage sizes achievable on 9402 systems.

While Model F06 systems can support one or two 8-MB main storage features, Model F06 systems are brought to their maximum of 40 MB by installing two 16 MB main storage features. Figure 2.11 shows the main storage sizes supported by 9402 systems.

## 9404 Main Storage Expansion

All AS/400 9404 systems come standard with two slots designed to accept the same main storage expansion cards: the 8-MB main storage feature (#3120) or the 32-MB main storage feature (#3122). Model F10 comes standard with 8 MB of memory. To get the maximum main storage size of 72 MB, you must install two 32 MB main storage features. Alternately, you can expand the main storage of an F10 by installing one or two 8 MB main storage features. Once the two slots are filled with 8 MB main storage features, you have 24 MB of main storage and no more slots. However, by adding one or two 8 MB main storage expansion features (#3121), which reside on the 8 MB main storage feature cards themselves, you can get to 40 MB of main storage.

The 9404 Models F20 and F25 come standard with 16 MB of main storage. To achieve the 80 MB maximum main storage size of an AS/400 9404, you must install two 32 MB main storage features in the available slots. However, if more incremental main storage expansion is preferred over maximum main storage size, you can install one or two 8 MB main storage features and one or two main storage expansion features as needed. Figure 2.12 shows the possible main storage configurations available in 9404 computers.

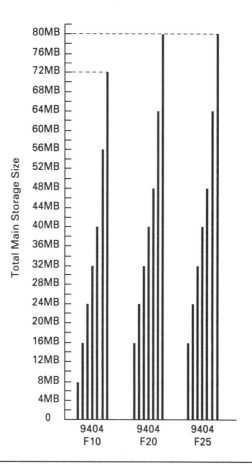

**Figure 2.12.** The possible main storage sizes achievable on 9404 systems.

## 9406 Main Storage Expansion

The main storage in 9406 computers can also be expanded through the addition of main storage feature cards. For 9406 Model F35 systems, there are three main storage expansion cards, with varying amounts of main storage, from which to choose. The 8 MB main storage card (#3119), the 16 MB main storage card (#3100), and the 32 MB main storage card (#3101) can be mixed and matched in these systems to provide the desired main storage size. Model F45 systems require faster memory cards: the 8 MB main storage card (#3140), the 16 MB main storage card (#3141), and the 32 MB main storage card (#3142). Model F50 systems use still faster main storage cards: the 16 MB main storage card (#3102) and the 32 MB main storage card (#3103). F60 systems use the 32 MB main storage card (#3130), the 64 MB main storage card (#3131), and the 128 MB memory card (#3132). Finally, for the F70, F80, F90, and F95 models, there are two main storage expansion cards: the 64 MB main storage card (#3133) and the 128 MB main storage card (#3134). In all cases, these cards can be used in any combination to achieve the desired main storage size. Figure 2.13 shows the possible main storage sizes achievable in the various 9406 computer systems.

## AUXILIARY STORAGE OPTIONS

As shown in Chapter 1, there are four basic types of auxiliary storage devices used with Application Systems:

- Diskettes
- Disk units
- Tape
- Optical

Let us look at the specific auxiliary storage options available for the Application Systems.

## Diskette Storage

Diskette storage is commonly used by many different types of computer systems. It provides a convenient way to transfer small amounts of information between computer systems. Although diskettes can also be used for making backup copies of the information stored on disk units, diskettes lack the storage capacity to make them effective for this, particularly for larger disk units.

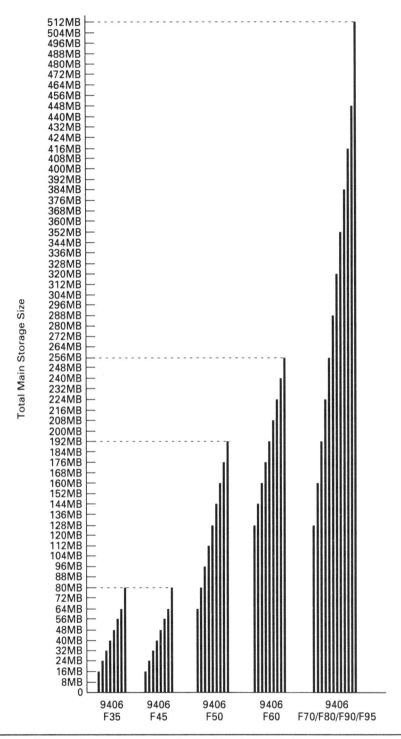

**Figure 2.13.** The possible main storage sizes achievable on 9406 systems.

The AS/Entry comes standard with a 5.25-inch diskette unit. AS/400 systems do not come standard with any diskette storage. There are, however, several options that allow the user to have diskette storage on AS/400 systems:

- Diskette Unit 5.25 Inches (9402 Models)
- Diskette Unit 5.25 Inches (9404 Models)
- Diskette Unit 8 Inches (9404 Models)
- 9331 Diskette Unit Model 1 (9406 Models)
- 9331 Diskette Unit Model 2 (9406 Models)

### Diskette Unit 5.25 Inches (9402 Models)

The optional 5.25-inch diskette unit (#6139) can be installed in the AS/400 9402 F Model System Units. It provides the ability to read and write 5.25-inch diskettes, each capable of holding 1.2 MB of information. It is useful for moving information between AS/400 9402 systems and AS/400 9404 systems equipped with a 5.25-inch diskette unit, AS/400 9406 systems equipped with a 9331 Model 2 Diskette Unit, AS/Entry 9402 Y10 systems, or earlier System/36 computers. This diskette unit, however, is not compatible with the 5.25-inch diskettes used by IBM Personal Computers.

### Diskette Unit 5.25 Inches (9404 Models)

The optional Diskette Unit 5.25 Inches (#6137) can be installed in an AS/400 9404 Model F10, F20, or F25 System Unit or the Expansion Unit (#7120) to provide diskette storage. It provides the ability to read and write 5.25-inch diskettes, each capable of holding 1.2 MB of information. It is useful for moving information between AS/400 9404 systems and AS/400 9402 systems equipped with a 5.25-inch diskette unit, AS/400 9406 systems equipped with a 9331 Model 2 Diskette Unit, AS/Entry 9402 Y10 systems, or earlier System/36 computers. This diskette unit, however, is not compatible with the 5.25-inch diskettes used by IBM Personal Computers.

### Diskette Unit 8 Inches (9404 Models)

The Diskette Unit 8 Inches (#6138) can be mounted in the AS/400 9404's System Unit or Expansion Unit (Figure 2.14). This diskette unit uses 8-inch diskettes that also store up to 1.2 MB of information. It is compatible with the 8-inch diskettes used in System/36 Models 5360, 5362, System/38 computers and with the 9331 diskette unit Model 1.

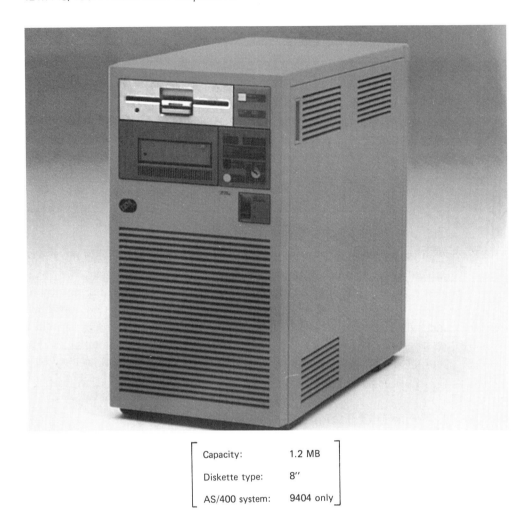

Capacity:         1.2 MB

Diskette type:    8″

AS/400 system:    9404 only

**Figure 2.14.** 8-Inch Diskette Unit for the AS/400 9404.

### 9331 Diskette Unit Model 1 (9406 Models)

The 9331 Diskette Unit Model 1 can be used with AS/400 9406 systems (Figure 2.15. This 8-inch diskette unit provides compatibility with the 1.2-MB diskettes used in System/36 Models 5360 and 5362, System/38 computers, and the 8-inch diskette units used with 9404 systems. The 9331 Model 1 can be used only with 9406 computers and attaches via the Magnetic Storage Device Controller (#6112). A maximum of two 9331s can be installed in a 9406 system (any mix of Models 1 and 2).

| Capacity: | 1.2 MB |
| --- | --- |
| Diskette type: | 8″ |
| AS/400 system: | 9406 only |

**Figure 2.15.** 9331 Diskette Unit Model 1 for the AS/400 9406 systems. This drive accepts 8-inch diskettes.

## 9331 Diskette Unit Model 2 (9406 Models)

The 9331 Diskette Unit Model 2 can be used with any AS/400 9406 system. This 5.25-inch diskette unit provides compatibility with the 1.2-MB diskettes used in the

AS/Entry, the System/36 Model 5364, and the 5.25-inch diskette units used with AS/400 9404 systems. The 9331 Model 2 also attaches to the 9406 through the Magnetic Storage Device Controller (#6112). A maximum of two 9331s can be installed on any 9406 (any mix of Models 1 and 2).

## Disk Storage

All Application Systems need disk storage, also called **direct access storage device (DASD)**, to be a complete computer system. We look at several options that allow the user to provide or expand the disk storage of Application Systems. Chapter 1 covered the standard and maximum disk storage configurations for all Application Systems. Here we look at the disk storage options themselves as follows:

- AS/Entry disk units
- AS/400 9402 disk units
- AS/400 9404 disk units
- 9337 direct access storage device

### AS/Entry Disk Units

All AS/Entry 9402 Y10 Systems come standard with 160 MB of disk storage mounted inside the System Unit. The disk storage of the Y10 can be expanded by adding either the additional 160-MB DASD (#2531) or the additional 200-MB DASD (#2532). Up to three of these additional disk units can be added to a Y10 system in any combination. In order to achieve the maximum disk storage capacity of a Y10 (760 MB), you must install three additional 200-MB DASD options.

The additional 160-MB DASD option has an average seek time of 12.5 ms and an average latency of 7.0 ms. The additional 200-MB DASD option has an average seek time of 11.5 ms with an average latency of 7.0 ms.

### AS/400 9402 Disk Units

All AS/400 9402 F models come standard with 988 MB of disk storage. The standard 988 MB of disk storage is made up of one 3.5-inch disk unit that resides in the System Unit. To expand disk storage in 9402 F02 systems, either a Single Disk Unit 400 MB (#6103) or a Single Disk Unit 988 MB (#6104) can be installed.

To expand the disk storage of 9402 F04 and F06 System Units, up to three more disk units can be installed. The disk unit options for F04 and F06 systems include Disk Unit 320 MB (#6102), Single Disk Unit 400 MB (#6103), and Single Disk Unit 988 MB (#6104). These disk units can be installed in any combination to achieve the desired amount of fixed disk storage. However, to achieve the F04 and F06 maximum System Unit disk storage configuration (3952 MB), you must install three Single Disk Unit 988 MB options. Three more disk units can be installed in the optional Expansion Unit (#7115) and attached to a 9402 F06 system. This means that a single 9402 F06 system can have up to 7904 MB of disk storage.

## AS/400 9404 Disk Units

The 9404 systems come standard with 988 MB of disk storage. The standard 988 MB of disk storage is made up of one 3.5-inch disk unit that takes one of the three spaces available for disk storage in the 9404 System Unit. The 988-MB disk unit can be upgraded with an Additional Dual Disk Unit (#6123) to provide 1976 MB of disk storage without consuming either of the two available spaces for additional disk units. Further disk storage expansion can be accomplished by installing any of the options listed in Figure 2.16. The two available disk positions provided in the 9404

| 9404 Disk Storage Option | Description | Comments |
| --- | --- | --- |
| Single Disk Unit 320 MB (#6105) | One 3.5-inch Disk Unit, Avg seek = 12.5 ms, data rate = 2 MB/second | Can be upgraded to a Dual Disk Unit 640 MB (#6108) |
| Single Disk Unit 400 MB (#6107) | One 3.5-inch Disk Unit, Avg seek = 11.5 ms, data rate = 2 MB/second | Can be upgraded to a Dual Disk Unit 800 MB (#6121) |
| Dual Disk Unit 640 MB (#6108) | Two 3.5-inch 320 MB Disk Units in a single housing, Avg seek = 12.5 ms, data rate = 2 MB/second | |
| Single Disk Unit 988 MB (#6109) | One 3.5-inch Disk Unit, Avg seek = 11.0 ms, data rate = 3 MB/second | Comes standard with 9404 systems. Can be upgraded to an Additional Disk Unit 1,976 MB (#6123) |
| Additional Dual Disk Unit 800 MB (#6121) | Two 3.5-inch 400 MB Disk Units in a single housing, Avg seek = 11.5 ms, data rate = 2MB/second | |
| Additional Disk Unit 1,976 MB (#6123) | Two 3.5-inch 988 MB Disk Units in a single housing, Avg seek = 11.0 ms, data rate = 3 MB/second | |

**Figure 2.16.** Disk units used to expand the disk storage of AS/400 9404 systems.

can accommodate any combination of these options. (Note the Feature Power Supply [#5133] if you install a disk unit in the third available position.) However, to achieve the maximum disk storage configuration of the 9404 System Unit, 1976-MB disk units must be installed.

Further disk storage expansion is possible on all 9404 F Models by adding the Expansion Unit (#7120) covered later in the chapter. The Expansion Unit can house up to three single or dual disk options. When three 1976-MB Dual Disk Units are installed in the 9404 System Unit and three 1976-MB Dual Disk Units are installed in the Expansion Unit, the maximum disk storage of 11,856 MB for 9404 F10 and F20 systems is achieved. The optional Storage Expansion Unit (#7203), supported only by the 9404 Model F25, provides for further disk storage expansion. The Storage Expansion Unit is a small box that is attached to the top of the 9404 System Unit and provides space to install one or two more disk units. If two 1976-MB Dual Disk Units are installed in the Storage Expansion Unit, the maximum disk storage configuration of 15,808 MB of the Model F25 is achieved.

### AS/400 9406 Disk Options

All AS/400 9406 models come standard with 1.97 GB of disk storage installed in the processor drawer itself. This internal disk storage can be expanded to 3.95 GB by installing the optional Internal DASD Book Adapter (#2801). The 9337 direct access storage device can be used to expand the disk storage capacity of any AS/400 9406 system beyond that of the internal disk storage.

There are six 9337 models: Models 10, 20, 40, 110, 120, and 140 (see Figure 2.17). The 9337 Model 10 consists of a 19-inch rack-mounted unit that contains two 542-MB disk units (1.08 GB) and space for up to five more 542-MB disk units (#1206). This means a single 9337 Model 10 can provide up to 3.79 GB of disk storage. The 9337 Model 20 consists of a 19-inch rack that contains two 970-MB disk drives (1.94 GB) and space for up to five additional 970-MB disk units (#1212). The maximum capacity of a 9337 Model 20 is therefore 6.79 GB. The 9337 Model 40 consists of a 19-inch rack that contains four 1967-MB disk drives (7.68 GB) and space for up to three additional 1967-MB disk units (#1220). The maximum capacity of a 9337 Model 40 is therefore 13.45 GB.

The 9337 Models 110, 120, and 140 are built using the same 542-MB, 970-MB, and 1967-MB disk units (respectively) housed in the same 19-inch rack mounted unit. However, the 9337 Models 110, 120, and 140 are configured as a **Redundant Array of Independent Disks (RAID)**. A RAID uses classical data detection and correction techniques to automatically re-create lost information should one of the disk units in the 9337 fail. Although, in the event of a disk unit

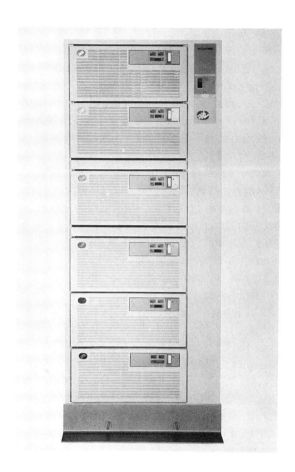

| | No Data Protection | | | Data Protection | | |
|---|---|---|---|---|---|---|
| | **9337 Model 10** | **9337 Model 20** | **9337 Model 40** | **9337 Model 110** | **9337 Model 120** | **9337 Model 140** |
| Standard Capacity: | 1.08 GB | 1.94 GB | 7.68 GB | 1.62 GB | 2.91 GB | 5.76 GB |
| Max Capacity: | 3.79 GB | 6.79 GB | 13.45 GB | 3.25 GB | 5.82 GB | 11.52 GB |
| Attaches to: | DASD Controller | DASD Controller | DASD Controller | DASD Controller | DASD Controller | DASD Controller |
| Actuators: | 2–7 | 2–7 | 4–7 | 4–7 | 4–7 | 4–7 |
| Avg seek time: | 9.8 ms | 9.8 ms | 9.8 ms | 9.8 ms | 9.8 ms | 9.8 ms |
| Avg latency: | 6.95 ms | 6.95 ms | 5.56 ms | 6.95 ms | 6.95 ms | 5.56 ms |
| Transfer rate: | 3.0 MB/second | 3.0 MB/second | 5.2 MB/second | 3.0 MB/second | 3.0 MB/second | 5.2 MB/second |

**Figure 2.17.** Rack containing six 9337 Direct Access Storage Devices.

failure, there will be a performance impact while the lost information is reconstructed, the users will be able to continue their work uninterrupted. The 9337 Models 110 and 120 must have at least four disk units installed to implement the RAID (level-5) data protection scheme. The Model 140 comes standard with four disk units installed. Dual power supplies are also provided in each 9337 Model 110, 120, or 140 to allow for uninterrupted operation in the event of one power failure. If a power supply does fail, it can be replaced without interrupting the operation of the 9337 Models 110, 120, and 140.

The same 3.5-inch disk units used in the 9337 Models 10, 20, and 40 are used in the 9337 Models 110, 120, and 140. However, each disk of the first four disk units must hold some error correction information not needed in the Model 10, 20, or 40. So the first four disk units in a Model 110 hold 406 MB each (rather than 542 MB), the first four disk units in a Model 120 hold 728 MB each (rather than 970 MB), and the first four disk units in a Model 140 hold 1475 MB (rather than 1967). The Models 110, 120, and 140 provide space for up to three more 542-MB, 970-MB, or 1475-MB disk units respectively. This means that a single 9337 Model 110 can provide up to 3.25 GB of RAID-5 protected disk storage, a 9337 Model 120 can provide up to 5.82 GB of RAID-5 protected disk storage, and a 9337 Model 140 can provide up to 11.52 GB of RAID-5 protected disk storage. The 9337 attaches to the AS/400 9406 system through the DASD Controller (#6500).

The older 9332, 9335, and 9336 DASDs used with earlier AS/400 systems can still be used with 9406 F models. However, the price/performance, cost-per-MB, storage density, and RAID-5 data protection of the 9337 DASDs make them the preferred DASD for new AS/400 9406 systems.

## Tape Storage

Computer systems are woven deeply into today's businesses and usually become the core of day-to-day operations. The information stored on the computer is in and of itself a valuable asset and therefore must be protected like any other asset. Magnetic tape storage provides a cost-effective and efficient means of backing up the information on the disk units of computer systems. Included among the tape storage options that can be used with IBM's Application Systems are the following:

- 1.2-GB 1/4-Inch Cartridge Tape Unit
- 525-MB 1/4-Inch Cartridge Tape Unit
- 120-MB 1/4-Inch Cartridge Tape Unit
- 7208 8mm Cartridge Tape Drives

- 9348 Tape Unit
- 3490 Tape Unit

### 1.2-GB 1/4-Inch Cartridge Tape Unit

The 1.2-GB 1/4-Inch Cartridge Tape Unit (#6348) reads and writes a 1/4-inch tape cartridge capable of holding up to 1.2 GB of information. It is an option for AS/400 9402, 9404, and 9406 systems. It supports burst data transfer at a rate of up to 300 KB/second. The 1.2-GB 1/4-Inch Cartridge Tape Unit can read and write the 120-MB and 525-MB tape cartridges used by the 120-MB and 525-MB 1/4-Inch Cartridge Tape Units, thus facilitating the transfer of programs and data between different Application Systems. It attaches to the Multi-Function I/O Processor provided as standard in AS/400 System Units. The Multi-Function I/O Processor in AS/400 F Models has circuitry that can perform data compression, allowing more information (up to two times more) to be stored on a tape cartridge.

### 525-MB 1/4-Inch Cartridge Tape Unit

This tape unit reads and writes a 1/4-inch tape cartridge capable of holding up to 525 MB. It is provided as standard equipment with AS/400 9402 and 9404 F Models. Also, a second 525-MB 1/4-Inch Cartridge Tape Unit (#6347) can be installed in the 9404 Expansion Unit (#7120).

The 525-MB Cartridge Tape Unit supports burst data transfer at a rate of up to 200 KB/second. The 525-MB Cartridge Tape Unit can read and write the 120-MB tape cartridges used by the 120-MB Cartridge Tape Unit, thus facilitating the transfer of programs and data between different Application Systems. It attaches to the Multi-Function I/O Processor provided as standard in the System Unit. The Multi-Function I/O Processor in 9404 F Models has circuitry that can perform data compression, allowing more information (up to two times more) to be stored on a tape cartridge.

### 7208 8mm Cartridge Tape Drives

A 7208 External Tape Drive is shown in Figure 2.18. These drives are 5.25-inch tabletop, medium-performance tape units that can be used with all AS/400 9402, 9404, or 9406 systems except the 9402 F02. They are self-contained devices that attache to the AS/400 via a cable to the Removable Media Device Attachment feature (#2621).

There are two 7208 models used with AS/400 systems. The 7208 2.3-GB 8mm External Tape Drive (Model 2) uses a tape cartridge capable of holding up to 2.3 GB

**Figure 2.18.** 7208 2.3-GB 8mm Tape Unit.

(over 2.3 billion bytes) of information (without compression). Information is transferred at a rate of 245 Kb/second. The 7208 5-GB External Tape Drive (Model 12) can store up to 5 GB of information (without compression) on a single tape drive. The Removable Media Device Attachment feature has circuitry designed to compress information (hardware compress/decompress function) as it is written to the tape cartridge. This effectively increases the capacity of each tape cartridge by as much as two times. The 7208 is primarily used for disk backup, data archiving, alternate IPL devices, information distribution, and the processing of large sequential files. It uses an 8mm tape cartridge like that used with 8mm video cameras, but of computer grade.

## 9348 Tape Unit

The 9348 Magnetic Tape Unit (Figure 2.19) is an intermediate performance streaming tape drive that uses 1/2-inch tape reels. It utilizes standard 9-track tape reels, which are automatically loaded and threaded. The 9348 is capable of reading/writing in either 1600 bpi at 200 Kb/second (PE mode) or 6250 bpi at 781 Kb/second (GCR mode). It has a 1-MB memory buffer (which will continue to accept information from the AS/400 system while the tape is being positioned, for example). This buffer helps improve the overall performance of the 9348 Tape Unit. There are two models of the 9348 used with AS/400 systems, differing only in their physical packaging. The 9348 Model 1 is packaged to mount in an AS/400 9406 rack, while the 9348

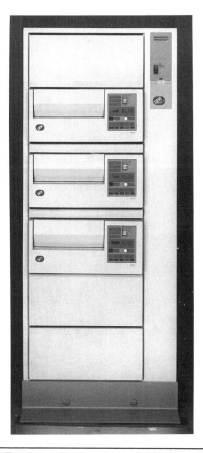

**Figure 2.19.** The IBM 9348 Tape Unit (three mounted in a rack).

Model 2 is a tabletop unit used with AS/400 9402 and 9404 systems. The 9348 Model 1 can be attached to AS/400 9406 systems through the Removable Media Device Attachment (#2621). The 9348 Model 2 can be attached to AS/400 9402 (but not the AS/Entry) and AS/400 9404 systems through the same attachment (#2621). In either case, the Removable Media Device Attachment provides an additional hardware compress/decompress function that increases the effective data rate of the 9348 and stores more information per inch of tape.

## 3490E Tape Unit

The 3490E Magnetic Tape Subsystem, shown in Figure 2.20, is currently the most powerful tape drive available for use with the AS/400 family. The 3490E utilizes a

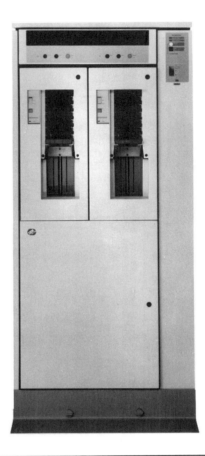

**Figure 2.20.** The IBM 3490E Tape Unit, mounted in a rack.

compact 1/2-inch cartridge tape. Information is read from or written to the tape cartridge at up to 3 Mb/second.

The newest models in the 3490E family are the Models C10, C11, and C22. These models use the Enhanced Capacity Cartridge capable of storing 800 MB of information. When the standard **Improved Data Recording Capability (IDRC)** function is enabled, a data compression technique is used to further increase tape capacity (by as much as 300 percent). These models can also read tapes that utilize the 200-MB and 400-MB cartridges used by earlier 3480 and 3490 tape drive models.

The C10 contains a single tape drive, the associated control circuitry, and the power supply. The C11 contains a single tape drive, control circuitry, the power supply, and an **Automatic Cartridge Loader**. The Automatic Cartridge Loader allows the operator to pre-mount up to six tape cartridges per tape drive. Then during the backup process, when one tape is full, it will be automatically removed from the 3490E and replaced with the next blank tape. The operator can load and unload the Automatic Cartridge Loader without interrupting the backup process. The C22 is just like the C11 except that the C22 has two tape drives built in, each with an Automatic Cartridge Loader.

The D41/D42 models of the 3490 can be used with AS/400 systems. The D41 contains a single tape drive, the associated control circuitry, and the power supply. The D42 is just like the D41 except that the D42 has two tape drives built in. Like the C10/C11/C22 models, the D41 and D42 use the Enhanced Capacity Cartridge System allowing a single cartridge to hold up to 800 MB of uncompressed data. The D41/D42 also support IDRC and have the ability to read the lower capacity tape cartridges used by 3480 and earlier 3490 tape drives. An optional Automatic Cartridge Loader can be added to any D41/D42 model. All 3490 Tape Units attach to the AS/400 9406 systems through the 3490 High Performance Magnetic Tape Attachment (#2644).

## 3995 Optical Library

For information that is not needed frequently but must be readily available when it is needed, **optical disk storage** should be considered. Unlike magnetic disks, which record information with magnetic fields, optical disks use plastic disks coated with a thin reflective alloy material and housed in a cartridge case. Information is stored on the plastic disk by actually burning holes into the reflective surface with a laser beam. The information can then be read back by the same laser beam (at a lower power). Once the surface is burned, it can be read as often as needed. However, since this surface cannot be "unburned," no other information can be written to that particular portion of the optical disk. Optical disks of this type are called "Write-Once-Read-Many" or WORM optical disk systems. This type of storage provides for extremely high data recording densities, which makes for relatively inexpensive storage. However, today's optical disk technology is slower than magnetic disk storage.

There are two models of the 3995 Optical Library Dataserver used with AS/400 systems: Model 042 and Model 142. The Model 042 (Figure 2.21) is a WORM drive used with AS/400 9402/9404/9406 systems (except the 9402 F02). It is a self-contained box that rests on the floor near the AS/400 System Unit. Inside the box are two optical disk drives and 32 storage cells that can each contain a removable optical disk cartridge. Also inside is a 300-MB magnetic disk unit for use by the additional AS/400 software needed to support the 3995.

**Figure 2.21.** The AS/400 Compact Optical Library Dataserver.

Each optical disk cartridge used in the 3995 can hold over 600 million bytes of information, so a fully loaded 3995 (i.e., with 32 optical disk cartridges loaded) can hold over 19.5 billion bytes of information. This means that a single 3995 can hold a digitized image of over 300,000 pieces of paper (assuming 50 KB/image). That many pieces of paper make a stack over 90 feet tall! Further, since you can attach up to fourteen 3995 units on the larger 9406 systems, you can have up to 270 billion bytes of information readily available, or enough to hold images of over 4,000,000 pieces of paper. That's a stack over *1200* feet tall!

The 3995 Optical Library Dataserver Model 142 offers a greater storage capacity using the same technology. The Model 142 can manage up to 144 optical disks, each holding over 600 MB of information. That makes a total storage capacity of over 94 billion bytes. That's enough storage to hold the images of over 1,342,177 pieces of paper, or a stack over 400 feet tall. Again, multiple 3995 Model 142 Optical Library Dataservers can be attached to a single AS/400 system, providing even more storage.

The 3995 attaches to the AS/400 system through the Removable Media Device Attachment feature (#2621). Also needed is the Optical Library Dataserver Support/400 program (PRPQ #5799-XBK). This program provides a programming interface for application programs to use when accessing information stored in the 3995. That is, the application program must be specially written to take advantage of the 3995 or else the information stored in 3995 will be unavailable to the application program. Chapter 4 will cover an example of an application program (Workfolder Application Facility) designed to take advantage of the 3995.

## Auxiliary Storage Controllers

As discussed in Chapter 1, all Application Systems have a multi-processor architecture that allows them to do work more efficiently. The **auxiliary storage controllers** manage the data flow between the computer system and the auxiliary storage devices. They are small, specialized processors that do most of their work independent of the system processor. They are installed in an expansion slot inside the System Unit of the computer and attach via cable to the auxiliary storage.

The AS/Entry System Units or their auxiliary storage options come standard with the necessary auxiliary storage controllers. The following auxiliary storage controllers are used with AS/400 systems and are purchased separately:

- Removable Media Device Attachment
- 3490 High Performance Magnetic Tape Subsystem Attachment
- Magnetic Storage Device Controller
- DASD Controller

### Removable Media Device Attachment

The Removable Media Device Attachment (#2621) is used in the AS/400 9402, 9404, and 9406 systems. It allows the attachment of one or two 7208 or 9348 tape units. It provides a hardware-implemented data compression/decompression function that is designed to increase the effective capacity of the attached tape subsystem. This attachment is also required to attach a 3995 Optical Library to an AS/400 system. One I/O slot is required for this feature.

### 3490 High Performance Magnetic Tape Subsystem Attachment

The 3490 Magnetic Tape Subsystem (#2644) is used exclusively with the AS/400 9406 systems. This attachment allows a 3490 Tape Subsystem to be attached to an AS/400 system. It also provides a hardware-implemented compression decompression that is designed to increase the effective capacity of the attached tape subsystem. This attachment consumes one I/O slot but cannot be installed in a Bus Extension Unit (#5040).

### Magnetic Storage Device Controller

The Magnetic Storage Device Controller (#6112) can support the 9336 DASD, the 9332 and 9335 DASDs, the 9331 Diskette Units, and the 9347 Tape Unit. It provides IBM's implementation of the industry-standard **ANSI IPI-3** interface. It uses one slot.

### DASD Controller

The DASD Controller (#6500) is used to attach 9337 DASD to AS/400 9406 systems. It uses the **Small Computer System Interface (SCSI)** which transfers information at an instantaneous rate of 5 Mb/second. It uses one slot.

## COMMUNICATIONS OPTIONS

Today's businesses are placing an increasing emphasis on computer communications. This section provides a quick communications tutorial and then an overview of some communications feature cards available for IBM's Application Systems. These feature cards may be complete communications subsystems, providing the communications controller and the necessary adapter on a single card, or the controller circuitry may be on a separate card designed to accommodate one of several different communications adapter cards, depending on the requirements. In either case, the cards are installed in one or more expansion slots to add some type of communications capability to the computer system. Through these communications options, IBM's Application Systems can be attached to each other, to larger computers (e.g., System/390), or to smaller computers (e.g., Personal System/2). Chapter 6 shows how to use these communications options to allow Application Systems to participate in various communication configurations. If your interest is in communications environments rather than the feature cards themselves, skip to Chapter 6.

As with main storage expansion options, internal differences sometimes prevent the interchange of communications feature cards between the various Application System types. We look at the following options in this section:

- AS/Entry Communications Subsystems
- AS/400 Communications Subsystems
- Modems
- 5394 Remote Workstation Controller

This chapter does not provide a comprehensive list of all communications options that are available for the Application Systems, but it does discuss representative options that fit the most common business needs.

As there are configuration limitations governing which and how communications options can be used together in a single computer system, the assistance of IBM or an authorized dealer should be sought when configuring systems.

## Communications Interfaces/Protocols—A Road Map

One of the easiest areas in which to get confused in today's computer environment is communications. This section serves as a quick communications tutorial, providing you with the background necessary to understand the differences among the various communications options covered in this chapter.

A **communications line** can be thought of as a cable between two or more computer systems. A single communications line can provide a connection to one other computer across the room or hundreds of other computers across global distances. By using multiple communications lines, a business can provide information from a single point to users in many locations.

To be attached to a communications line, the Application Systems must first have the proper electrical **interface**. The term "interface" refers collectively to the connector, electrical voltage levels, connector pin functions, and so on, that are provided for the physical attachment to a communications line. We will discuss options that use either the **232/V.24, V.35, token-ring, Ethernet (802.3), X.21, ISDN,** or **FDDI** interfaces. For our purposes, it is not necessary to understand exactly what all these cryptic names mean. It is enough to know that there are different types of interfaces necessary to support different types of communications. The interface may be provided by a separate adapter card working with a communications controller card, or it may be built onto the same card with the communications controller circuitry.

In addition to the different interfaces, you must also know about **communica-**

**tions protocols** to be conversant in computer communications. Just as there are different rules of grammar and punctuation in English, French, and other languages, there are different rules for various types of computer communications. In computer communications, a set of rules is called a *communications protocol.* The protocols of most interest for our purposes are **Async, Bisync, SDLC, token-ring, Ethernet (802.3), X.25, IDLC,** and **FDDI (ISO 9314).** Each of these different protocols has the same basic goal of moving information from one place to another efficiently and reliably, and each has advantages and disadvantages. The one you use will depend on your requirements in the areas of transmission speed, cost, and compatibility with the other device(s) in the network. At all times, however, each device using a given communications line must be using the same protocol.

The Async (short for asynchronous) protocol is a low-speed, low-cost communications method commonly used by many devices. With Async, individual bytes of information are transmitted (one bit at a time) with no fixed relationship between bytes. Figure 2.22 shows one way a byte might be packaged before it is sent over an Async communications line. The start bit tells the receiving end that information is coming down the line. The user's data follow the start bit. The parity bit is used by the receiving end to check for transmission errors in the user's data. Finally, the stop bit signifies the end of the transmission of the character. This is just one example of how information might be transmitted over an Async line. The user can select other organizations—including eight-user data bits, no parity bits, and two- stop bits. These different organizations exist primarily because of the many types of equipment that have used this protocol over the years. The specific organization used must be established at both ends of the communications link before communications can begin.

Next is the Bisync protocol (short for *bi*nary *synch*ronous communications, or BSC). The "synchronous" in "Bisync" means that a special character preceding the information synchronizes the receiver with the incoming information. This synchronization allows many bytes of information to be sent as a single block—in contrast to the asynchronous protocol, in which a single byte is sent at a time. The ability to send blocks of characters makes Bisync more efficient than the asynchronous proto-

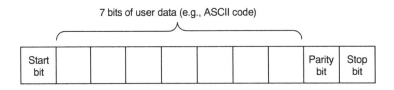

**Figure 2.22.** Example Async protocol data organization.

col. Bisync is an older communications protocol used by terminals and other equipment to exchange information with many different types of computers—including IBM's System/360, System/370, and System/390 mainframes. As a result of its past popularity, many of today's computer systems still use this protocol.

The Synchronous Data Link Control (SDLC) protocol is basically an updated version of Bisync. As with Bisync, SDLC is a synchronous communications protocol. However, SDLC is a more flexible protocol that is part of IBM's Systems Network Architecture (SNA). SNA is a set of communications standards published by IBM and used as a road map to ensure that compatible communications are provided for current and future computer systems and software. SNA is discussed further in Chapter 6.

The Token-Ring Network is another type of communications configuration that allows for a collection of different computer systems within a small area (e.g., in the same building) to communicate very efficiently. The protocol used by the Token-Ring Network is the **token-ring protocol**, Basically, packets of information are passed around the ring from node to node in a continuous circle. These packets are called **message frames**. A unique frame called a **token frame** controls access to the ring. When a node receives a frame, it checks to see if it is a message or a token frame. If it is a message frame, it examines the destination address (see Figure 2.23) to see if the message is intended for that node. If the message is not intended for that node, the message frame is passed on unchanged to the next node in the ring. If the frame received by a node is a token frame, the node knows that the network is idle and that it may send a message frame if it has information to transfer. After it sends a message frame, the node then sends a token frame to indicate that the ring is again inactive and ready to carry information.

Another type of Local Area Network popular today is the Ethernet LAN (IEEE 802.3). With Ethernet, each computer is attached as a tap off of a common cable or **bus**. For this reason, Ethernet is called a **bus wired network**. Thus, an Ethernet LAN is basically a party line on which all computers can transmit a message for all other computers to hear. Every computer has equal access to the cable and can send a message at any time without warning. To ensure that only one computer transmits at a time, there is a protocol that each node follows when transmitting messages. This protocol is called *Carrier Sense Multiple Access/Collision Detect (CSMA/CD)*. It's a mouthful, but really it's a quite simple protocol. In fact, we follow this protocol in our everyday telephone conversations. Here, too, only one person can speak at a time or neither is clearly understood. One party waits for the other to finish before beginning to speak. Thus the phone line only carries one party's voice at a time and the message is clear. This is the "CSMA" part of CSMA/CD. The "CD" part of the protocol handles the times when two nodes start transmission simultaneously. To understand this part of the protocol, think of what you do during a telephone conver-

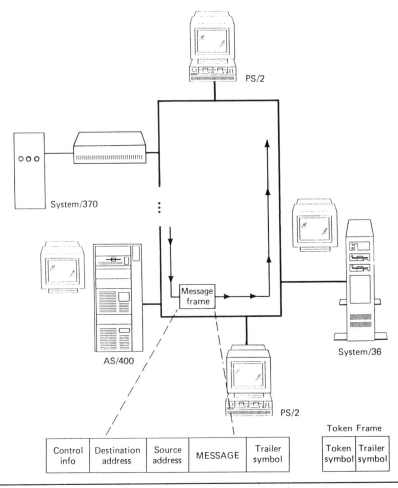

**Figure 2.23.** Token-passing protocol used on IBM Token-Ring Network.

sation, when you begin talking at the same time as the other party. Typically, you both stop talking and begin again a few moments later, hoping that this time one of you begins sooner than the other. This is exactly analogous to the situation with CSMA/CD. If two (or more) nodes begin transmitting at the same time, the messages "collide" on the network. The nodes monitor for such a collision and when it is detected, all nodes stop transmitting and begin again after a pause of random length. Usually, one node will begin its retransmission before the other, thus gaining control of the network.

The X.25 protocol is an industry standard used in the relatively new **packet switched** networks available to the public today. Although more traditional communications networks are based on **analog** or voice-type communications signals, packet switched networks use **digital** or computerlike communications signals. Each packet is then sent to its destination elsewhere in the network through the most economical and available route. Since each packet is routed in the most efficient way, overall information flow is improved over conventional techniques. X.25 is fully supported in IBM's Systems Network Architecture.

The IDLC Protocol is similar to SDLC, except that with IDLC the other computers on the network need not wait to be **polled** by the computer in charge of the network, as with the SDLC protocol. Instead, all computers have an equal ability to transmit messages to and receive messages from any other computer on the network. The IDLC protocol is used by the AS/400 to communicate over **Integrated Services Digital Networks (ISDNs)**.

Integrated Services Digital Networks are another type of digital network that fits more naturally with computer communications than do the traditional analog communications used with telephone communications. Currently more popular in Europe and Japan, ISDN communications services are starting to become more common in the United States. Computers attach to ISDN with a digital connection, eliminating the need for the conversion to analog signals. There are different levels of ISDN service, which correspond to different transmission speeds. AS/400 systems can currently participate in the slower or **basic rate** of ISDN service. Even though this is the slowest ISDN service level, information is transferred at up to 64,000 bits per second. Fiber Distributed Data Interface (FDDI) networks are high-speed (100 Mb/second) local area networks. FDDI networks utilize fiber optic cable or twisted pair cable to move information at a rate of 100 Mb/second between the computer systems participating in the network. Using light signals transmitted through the fiber optic cable, FDDI networks can move information more quickly and with greater immunity from electrical interference than electrical networks. The protocol used on FDDI networks is an enhanced version of the token-passing protocol described for the Token-Ring Network above. With this understanding of interfaces and protocols, let us look at the specific communications options available for Application Systems.

## AS/Entry Communications Subsystems

Unlike AS/400 systems, the standard AS/Entry configuration does not include a communications line. There are several options from which to choose when adding communications lines to AS/Entry systems. By also equipping the AS/Entry with the proper communications adapter(s), the AS/Entry can support up to three communications lines and participate in many different communications environments.

## Basic Communications Adapter

The Basic Communications Adapter (#2616) can be installed in an AS/Entry system to provide a single EIA 232 communications line. This line can support SDLC, Bisync, or Async communications protocols at speeds of up to 9600 bps. Only one Base Communications Adapter can be installed per AS/Entry system.

## Expanded Communications Adapter

The Expanded Communications Adapter (#2627) is a controller used with AS/Entry systems that supports SDLC, Bisync, Async, or X.25 communications protocols. The programming that determines and performs the proper protocol functions is loaded into the Expanded Communications Adapter during initialization. This controller must work with one of two adapters (which provide the electrical interface) in order to make a complete communications line: EIA Line Interface (#2630) or V.35 High-Speed Line Interface (#2645). One or two EIA Line Interface adapters or one V.35 High-Speed Line Interface adapter can be installed with a single Expanded Communications Adapter. However, the EIA Line Interface and V.35 High-Speed Line Interface cannot both be installed on the same Expanded Communications Adapter. The Processor Expansion feature (#2602) is a prerequisite for the Expanded Communications Adapter.

## EIA Line Interface

The EIA Line Interface (#2630) allows the AS/Entry to communicate over an EIA 232/V.24 electrical interface. In conjunction with the Expanded Communications Adapter (#2627), this interface adapter provides support for SDLC communications at speeds up to 19,200 bits per second (bps), Bisync or Async communications at speeds up to 9600 bps, or X.25 communication at speeds up to 9600 bps **full duplex** (i.e., communication occurs in both directions at once).

## V.35 High-Speed Line Interface

The V.35 High-Speed Line Interface (#2645) allows the AS/Entry to attach to perform communications over a V.35 electrical interface. This interface, in conjunction with the Expanded Communication Adapter (#2627), allows for communications at higher speeds than are possible with the EIA Line Interface. With the V.35 High-Speed Line Interface, SDLC communications can operate at up to 64,000 bps in **half-duplex** mode (i.e., communication occurs one way at a time).

## *16/4 Mbps Token-Ring Network Adapter*

The 16/4 Mbps Token-Ring Network Adapter (#2634) allows the AS/Entry to participate in a Token-Ring Network. Some Token-Ring Networks operate at 4 Mb/second while others operate at 16 Mb/second. This adapter can operate at either speed — determined by a hardware switch preset at the factory based on the user's request. This switch can be changed by IBM Service personnel in the field if need be. Only one of these adapters can be installed in an AS/Entry. The Processor Expansion feature (#2602) is required for this option.

## AS/400 Communications Subsystems

Every AS/400 system comes standard with a multi-function input/output (I/O) processor, which is a specialized computer on a card that works in concert with the AS/400's system processor. In addition to managing the standard disk unit and tape unit, the multi-function I/O processor can do the processing necessary to handle up to two communications lines. Also provided as standard on all AS/400 systems (except the 9402 F02 where it is an option) is one EIA 232/V.24 adapter. This adapter provides the electrical interface necessary to attach the AS/400 system to a communications network. Although this standard communications line can be used for any purpose, it is provided as standard with the intent that it be used with IBM's Electronic Customer Support communications network (see Chapter 7).

A second optional communications adapter can be added to the standard multi-function I/O processor, providing a second communications line: the EIA 232/V.24 One-Line Adapter, the X.21 One-Line Adapter, or the V.35 One-Line Adapter. On 9402 F02 systems, the Multi-Function I/O Processor Expansion (#3116) adds memory to the multi-function I/O processor, which is necessary to support a second communications line.

## *EIA 232/V.24 One-Line Adapter*

The EIA 232/V.24 One-Line Adapter provides an interface to the communications line compatible with the EIA 232 and V.24 industry standards. It provides one communications line operating with the Async, Bisync, SDLC, or X.25 protocol. The line speeds can be up to 19,200 bps for Async, Bisync, or SDLC protocols and up to 9600 for X.25. The EIA 232/V.24 One-Line Adapter comes standard with one of four cables, depending on what type of modem you intend to use and the length of cable you want (#6155 — Adapter plus 20-foot cable; #6154 — Adapter plus 20-foot enhanced cable; #6175 — Adapter plus 50-foot cable; #6174 — Adapter plus 50-foot enhanced cable).

### X.21 One-Line Adapter

The X.21 One-Line Adapter provides an interface to the communications line compatible with the X.21 industry standards currently more common in networks in Europe. It provides one X.21 communications line operating with either the SDLC or X.25 protocols. Line speed can be up to 64 Kbps for either protocol. The X.21 One-Line Adapter comes standard with one of two cables, depending on what length of cable you want (#6151 – Adapter plus 20-foot X.21 cable; #6171 – Adapter plus 50-foot X.21 cable).

### V.35 One-Line Adapter

The V.35 One-Line Adapter provides an interface to the communications line compatible with the V.35 industry standard. When attached to the multi-function I/O processor provided as standard with all AS/400 systems, it provides one communications line operating with the SDLC protocol. The V.35 One-Line Adapter can also be attached to the Six-Line Communications Controller (#2623) used in the AS/400 9404 and 9406 systems. When attached to a Six-Line Communications Controller, the V.35 One-Line Adapter provides one communications line operating with the Bisync, SDLC, or X.25 protocols. One SDLC line per Six-Line Communications Controller can operate at up to 640 Kbps (SDLC). The V.35 One-Line Adapter comes standard with one of two cables – depending on what length of cable you specify (#6153 – Adapter plus 20-foot V.35 cable; #6173 – Adapter plus 50-foot V.35 cable).

### Six-Line Communications Controller

The Six-Line Communications Controller (#2623) is a specialized computer on a card (I/O processor) that can handle the traffic of up to six independent communications lines. It requires a separately purchased interface adapter for each line. The adapters that can be used with the Six-Line Communications Controller include the EIA 232/V.24 Two-Line Adapter, the X.21 Two-Line Adapter, and the ISDN Basic Rate Adapter.

### EIA 232/V.24 Two-Line Adapter

The EIA 232/V.24 Two-Line Adapter provides an interface to the communications line compatible with the EIA 232 and V.24 industry standards. It provides two communications lines operating with the Async, Bisync, SDLC, or X.25 protocols. Line speeds up to 19,200 bps are supported. The EIA 232/V.24 Two-Line Adapter comes standard with one of four cables, depending on what type of modem you intend to use and the length of cable you want (#2655 – Adapter plus two 20-foot cables;

#2654—Adapter plus two enhanced 20-foot cables; #2658—Adapter plus two 50-foot cables; #2657—Adapter plus two enhanced 50-foot cables).

### X.21 Two-Line Adapter

The X.21 Two-Line Adapter provides an interface to the communications line compatible with the X.21 industry standards currently more common in packet switching networks in Europe. It provides one X.21 communications line operating with either the SDLC or X.25 protocols. The line speed can be up to 64,000 bps when used with the SDLC or X.25 protocols. The X.21 Two-Line Adapter comes standard with one of two cables, depending on what length of cable you want (#2656—Adapter plus 20-foot X.21 cable; #2659—Adapter plus 50-foot X.21 cable).

### ISDN Basic Rate Interface Adapter

The Integrated Services Digital Network (ISDN) Basic Rate Interface Adapter (#2605) provides an interface to the communications line compatible with the ISDN standards. ISDN is becoming prevalent in Europe and Japan and beginning to become more available in the United States. Like X.21, ISDN uses a digital interface to transfer information, improving the overall efficiency of the information transfer and eliminating the need for a conversion to traditional analog communications.

Each ISDN Basic Rate Interface Adapter supports two 64,000 bits/second "streams of information" over an ISDN communications link (full duplex). Each of these "streams of information" is called a **B Channel**. In addition, each ISDN Basic Rate Interface Adapter supports one 16,000 bits/second "stream of information" over that same ISDN communications link—called a **D Channel**. Up to two ISDN Basic Rate Interface Adapters can be used with every Six-Line Communications Controller—but no other adapters may be used with that Six-Line Communications Controller. It supports the ISDN Data Link Control (IDLC) protocol for communications over ISDN lines. A maximum of two ISDN adapters are supported per Six-Line Communications Controller.

### 16/4 Mbps Token-Ring Network Adapters

All of IBM's AS/400 systems can participate in a **Token-Ring Network**. This is a communications network that allows different computers in close proximity to one another (e.g., in the same building or campus) to easily share information, programs, and computer hardware. In fact, the Token-Ring Network is the preferred method of attaching local Application Systems together. Information flows at either 4,000,000 bits/second or 16,000,000 bits/second—depending on the version of the Token-Ring Network. At either speed, the Token-Ring Network represents a significantly faster communications link than any other discussed in this chapter so far. What you sacrifice for this speed is distance, in that all systems on the Token-Ring Network must be near each other (e.g., the same building or campus). Computers of all sizes (e.g., Personal System/2s, AS/400s, and System/390s) can participate in a single Token-Ring Network. Chapter 6 discusses Token-Ring Networks further.

We will consider three Token-Ring Network Adapters used with AS/400 systems: the 16/4 Mbps Token-Ring Network Adapter (#2636), the 16/4 Mbps Token-Ring Network Adapter (#2626), and the 16/4 Mbps Token-Ring Network Adapter/A (#2619). Any of these adapters consists of a combined controller and adapter that allows AS/400 systems to participate in a Token-Ring Network. The Token-Ring protocol processing, adapter programming, and electrical interface (IEEE 802.2 and 802.5) are all provided with these adapters. They each use one expansion slot and come with an 8-foot cable.

The #2626 version of the 16/4 Mbps Token-Ring Network Adapter is functionally equivalent to the #2636 version; however, the #2626 is built around a faster microprocessor chip, resulting in a performance improvement. That is, the overall amount of information that can move through the Token-Ring Network Adapter is greater (up to twice as much information in the same amount of time).

The #2619 version of the 16/4 Mbps Token-Ring Network Adapter is functionally equivalent to the #2636 version; however, the #2619 is built around a faster microprocessor chip, resulting in a performance improvement. That is, the overall amount of information that can move through the Token-Ring Network Adapter is greater (up to three and one half times as much information in the same amount of time when compared to a #2626). However, the #2619 version of the adapter is not supported in the AS/400 9402 F02 model. Only one #2636 or #2626 adapter is supported in an AS/400 9402 F02 system. An Expansion Gate is a prerequisite in all 9402 systems. Up to two Token-Ring Network Adapters (one in the System Unit and one in an Expansion Unit) can be installed in a 9404 system, and up to four can be installed in any 9406 system. This allows a single AS/400 system to participate in multiple Token-Ring Networks.

## Ethernet/IEEE 802.3 CSMA/CD LAN Adapters

All of IBM's AS/400 systems can participate in an **Ethernet network**. Like the Token-Ring Network, Ethernet networks allow different computers in close proximity to one another (e.g., in the same building or campus) to easily share information, programs, and computer hardware. In Ethernet networks, information is transferred at 10,000,000 bits per second using the CSMA/CD protocol discussed earlier. Computers of all sizes and brands can participate in a single Ethernet network. Chapter 6 discusses Ethernet networks further.

There are two different Ethernet adapters that allow AS/400 systems to participate in an Ethernet network: the Ethernet/IEEE 802.3 CSMA/CD LAN Adapter and the Ethernet/IEEE 802.3 Adapter/HP.

The Ethernet/IEEE 802.3 CSMA/CD LAN Adapter (#2625) is used to allow AS/400 systems to participate in an Ethernet network (version 2). This adapter consists of a combined controller that provides the Ethernet protocol processing, adapter programming, and electrical interface (IEEE 802.3). It uses one expansion slot in the 9404/9406 system and requires the Expansion Gate in AS/400 9402 systems.

The Ethernet/IEEE 802.3 Adapter/HP (#2617) offers higher performance (up to six times the throughput) than the Ethernet/IEEE 802.3 CSMA/CD LAN Adapter. This is because of the faster microprocessor and larger memory used in the #2617 adapter. The Ethernet/IEEE 802.3 Adapter/HP also has the ability to communicate using both the Ethernet Version 2 and IEEE/802.3 protocols simultaneously over the same LAN. This is helpful to those migrating from the Ethernet Version 2 protocol to the newer IEEE/802.3 protocol.

All of IBM's AS/400 systems can participate in Fiber Distributed Data Interface (FDDI) networks. These are high-speed (100 Mb/second) local area networks that utilize fiber optic or twisted pair cable to move information between the computer systems participating in the network.

For FDDI networks using fiber optic cable, an AS/400 must be equipped with a Fiber Distributed Data Interface Adapter (#2618). For FDDI networks constructed from shielded twisted pair, the AS/400 must be equipped with the Shielded Twisted Pair Distributed Data Interface (#2665).

## Modems

A **modem** is a device that converts computer information into communications signals and transmits them over the telephone lines (i.e., it *mod*ulates the computer information). It is also a modem, at the receiving end, that converts the telephone line signals back into computer information (i.e., it *dem*odulates the telephone line signal). The term "modem" is a combination of the terms *mod*ulate and *dem*odulate. Why do computers need a modem for telephone line communications? Telephone lines are designed to carry electronically encoded voice messages from one point to another. A device (the telephone) is therefore necessary to convert the speaker's voice into electronic signals suitable for phone line transmission. Although the information in a computer is already electronically encoded, it is not in a form that can be transmitted over the phone lines. For this reason, a device is needed to convert the electronically encoded computer information into electronic signals suitable for telephone line transmission. A modem can be thought of as a telephone for a computer. Just as both parties need their own telephone to hold a conversation, both computers must have their own modem to transfer information over the phone lines. This section looks at some representative modems available for IBM's Application Systems.

### 5853 Modem

The 5853 Modem, shown in Figure 2.24, is a standalone unit designed to sit on a desktop near the computer system. It is attached to the computer system through a 232/V.24 interface and an appropriate cable. The 5853 supports communications speeds of up to 2400 bps over **public switched telephone (PST)** lines. PST lines, also called "switched lines," are the type of line used for voice communications. They are called "switched" lines because the modem must dial a number as would a telephone user to establish the proper connection. The 5853 is compatible with the Bell 103 (0 to 300 bps), Bell 212A (300 and 1200 bps), and V.22bis (1200 and 2400 bps) industry standards pertaining to modem operation. For perspective, 1200 bps is about 120 alphanumeric characters per second. The average adult reads at a rate of about 20 or 30 characters per second. The 5853 can transmit information at the same time it is receiving other information. This is called **full duplex** operation.

The 5853 is said to be "intelligent" because a built-in microprocessor interprets high-level commands (from a computer program) to perform various modem functions.

**Figure 2.24.** 5853 Modem.

For example, the modem can be instructed to automatically place or answer a telephone call. These capabilities are called **auto-originate** and **auto-answer**, respectively. This modem uses the "IBM" and "Attention" command sets to control these functions, providing compatibility with programs and systems that use these commands. When the 5853 answers an incoming call, it senses the kind of communications being sent (e.g., 212A/103 or V.22bis, 300 or 1200 bps) and automatically adapts to the proper operating mode. Pulse or tone dialing is supported and the built-in speaker allows you to hear the call progress tones as the link is being established. The modem's built-in test programs check the health of the modem every time power is turned on.

### 786X Modem

The 786X family of modems, shown in Figure 2.25, provides various models all designed to work over **leased lines**. Unlike the "switched" lines used by the 5853 Modem discussed earlier, leased lines maintain a constant communications link. You need not dial a telephone number to establish the connection; leased lines are always connected. They are called "leased" because the user pays for exclusive rights to use the line continuously.

All 786X modems can also use **voice-grade** telephone lines as does the 5853. "Voice-grade" means that the modems can operate over a standard telephone line rather than a specially **conditioned** line. All 786X modems are microprocessor-based and have a 20-key key-pad with a 16-character display for operator interaction. Many functions in the modems can also be manipulated remotely through network management programs. They have built-in diagnostic and test functions, including detailed measurements of communications line parameters. When the

**Figure 2.25.** 786X Modem.

modem is receiving a transmission, it automatically adjusts to the speed of the transmitting modem. These modems can be used to communicate from one computer to another (**point-to-point**) and as the controlling or subordinate modem on a single communications line with multiple modems attached (**multipoint**). This multipoint capability allows multiple devices to share a single communications line.

The 7861 and 7868 modems (each with multiple models) are the two basic types of modems in the 786X family. The 7868 series are simply versions of the 7861, designed to be rack-mounted. Since the 7868 series is functionally identical to the 7861, we focus on the latter.

The 7861 modems operate at from 4800 to 19,200 bps, depending on the model and the telephone line quality. All models support the enhanced link problem determination aid (LPDA). LPDA is very helpful when isolating problems in a large communications network consisting of many modems, workstations, and computers. They also provide four interfaces allowing up to four workstations to be cabled to a single modem. This is called **fan-out**. Alternately, these four ports can be used to attach the modem to two control units for backup purposes. This is called **fan-in.** An optional switch network backup (SNBU) feature allows the modem to establish a communications link over a switched line if the leased line connection fails. Through **data multiplexing** the 7861 Modem allows synchronous and asynchronous devices transmitting at different speeds to share a single communications line.

### 7855 Modem

Figure 2.26 shows the 7855 Modem. This modem is designed to operate over either public switched or leased lines using either asynchronous or synchronous protocols. Unlike the "public switched" lines, leased lines maintain a constant communications link. That is, you need not dial a telephone number to establish the connection, leased lines are always connected. They are called "leased" because the user pays for exclusive rights to use the line continuously.

When operating in asynchronous mode, transmission speeds of 9600 bits/sec are supported over "voice-grade, public switched" telephone lines (up to 12,000 bits/sec can be achieved if line quality is good). Further, transmission speeds of up to 19,200 bits/sec can be achieved if the information being transmitted lends itself to data compression techniques used by the 7855 (compatible with class 5 of Microcom Networking Protocol). This represents transmission speeds up to five times faster than possible with the 5853 Modem covered earlier. If telephone line quality is poor, the 7855 Modem will automatically reduce its transmission speed as necessary. The 7855 automatically adapts if necessary to accommodate the transmission speed and character formatting being used by the modem on the other end of the communications line.

**Figure 2.26.** 7855 Modem.

The 7855 Modem also supports full duplex communications at speeds of up to 12,000 bits/sec using synchronous protocols (e.g., Bisync or SDLC). It provides compatibility with the IBM 5841, 5842, and 5853 modems except that the 7855 does not support the IBM command set. Instead, the 7855 supports the popular Enhanced Attention (AT) command set to control basic modem operations under program control. A microprocessor chip provides intelligence to the modem, allowing for functions such as autodial and auto-answer. The 7855 performs a self-test every time it is turned on to help detect any problems.

When the 7855 is used with a leased telephone line and the line goes down for some reason, the 7855 can be programmed to automatically dial a predefined telephone number and establish a public switched telephone line communications link. This feature, called **switched network backup utility** (**SNBU**), allows communications to continue in the event of a leased line failure. The 7855 can be configured either locally or remotely via a communications line. Once the modem is configured, a password security feature can deter others from changing that configuration. Standards supported by the 7855 Modem include CCITT V.32, V.22 bis, V.22, V.24, V.28, V.54, Bell 212, and Bell 102. The 7855 attaches to an EIA 232/V.24 port on an AS/400. A built-in speaker allows the user to monitor call progress tones.

The ability to use this type of communications speed over switched phone lines is helpful in situations where there is an irregular need to transfer large amounts of information to remote computer systems. Some examples of such situations would include the distribution of programs, program modifications, graphics files, image files, digitized voice messages, and so on.

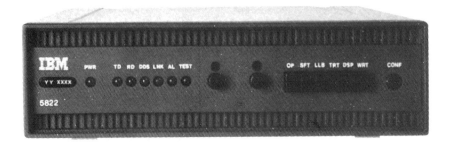

**Figure 2.27.** 5822 Digital Service Unit/Channel Service Unit.

## *5822 Digital Service Unit/Channel Service Unit (DSU/CSU)*

The 5822 Digital Service Unit/Channel Service Unit (DSU/CSU) is shown in Figure 2.27. The 5822 can be thought of as a modem used with digital communications networks rather than the telephone-type communications lines discussed so far. Since information inside a computer system is in digital form, digital networks are better suited to transmit computer information and can do so at higher speeds and more reliably. It supports transmission speeds up to 56,000 bps over digital data service networks (based on standards published in the Bell Systems Technical Reference PUB 62310). The 5822 attaches to a 232/V.24 or V.35 interface of a computer on one side and to the digital network on the other side. The attachment can be in either a point-to-point or multipoint configuration. The 5822 provides network management functions as the 586X modems discussed above.

## Remote Workstation Controllers

All local workstations (e.g., those in the same building as the computer system) are attached to IBM's Application Systems through one of the workstation controllers discussed earlier in this chapter. The Application Systems can also have remote workstations—for example, in a different state from the computer system. These workstations are attached to the computer using communications equipment and lines. Earlier in the chapter we discussed options necessary to attach Application Systems to communications lines. In this section, we look at devices needed at the remote workstation end of the communications link called **remote workstation controllers**. These devices perform basically the same function as the workstation controllers we have already discussed in that they are cabled directly to workstations and manage the workstation traffic for the computer system. The difference is that remote workstation controllers attach to the computer via a communications line as opposed to the local workstation controller, which is a card installed directly in the System Unit of the computer. Remote workstation controllers allow terminals and printers to be located at remote locations, giving distant users access to the Application Systems. Chapter 6 shows just how remote workstation controllers are used to attach remote workstations.

### 5394 Remote Workstation Controller

Figure 2.28 shows a 5394 Remote Workstation Controller. This device, with the help of modems, is used to attach distant workstations to Application Systems via telephone lines. This is an updated version of the 5294 used with earlier System/3X computers (the 5294 can also be used with AS/400 systems). The 5394 comes standard with many features that were optional with the 5294. These include functions such as local screen printing and Enhanced Keyboard support. Other functions such as reversed video and file transfer through the PC Support Program are also standard with the 5394 but not available with the 5294. The 5394 can operate in 5294 mode, which allows it to be attached to a System/36 or System/38. While in 5294 mode, however, only eight workstations can be supported. When attached to AS/400 systems, the 5394 operates in its normal or native mode, supporting up to 16 workstations. In either case, the workstations can be up to 5000 feet from the

**Figure 2.28.** 5394 Remote Workstation Controller.

5394, using twinaxial cable and "cable-thru." Recent enhancements made in the programming of 5394s also allow them to more actively participate in communications networks (SNA networks) commonly used with larger IBM systems (e.g., S/390 computers).

There are 4 models of the 5394. The Models 01A and 02A support up to 4 workstations, and Models 01B and 02B support up to 16 workstations distributed over 3 ports. Models 01A and 02A can be upgraded to 01B and 02B in the field when more than 4 workstations are needed. The models with the "1" in their designation come with a 232/V.24 interface for attaching the appropriate modem and communicate at speeds from 2400 to 19,200 bps. The "2" models provide an X.21 electrical interface and operate at from 2400 to 64,000 bps. Model "1"s can be field-upgraded to model "2"s at any time.

### 5494 Remote Workstation Controller

The 5494 Remote Workstation Controller can be thought of as the big brother to the 5394 Workstation Controller. There are two models of the 5494: Model 001 and Model 002.

Model 001 can support up to 28 twinaxial attached workstations spread over four ports and provides all of the function of the 5394. The 5494 has some other niceties, including the ability to be configured more easily than the 5394 via an attached PS/2 or PC.

The Model 002 can do everything Model 001 can and has the capability to attach directly to a Token-Ring Network. This allows for some new configurations. For example, the 5494 Model 002 could be attached to a Token-Ring Network of PS/2s and to an AS/400 over a communications line, providing the PS/2 users with access to the AS/400. At the same time, twinaxial-attached workstations could be attached to the 5494 so that they also have access to the AS/400. Alternately, the 5494 Model 002 could be attached to from one to five AS/400 systems over a Token-Ring Network and twinaxially attached to the users' workstations. Only one Token-Ring Network attachment is allowed per 5494 Model 002 and the total number of workstations supported cannot exceed 40 (up to 28 twinaxial attached and the rest Token-Ring Network attached devices). The 5494 (Release 1.1) also supports the 5250 data stream extensions. These extensions attach InfoWindow II displays to present the Enhanced User Interface. As we saw earlier, this allows the user to interact with some application programs (specially written or used in conjunction with the IBM WindowTool™/400 product [5798-RYF]) using a mouse and special graphical items (e.g., pop-up windows, scroll bars, radio buttons, push-buttons, check boxes, and continuous window frames) to ease the user's interaction with application programs.

## OTHER OPTIONS

Before concluding the chapter, we cover a few other options for Application Systems:

- AS/Entry Processor Expansion
- 9402 Battery Power Unit
- 9402 Expansion Gate
- 9402 Card Expansion
- 9402 Expansion Unit
- 9404 Expansion Unit
- 9404 Feature Power Supply
- 9406 System Unit Expansion
- 9406 Bus Extension Unit
- Cryptographic Processor
- 5259 Migration Data Link
- 5299 Terminal Multiconnector and the TTPA

### AS/Entry Processor Expansion

The Processor Expansion Feature (#2602) is exclusively used with the AS/Entry. It provides the additional electrical power and board space necessary to support communications options.

### 9402 Battery Power Unit

The Battery Power Unit option (#1102) is used exclusively with the AS/Entry Y10 and AS/400 9402 systems. It is installed in the System Unit and provides up to five minutes of battery power in the event of a power failure. During that five minutes, the Battery Power Unit supplies power to the entire System Unit (i.e., processors, disk units, tape unit, diskette). If power is not restored within a user-specified time period or before the battery begins to run down, circuitry in the Battery Power Unit causes the 9402 system to perform an **orderly shutdown**. In other words, the system performs "clean-up tasks" like closing any open files and saving the state of the system in preparation for shutting down. This preserves the integrity of the information stored in the computer system.

## 9402 Expansion Gate

The Expansion Gate (#7107) is used with AS/400 9402 F04 and F06 systems only. It provides three card slots (one slot for Main Storage Expansion or I/O devices and two for I/O devices only) that accommodate other options covered in this chapter like the Removable Media Device Attachment (#2621), the 4 MB Main Storage Card (#4104), or the Six-Line Communications Controller (#2623).

## 9402 Card Expansion

The Card Expansion option (#7106) is used with AS/400 9402 F02 systems only. It provides one card slot that can accommodate various adapters including workstation controllers, communications adapters, tape drive adapters, optical library adapters, LAN adapters, and so on.

## 9402 Expansion Unit

The 9402 Expansion Unit (#7115) expands the 9402 Model F06 systems in the areas of auxiliary storage and I/O expansion slots. It has four compartments for disk storage that can each house additional disk units. In addition to disk storage, the 9402 Expansion Unit provides four additional I/O expansion slots.

## 9404 Expansion Unit

Figure 2.29 shows an AS/400 9404 System Unit and a 9404 Expansion Unit (#7120) with a Storage Expansion Unit on top. This option expands the 9404 systems in the areas of auxiliary storage and I/O expansion slots. It has three compartments for disk storage that can each house additional disk units. In addition to disk storage, the 9404 Expansion Unit provides five additional I/O expansion slots and can hold a 525-MB or 1.2-GB 1/4-Inch Tape Unit and a diskette unit (5.25-inch or 8-inch). Data compression hardware is provided with the 9404 Expansion Unit that can up to double the effective capacity of the cartridges used with the 1/4-inch tape units. A Battery Power Unit is provided as standard for the Expansion Unit as is an uninterruptible power supply interface.

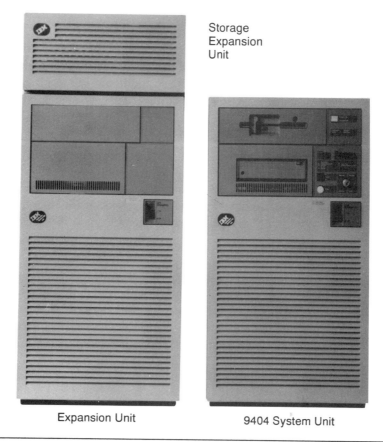

Storage
Expansion
Unit

Expansion Unit                    9404 System Unit

**Figure 2.29.** 9404 Expansion Unit and Storage Expansion Unit with a 9404 System Unit.

## 9404 Feature Power Supply

The Feature Power Supply option (#5133) provides the electrical power necessary to support the third disk unit in either the AS/400 9404 System Unit or the 9404 Expansion Unit. That is, if you install a disk in the third position provided in the 9404 System Unit, you must also install a 9404 Feature Power Supply in the System Unit. Likewise, if you install a disk unit in the third position provided in the 9404 Expansion Unit, you must also install a 9404 Feature Power Supply in the Expansion Unit.

## 9406 System Unit Expansion

The System Unit Expansion option (#5042) is used exclusively with AS/400 9406 models F50 through F95. This feature comes in its own rack and actually adds two additional system I/O busses with six additional I/O expansion slots each. The rack also provides space for auxiliary storage devices such as 9331 diskette units, 9348 tape units, or 9337 DASD units (disk storage). Also included in the Bus Expansion Unit is a battery power unit capable of sustaining power to critical components during short power outages. As with the optional Battery Power Unit for the Processor Rack, this battery power unit allows the system to ride out short power outages and perform an orderly shutdown if power is not restored before the batteries begin to run down. The rack containing the Bus Expansion Unit also contains an interface for connection of an uninterruptible power source. As was discussed in Chapter 1, more I/O busses often mean an overall improvement in information movement within the system and thus an increase in overall system performance.

Since the System Unit Expansion is attached to the 9406 System Unit via a laser-driven optical fiber cable, the System Unit Expansion can be located up to 10 or 20 meters away from the rest of the 9406 system. For the sake of configuration flexibility when adding tape and DASD devices to the system, IBM recommends that the System Unit Expansion options be added to the F50–F95 systems before adding the 9406 Bus Extension Unit (covered next).

## 9406 Bus Extension Unit

The Bus Extension Unit (#5040) is used exclusively with AS/400 9406 systems. It provides 11 additional I/O expansion slots to one of the system's I/O busses. It comes mounted in its own separate rack and provides space for auxiliary storage devices such as 9331 diskette units, 9348 tape units, or 9337 DASD units (disk storage). Also included in the rack provided with the Bus Extension Unit is a battery power unit capable of sustaining power to critical components housed in the rack for at least five minutes in the event of a power failure. Alternately, an uninterruptible power supply interface is also provided.

## Cryptographic Processor

The Cryptographic Processor (#2620) helps improve the security of an AS/400 system by encoding information using cryptographic techniques (ANSI Data Encryption Standard [DES]). That is, AS/400 resident information can be scrambled via encryption keys, making it meaningless to anyone except those who have the key. This capability is particularly beneficial where valuable AS/400 information might be exposed to unauthorized access via a communications network.

The 4754 Security Interface Unit (SIU) is an optional device that attaches to the Cryptographic Processor and allows the user to enter cryptography keys by sliding a Personal Security Card through a reader.

## 5259 Migration Data Link

Current System/36 and System/38 users can use the 5259 Migration Data Link to ease the transition from these earlier systems to AS/400. The 5259 is a standalone device that allows an S/3X to be attached to an AS/400 through their local workstation controllers as shown in Figure 2.30. This physical connection along with the System/36 or System/38 migration aids and OS/400 allows the operator to efficiently transfer information from one system to the other at twinaxial cable speeds

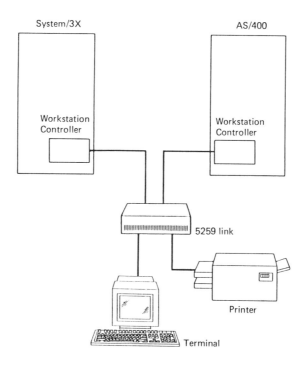

**Figure 2.30.** Example of a 5259 Migration Data Link configuration.

(over 1 million bps). This provides an alternative to using the time-consuming and error-prone diskette or tape method of transferring information between systems. The 5259 may be the only alternative for information transfer if the two systems are not configured with compatible tape or diskette devices.

Local workstations can also be attached to the 5259, allowing them to access either system from a single terminal. The users simply hit a simple keystroke sequence to switch from one system to the other. Printers attached to the 5259, however, must be dedicated to one system or the other.

The 5259 attaches to one workstation controller port on each system, providing seven addresses from each system. These seven addresses can be dedicated to information transfer between systems, workstation support, or any combination of the two. Usually, the more addresses assigned to transferring information between the two systems, the higher the transfer rate.

## 5299 Terminal Multiconnector and the TTPA

The most common way to attach local workstations to Application Systems is through twinaxial cable. The 5299 Terminal Multiconnector and the Telephone Twisted Pair Adapter (TTPA) shown in Figure 2.31 provide another wiring alternative. With the TTPA, you can make use of unused telephone twisted pair wiring that may already be installed in your building, as long as it conforms to IBM Type 3 Media specifications. This makes for reduced wiring costs at the expense of the maximum distance allowable from the computer or remote workstation controller to any workstation. With twinaxial cable this distance is 5000 feet, and with the less expensive twisted pair it is 1000 feet. The 5299 provides 10 telephone connectors that are used to attach up to 7 workstations and one computer system (two connec-

**Figure 2.31.** 5299 Terminal Multiconnector and Telephone Twisted Pair Adapter.

tors are used for problem determination procedures). The 5299/TTPA connections can coexist with twinaxial attached workstations on other ports of the computer system. The 5299 and TTPA do not require any power to operate.

## OPTION COMPATIBILITY MATRIX

With the many options and peripherals available for AS/400 computers, users can easily become confused as to what options work with which computers. Figure 2.32 summarizes what works with what for planning purposes. Appendix A lists some other devices supported (and not supported) by Application Systems. Because of complexities and various configuration limitations not addressed in this book, the assistance of IBM representatives and authorized dealers should be sought before finalizing any Application Systems configuration.

| | AS/Entry | 9402 | 9404 | 9406 |
|---|---|---|---|---|
| **Workstations** | | | | |
| 3486 Display Station | yes | yes | yes | yes |
| 3487 Display Station | yes | yes | yes | yes |
| 3855 Display Station | yes | yes | yes | yes |
| PS/2 as Display Station | yes | yes | yes | yes |
| **Printers** | | | | |
| 4230 Printer | yes | yes | yes | yes |
| 4224 Printer | yes | yes | yes | yes |
| 4234 Printer | yes | yes | yes | yes |
| 6252 Printer | yes | yes | yes | yes |
| 6262 Printer | yes | yes | yes | yes |
| 3816 Printer | yes | yes | yes | yes |
| 3825 Printer | yes | yes | yes | yes |
| 3835 Printer | yes | yes | yes | yes |
| 3827 Printer | yes | yes | yes | yes |
| **Workstation Controllers** | | | | |
| Workstation Expansion (#2551) | yes | no | no | no |
| First Workstation Att. (#6143/6145) | no | yes | no | no |
| Base Twinax Support (#9146/9148) | no | yes | no | no |
| Twinax W.S. Controller (#9050) | no | no | yes | yes |
| Twinax W.S. Controller (#6050) | no | F04/F06 | yes | yes |

*(Continued)*

**Figure 2.32.** Option compatibility matrix indicating which options discussed in the chapter work with which computer systems.

|  | AS/Entry | 9402 | 9404 | 9406 |
|---|---|---|---|---|
| **Workstation Controllers** *(Continued)* | | | | |
| Base ASCII Support (#9145/9147) | no | yes | no | no |
| ASCII Workstation Expansion (#6144) | no | yes | no | no |
| ASCII W.S. Controller (#9141) | no | no | yes | yes |
| ASCII W.S. Controller (#6141) | no | F04/F06 | yes | yes |
| 12-Port ASCII W.S. Attachment (#6142) | no | F04/F06 | yes | yes |
| **Protocol Converters** | | | | |
| 5208 Link Protocol Converter | yes | yes | yes | yes |
| 5209 Link Protocol Converter | yes | yes | yes | yes |
| **Main Storage Expansion** | | | | |
| AS/Entry Main Storage Expansion (#2585) | yes | no | no | no |
| 8 MB Main Storage (#3117) | no | yes | no | no |
| 16 MB Main Storage (#3118) | no | yes | no | no |
| 8 MB Main Storage (#3120) | no | no | yes | no |
| 8 MB Main Storage Expansion (#3121) | no | no | yes | no |
| 32 MB Main Storage Expansion (#3122) | no | no | yes | no |
| 8 MB Main Storage Card (#3119) | no | no | no | F35 |
| 16 MB Main Storage Card (#3100) | no | no | no | F35 |
| 32 MB Main Storage Card (#3101) | no | no | no | F35 |
| 8 MB Main Storage Card (#3140) | no | no | no | F45 |
| 16 MB Main Storage Card (#3141) | no | no | no | F45 |
| 32 MB Main Storage Card (#3142) | no | no | no | F45 |
| 16 MB Main Storage Card (#3102) | no | no | no | F50 |
| 32 MB Main Storage Card (#3103) | no | no | no | F50 |
| 64 MB Main Storage Card (#3104) | no | no | no | F50 |
| 32 MB Main Storage Card (#3130) | no | no | no | F60 |
| 64 MB Main Storage Card (#3131) | no | no | no | F60 |
| 128 MB Main Storage Card (#3132) | no | no | no | F60 |
| 64 MB Main Storage Card (#3133) | no | no | no | F70-F95 |
| 128 MB Main Storage Card (#3134) | no | no | no | F70-F95 |
| **Diskette Storage Expansion** | | | | |
| Diskette Unit 5.25" (#6139) | no | yes | no | no |
| Diskette Unit 5.25" (#6137) | no | no | yes | no |
| Diskette Unit 8" (#6138) | no | no | yes | no |
| 9331 Diskette Unit Model 1 (8") | no | no | no | yes |
| 9331 Diskette Unit Model 2 (5.25") | no | no | no | yes |

**Figure 2.32.** (Continued)

| | AS/Entry | 9402 | 9404 | 9406 |
|---|---|---|---|---|
| **Fixed Disk Storage Expansion** | | | | |
| Additional 160 MB Disk Drive (#2531) | yes | no | no | no |
| Additional 200 MB Disk Drive (#2532) | yes | no | no | no |
| Single Disk Unit (320 MB) (#6102) | no | F04/F06 | no | no |
| Single Disk Unit (400 MB) (#6103) | no | yes | no | no |
| Single Disk Unit (988 MB) (#6104) | no | yes | no | no |
| Single Disk Unit (320 MB) (#6105) | no | no | yes | no |
| Single Disk Unit (400 MB) (#6107) | no | no | yes | no |
| Single Disk Unit (988 MB) (#6109) | no | no | yes | no |
| Dual Disk Unit (800 MB) (#6121) | no | no | yes | no |
| Dual Disk Unit (1,976 MB) (#6123) | no | no | yes | no |
| Storage Expansion Unit (#7203) | no | no | F25 | no |
| Internal DASD Book Adapter (#2801) | no | no | no | yes |
| 9337 DASD (All models and features) | no | no | no | yes |
| **Tape Storage Expansion** | | | | |
| 1.2 GB Cart.Tape Unit (#6343/6348/6368) | no | yes | yes | yes |
| 525 MB Cart.Tape Unit (#6342/6347/6367) | no | standard | standard | yes (PRPQ) |
| 7208 2.3 GB 8mm Tape Unit | no | F04/F06 | yes | yes |
| 9348 Tape Unit | no | F04/F06 | yes | yes |
| 3490E Tape Unit | no | no | no | yes |
| **Optical Storage** | | | | |
| 3995 Optical Library | no | F04/F06 | yes | yes |
| **Storage Controllers** | | | | |
| Removable Media Dev. Attchmt. (#2621) | no | F04/F06 | yes | yes |
| 3490 High Perf. Mag Tape Attch. (#2644) | no | no | no | yes |
| Magnetic Storage Device Cntrl. (#6112) | no | no | no | yes |
| DASD Controller (#6500) | no | no | no | yes |
| **Communications Options** | | | | |
| Basic Communications Adapter (#2616) | yes | no | no | no |
| Expanded Communications Adapter (#2627) | yes | no | no | no |
| EIA Line Interface (#2630) | yes | no | no | no |
| V.35 High-Speed Line Interface (#2645) | yes | no | no | no |
| 16/4 Mbps Token-Ring Adapter (#2634) | yes | no | no | no |
| Multi-function I/O Proc. Expan. (#3116) | no | yes | no | no |
| EIA 232/V.24 One-Line Adapter (#6155/6154/6175/6174) | no | yes | yes | yes |
| X.21 One-Line Adapter (#6151/6171) | no | yes | yes | yes |
| V.35 One-Line Adapter (#6153/6173) | no | yes | yes | yes |

*(Continued)*

**Figure 2.32.** (Continued)

| | AS/Entry | 9402 | 9404 | 9406 |
|---|---|---|---|---|
| **Communications Options *(Continued)*** | | | | |
| Six-Line Communications Cntrl.(#2623) | no | yes | yes | yes |
| EIA 232/V.24 Two-Line Adapter (#2655/2654/2658/2657) | no | yes | yes | yes |
| X.21 Two-Line Adapter (#2656/2659) | no | yes | yes | yes |
| ISDN Basic Rate Adapter (#2605) | no | yes | yes | yes |
| 16/4 Mbps Token-Ring Adapter (#2636) | no | yes | yes | yes |
| 16/4 Mbps Token-Ring Adapter (#2626) | no | yes | yes | yes |
| 16/4 Mbps Token-Ring Adapter/HP (#2619) | no | F04/F06 | yes | yes |
| Ethernet LAN Adapter (#2625) | no | yes | yes | yes |
| Ethernet LAN Adapter/HP (#2617) | no | F04/F06 | yes | yes |
| FDDI Adapter (fiber) (#2618) | no | yes | yes | yes |
| FDDI Adapter (twisted pair) (#2665) | no | yes | yes | yes |
| **Modems** | | | | |
| 5853 Modem | yes | yes | yes | yes |
| 786X Modem | yes | yes | yes | yes |
| 7855 Modem | yes | yes | yes | yes |
| 5822 Digital Service Unit | yes | yes | yes | yes |
| **Remote Workstation Controllers** | | | | |
| 5394 Remote Workstation Controller | emulating 5294 | yes | yes | yes |
| **Other Options** | | | | |
| AS/Entry Processor Expansion (#2602) | yes | no | no | no |
| 9402 Battery Power Unit (#1102) | yes | yes | no | no |
| 9402 Card Expansion (#7106) | no | F02 | no | no |
| 9402 Expansion Gate (#7107) | no | F04/F06 | no | no |
| 9404 Expansion Unit (#7115) | no | F06 | no | no |
| 9404 Expansion Unit (#7120) | no | no | yes | no |
| 9404 Feature Power Supply (#5133) | no | no | yes | no |
| 9406 System Unit Expansion (#5042) | no | no | no | F50-F95 |
| 9406 Bus Extension Unit (#5040) | no | no | no | yes |
| Cryptographic Processor (#2620) | no | no | no | yes |
| 5259 Migration Data Link | yes | yes | yes | yes |
| 5299 and TTPA | yes | yes | yes | yes |

**Figure 2.32.** (Continued)

# 3

# Using Your AS/400

The previous chapters closely examined the System Units and optional equipment of the Application Systems. This chapter begins the discussion of how that hardware is put to work, namely, the all-important **software**. Software is a general term for the many programs that execute in computers. It is software that harnesses the Application Systems' computational power and allows you to perform many diverse and useful tasks. The chapter begins by taking you step by step through some "hands-on" interaction with an AS/400 system. This serves as a good introduction to the system and allows you to actually use the computer even if you never have before.

Later in the chapter, you are introduced to the kinds of software used to actually perform useful work with Application Systems. The three general categories of software along with the job each performs are discussed. Finally, AS/400's compatibility with software written for System/3X computers is discussed.

## GETTING YOUR FEET WET

One easy way to start learning about an AS/400 system is to sit down and start using one. The steps that follow in this section and throughout the remainder of this chapter help you learn by doing just that. If you are nervous about working with computers, remember that you cannot damage the computer system no matter how many mistakes you may make. Start with an open mind and you will likely be surprised at how easy AS/400s are to use.

To perform the exercises in this chapter, you need a user identification (user ID) and, if security has been activated on your system, a password. The user ID and password are given to you by the person designated as the **security officer** for your system. By providing the AS/400 system with your user ID and password, you are identifying yourself to the system and allowing it to verify that you are an authorized

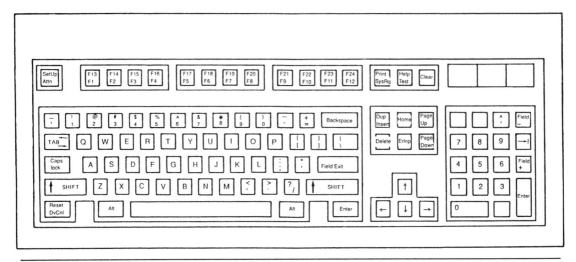

**Figure 3.1.** IBM enhanced keyboard layout.

user. If you do not have a user ID and password, now would be a good time to get them. If you cannot get them right now or if you do not have immediate access to a system, simply read along.

For your convenience, all keys referred to in the procedures that follow are labeled in Figure 3.1. However, since several different keyboard layouts are used with AS/400 workstations, yours may be different from the one shown. If you have difficulty locating the corresponding keys on your keyboard, see the "AS/400 Display Station User's Guide (#SC21-9744)" provided with the system. If your computer does not respond screen for screen with the procedures that follow, don't be concerned. Your security level, user profile, operating system level, and other things may cause your system to present an extra screen here or skip a screen there. If this happens, just follow the directions that appear on your screen and you should find yourself right back in step with these procedures.

## Signing On

Figure 3.2 shows the **sign-on screen** presented by the AS/400 system. This is the first screen a user sees when sitting before an active AS/400 terminal. In the upper-right corner, information about the AS/400 system is displayed. First, the AS/400 system's name is displayed. This is helpful when a business has two or more Application Systems because it may not be obvious which workstation is attached to which system. Next, the subsystem's name is displayed. Subsystems provide a way for the system's operator to subdivide the computer system for different types of activities (batch jobs, interactive sessions, etc.). The system operator may also assign different workstations to different printers according to their location, for example. However, typical systems have all workstations assigned to the same subsystem, in which case this information is not of much interest to the users. Finally, the name given by the AS/400 system to that particular workstation is displayed. All work done at a given workstation (printouts, for example) is labeled with that workstation's name.

The other area in the display is used to input information into the AS/400 system. By entering the requested information in the proper input area (called a **field**), you are identifying yourself to the system and may also initiate tasks. The first field is where you enter your **user identification (user ID)**, which is simply the name you use when interacting with the computer system. Associated with each user ID is a set

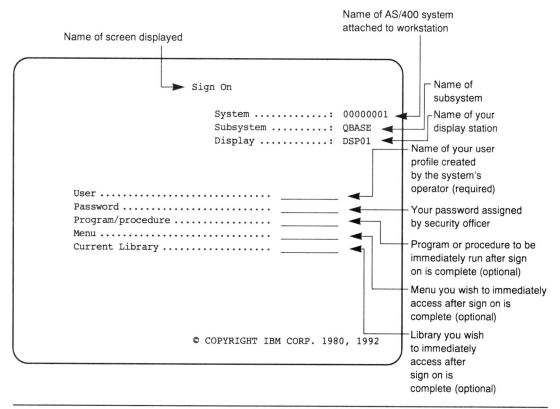

**Figure 3.2.** The sign-on screen presented by an AS/400 system.

of information called the **user profile**. This is created by the system operator for each user ID and contains information such as the tasks you can or cannot do, programs that automatically run, and menus you wish to have appear automatically after you sign on.

Next is the **password** field. This is a unique and secret code that must be entered every time the user signs on to the system. The purpose of the password is to prevent someone else from signing on to the system under your user ID. The password field may or may not be present on your screen, depending on whether the system operator has activated password security.

Below the password field is the **program/procedure** prompt. This is where you tell the system that you want to execute a particular program (or series of predefined commands called a **procedure**) automatically after you have signed on. If you leave this field blank, the system does what your user profile tells it to do when you sign on. If you enter a program name here, the system overrides what the user profile says to do unless the system's operator has disabled this function. Similarly, the **menu** field enables you to tell the system (if not disabled by the system's operator) to automatically present you with a particular menu when you sign on. Again, if you leave this field blank, the system will do what your user profile tells it to do when you sign on.

Finally, the **current library** field allows you to request access to libraries other than those normally available to you. A library can be thought of as a collection of similar items; for example, one library may contain all accounting programs. Every user has access to certain libraries, but by specifying a current library on the sign-on screen, you gain immediate access to a library if you are so authorized.

Armed with this information, you are now ready to sign on to an AS/400 system:

⇒ Locate the blinking or otherwise highlighted spot on the screen (called a **cursor**). If it is not located at the *user* field, repeatedly press the Tab key until it is.

⇒ Type your user ID in the field and press the Tab key.

⇒ If necessary, type your password and press the Tab key.

⇒ Press the Tab key to skip the *program/position* field and position the cursor at the *menu* field.

⇒ Type *MAIN* in the *menu* field.

⇒ Press the Enter key.

After the system verifies that you are an authorized user, the display shown in Figure 3.3 appears. You are now signed on to the AS/400 system. You were taken directly to the *AS/400 main menu* because you entered *main* in the menu field when you signed on. While you are still signed on, proceed to the next section to learn about AS/400's on-line help.

```
MAIN                        AS/400 Main Menu
                                                    System:   SYS400C2
   Select one of the following:

         1. User tasks
         2. Office tasks
         3. General system tasks
         4. Files, libraries, and folders
         5. Programming
         6. Communications
         7. Define or change the system
         8. Problem handling
         9. Display a menu
        10. User support and education

        90. Sign off




        Selection or command
        ===>_____

        _____


        F3=Exit    F4=Prompt   F9=Retrieve   F12=Cancel   F13=User support
        F23=Set initial menu
```

**Figure 3.3.** AS/400 main menu.

## Using On-Line Help

Any time you are using your AS/400 system and you are not sure how to proceed, try using the **on-line help** function. On-line help can be thought of as a built-in teacher always ready to assist you.

There are two different types of help available in AS/400 systems. First, by pressing the **Help key** (labeled "F1") you are presented with textual information pertaining to the task you are performing. Let us see how this type of help works:

- If you are still signed on to the AS/400 system, you should see the AS/400 main menu screen shown in Figure 3.3.

- If you are not signed on, follow the procedure previously given for *signing on* to get to this screen.

From the AS/400 main menu, you can get to any operating system task for which you are authorized. For example, suppose you would like to change your password. Although we will not actually change your password in this exercise, we will see how it is done. Since the AS/400 main menu makes no mention of passwords, we use OS/400's on-line help facility to see how to proceed.

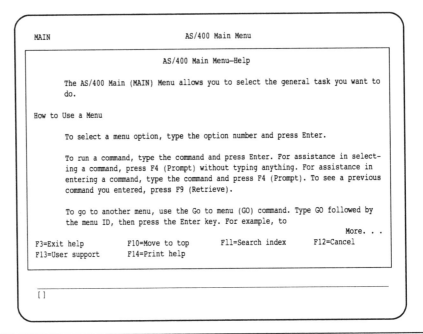

```
 MAIN                            AS/400 Main Menu

 ┌──────────────────────────────────────────────────────────────────┐
 │                       AS/400 Main Menu─Help                        │
 │                                                                    │
 │      The AS/400 Main (MAIN) Menu allows you to select the general task you want to │
 │      do.                                                           │
 │                                                                    │
 │  How to Use a Menu                                                 │
 │                                                                    │
 │      To select a menu option, type the option number and press Enter. │
 │                                                                    │
 │      To run a command, type the command and press Enter. For assistance in select- │
 │      ing a command, press F4 (Prompt) without typing anything. For assistance in │
 │      entering a command, type the command and press F4 (Prompt). To see a previous │
 │      command you entered, press F9 (Retrieve).                     │
 │                                                                    │
 │      To go to another menu, use the Go to menu (GO) command. Type GO followed by │
 │      the menu ID, then press the Enter key. For example, to        │
 │                                                            More. . . │
 │  F3=Exit help          F10=Move to top      F11=Search index    F12=Cancel │
 │  F13=User support      F14=Print help                              │
 └──────────────────────────────────────────────────────────────────┘

   ───────────────────────────────────────────────────────────────────
   [ ]
```

**Figure 3.4.** Help text for the AS/400 Main Menu.

⇒ Press the Help key ("F1" key).

You are now presented with the text shown in Figure 3.4. This provides general information about the screen we were on when we hit the Help key (the AS/400 main menu). The system recognized that the user was on the AS/400 main menu and presented specific information pertaining to that screen. This is called **contextual help**. Additional help information is available as indicated by the *More . . .* message at the bottom of the help screen.

⇒ Press the PgDn key.

You are now presented with the additional help text shown in Figure 3.5 pertaining to the AS/400 main menu. This page of help text starts to explain menu item 1: *User tasks* on the AS/400 main menu. To finish reading about item 1:

⇒ Press the PgDn key again.

You are now presented with the rest of the help text that explains menu item 1 as shown in Figure 3.6.

Notice that menu item #1 allows you to change your password, so this is the

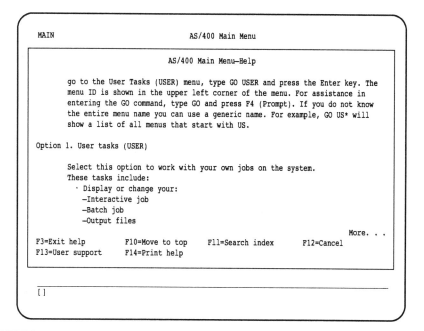

**Figure 3.5.** Second page of help text for the AS/400 Main Menu.

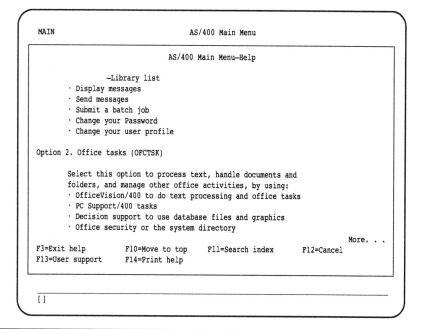

**Figure 3.6.** Third page of help text for the AS/400 Main Menu.

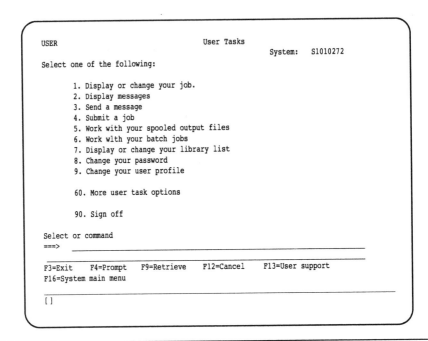

```
USER                              User Tasks
                                              System:    S1010272
Select one of the following:

        1. Display or change your job.
        2. Display messages
        3. Send a message
        4. Submit a job
        5. Work with your spooled output files
        6. Work wlth your batch jobs
        7. Display or change your library list
        8. Change your password
        9. Change your user profile

        60. More user task options

        90. Sign off

Select or command
===>  _____

       _____
F3=Exit    F4=Prompt    F9=Retrieve    F12=Cancel    F13=User support
F16=System main menu

       _____
[ ]
```

**Figure 3.7.** The user tasks menu provides an option for changing your password.

menu item we need. We have learned what we needed to know, so it is time to exit help and get back to the AS/400 main menu:

⇒ Press the F3 key.

Because we learned that menu item 1, *User Tasks*, allows us to change our password,

⇒ Type 1 and press the Enter key to select the *User Tasks* menu item. This takes you to the user tasks menu shown in Figure 3.7. Selecting menu item 8, *Change your password*, would allow you to do just that:

⇒ Type *8* and press the Enter key to select the *Change your password* menu item.

Figure 3.8 shows the change password screen that lets you change your password. Notice that the cursor is located on the current password field. It is asking you to enter your current password. The other two input fields are for your new password (they ask you to type it in twice to avoid typing errors when entering your new password). Let us see what pressing Help does now.

⇒ Press the Help key.

Figure 3.9 shows the resulting help text. Notice that since the cursor was at the current password field, help text specific to that field is presented. This is a more spe-

```
                          Change Password

Password last changed..........................:08/05/99

Type choices, press Enter.

     Current password ..........................:

     New password ..............................:

     New Password (to verify) ..................:




F3=Exit                        F12=Cancel
_____
[ ]
```

**Figure 3.8.** Screen used to change your password.

```
                          Change Password

Password last changed..........................:08/05/99

Type choices, press Enter.

     Current password ..........................:
                     +------------------------------------------------+
     New password    |          Current Password—Help                 |
                     |                                                |
     New password    | Type the password you currently use to sign on the sys- |
                     | tem.                                           |
                     |                                        Bottom  |
                     | F2=Extended help   F10=Move to top   F11=Search index |
                     | F12=Cancel         F13=User support  F24=More keys |
                     +------------------------------------------------+


F3=Exit                        F12=Cancel
_____
[ ]
```

**Figure 3.9.** Help text for the current password field of the change password screen.

cific example of contextual help. Since you are not actually going to change your password, return to the AS/400 main menu.

⇒ Press the F3 key to get back to the change password screen.

⇒ Press the F3 key again to get back to the user tasks menu.

⇒ Press the F3 key again to get back to the AS/400 main menu.

Contextual help is very useful when you are in the middle of a task and you get stuck. But what if you just want information about some specific OS/400 task or topic? Another function of AS/400's on-line help, called **index search**, can be employed. This is a concept very similar to the index in the back of a book or manual. You look up a term, turn to the proper page in the book, and then read information about that term. With AS/400's index search, however, the computer system looks up the information for you and presents it on the screen. Let us see how this function works. Suppose we want to know more about the AS/400 term *job*. As before, we start by pressing the Help key.

⇒ Press the Help key.

This presents us with the help text shown in Figure 3.10. This time, however, we

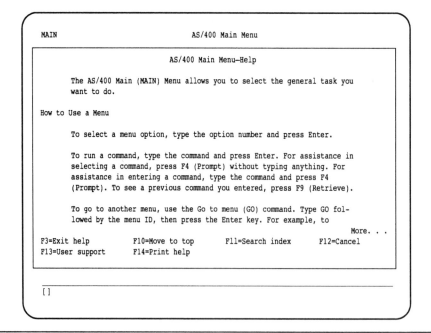

**Figure 3.10.** Help text for AS/400 main menu.

```
                          Search Help Index

Index Search allows you to tell the system to search for specific
Information. To use Index Search, do the following:

        1. Type the phrase or words to search for.

        2. Press Enter.

When you press Enter, the system searches for topics related to the words you
supplied and displays a list of topics found.

If you press Enter without typing anything, the system displays a list of all
available topics.




Type words to search for, press Enter
_____



F3=Exit help        FS=All topics        F12=Cancel F13=User support
[ ]
```

**Figure 3.11.** Screen used to look up information in the AS/400 help index.

ignore the help text and use the index function. Notice the *F11=Search index* message at the bottom of the help screen:

⇒ Press F11.

Figure 3.11 shows the search help index screen. From this screen, you can type in a term and ask the computer to search its help index for any information related to that term. We were interested in the term *job queues*.

⇒ Type in *job* and press the Enter key.

Figure 3.12 shows the kind of result you will get. The AS/400 system has searched the OS/400 help index for all information or **topics** related to the term *job*. There is more than one topic that is related to the term *job*, but the first one, *About job queues, output queues, and priority*, looks as if it contains the basic definition. Since the cursor is already positioned at that topic,

⇒ Type *5* and press the Enter key to display the topic.

You are presented with the information shown in Figure 3.13 and you can read about job queues. Thus, the system automatically looks up information for you on any topic contained in the index. This is faster than locating the appropriate AS/400

```
                      Main Help Index for AS/400

Type options, press Enter.
   5=Display topic     6=Print topic

Option Topic
        About job queues, output queues, and priority
        About jobs, job descriptions, and job logs
        About your work on the system
        Acknowledgment character
        Active job, file, record
        Add autostart job entry (ADDAJE) command
        Add forms control table entry (ADDFCTE) command
        Add job queue entry (ADDJOBQE) command
        Add job schedule entry (ADDJOBSCDE) command
        Add network job entry (ADDNET JOBE) command
        Add prestart job entry (ADDPJE) command
        Add RJE communications entry (ADDRJECMNE)
                                                           More  . .
Or to search again, type new words and press Enter.
job _____


F3=Exit help     FS=All topics     F12=Cancel     F13=User support
  _____
[ ]
```

**Figure 3.12.** List of help index topics related to the term "job."

```
                    About job queues, output queues, and priority
   Help
           A queue is a waiting list. It may be a list of people waiting to be seated in
           a restaurant, a list of jobs waiting to be processed by a computer, or a list
           of reports waiting to be printed on a printer.

           The items on a queue receive service in the same order as listed on the queue.
           For example, the first name on the restaurant waiting list is the first person
           to be seated. Each time a person is seated, his or her name is removed from
           the list and the remaining names move up one step in the list.

           A job queue is a set of one or more jobs that have been grouped together and
           are waiting their turn to run. In general, when a job reaches a queue, it is
           put at the end of the line and as jobs leave the queue it moves towards the
           front.

           Job queues have a status of Ready when they are operational and Held when they
           have been stopped. Tasks related to job queues can be performed on the Work
           with Job Queues display. To get to the Work
                                                           More. . .
F3=Exit help     F1O=Move to top     F12=Cancel     F13=User support
F14=Print help
   _____
[ ]
```

**Figure 3.13.** Text from the help index topic "About job queues, output queues, and priority."

manual and leafing through it page by page. Computers are very good at handling large amounts of information. Why not apply this strength to handling information about the computer itself? When you are done reading the help text, go back to the AS/400 main menu:

⇒ Press the F3 key repeatedly until you see the AS/400 main menu.

Feel free to use this contextual help function at any time during your interaction with any AS/400 system (including the rest of the procedures in this book).

## Signing Off

When all tasks are complete, you can sign off the system in one of two ways. First, you can select a *90. Sign off* menu item like the one shown in Figure 3.3. The other way to sign off is to type in *signoff* at any command prompt. Let us try the latter:

⇒ Locate the blinking cursor. If it is not located at the "⇒" command prompt near the bottom of the display, repeatedly press the Tab key until it is.

⇒ Type *signoff* and press the Enter key.

The system returns you to the sign-on screen.

## Using AS/400 On-Line Education

Every AS/400 system comes with a group of self-study tutorial programs that together make up AS/400's **on-line education**. As the term *on-line* implies, the educational information is presented on an AS/400 workstation in an interactive learning session. The student is presented with visual information, asked to provide simple responses, and informally quizzed on the topics presented (the quiz results are not recorded). Before any of the on-line education can be accessed, the user must first be **enrolled** in the on-line education system. This is a simple process that involves entering the user's first and last names.

The educational information is organized as **courses, modules, topics**, and **subtopics** as illustrated in Figure 3.14. After being enrolled, the user can select a course for study. One module provided by IBM with every AS/400 system is **How to Use AS/400 Online Education**, which can be found in the **Tutorial System Support for AS/400 (TSS)** course. This first module introduces the concept of computer-based education and teaches the user how to work with the courses, modules, and topics.

Rarely will a single user need to take every module in a course. For example, a clerical worker need not take the module on command language programming in the

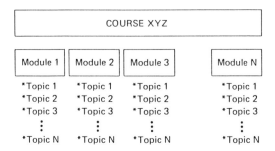

**Figure 3.14.** AS/400 on-line education is organized into courses, modules, and topics, as shown.

TSS course. This is where the **audience path** comes in. Once the user selects a particular course, the AS/400 system recommends a customized sequence of modules from that course based on the user's job needs. These needs can be defined by the user or the education administrator. IBM has provided some predefined audience paths that cover many users (e.g., a systems operator and secretarial audience paths are included). The education administrator can also create additional audience paths if necessary to accommodate the user's educational needs. Finally, tools are available that allow a business to design its own on-line education courses covering virtually any topic (loan processing, company policy, hotel check-in procedures). These specially designed courses then become additions to the AS/400 on-line education system.

It is strongly recommended that the user take the *How to Use AS/400 Online Education* course before taking any of the others. The next section guides the first-time user through this first course to provide a starting point.

### What You Need Before You Start

The only thing you need to use the AS/400 on-line education system is your user ID (and a password if security is activated on your system). Once you have these, find any workstation (terminal) and start.

### Taking the First Course in AS/400 On-Line Education

As with any AS/400 task you wish to perform, the first step in the process is to sign on to the system, as done previously in this chapter.

⇒ Locate the blinking cursor on the screen. If it is not located at the user field, repeatedly press the Tab key until it is.

⇒ Type your user ID in the field and press the Tab key.

⇒ If necessary, type your password and press the Tab key.

```
MAIN                        AS/400 Main Menu
                                                        System:    SYS400C2
Select one of the following:

        1. User tasks
        2. Office tasks
        3. General system tasks
        4. Files, libraries, and folders
        5. Programming
        6. Communications
        7. Define or change the system
        8. Problem handling
        9. Display a menu
       10. User support and education

       90. Sign off


Selection or command
===>


F3=Exit  F4=Prompt  F9=Retrieve  F12=Previous  F13=User support
F23=Set initial menu
```

**Figure 3.15.** AS/400 main menu.

⇒ Press the Tab key to skip the program/position field and position the cursor at the menu field.

⇒ Type *MAIN* in the menu field and press the Enter key.

After the system verifies that you are an authorized user, the AS/400 main menu shown in Figure 3.15 appears. You are now signed on to the AS/400 system. To get to the on-line education, use the user support function key:

⇒ Press the 1 key then the 0 key and then press the Enter key.

This presents you with the user support menu shown in Figure 3.16.

⇒ Press the 9 key to select the on-line education menu item.

Depending on your authorization level, you may or may not get the screen shown in Figure 3.17.

⇒ If you see the screen shown in Figure 3.17, press the 3 key and the Enter key to *work as a student*.

⇒ If you are presented with the student enrollment screen shown in Figure 3.18 you must enroll:

⇒ Type in your first name.

```
SUPPORT                    User Support

Select one of the following:

        1. How to use help
        2. Search system help index
        3. How to use commands
        4. Question and answer
        5. AS/400 publications
        6. IBM product information
        7. How to handle system problems
        8. Problem handling
        9. Online education


Selection or command
===>_____
    _____

F3=Exit  F4=Prompt  F9=Retrieve  F12=Previous  F16=System main menu
    _____

    [ ]
```

**Figure 3.16.** The user support menu provides access to AS/400's on-line education.

```
                         Start Education Administration

Select one of the following:

        1. Work with student information
        2. Work with courses
        3. Work as student








Selection






F3=Exit  F12=Previous
    _____

    [ ]
```

**Figure 3.17.** This screen is presented if you do not have the security clearance necessary to act as an education administrator. If it appears, choose the *work as student* option.

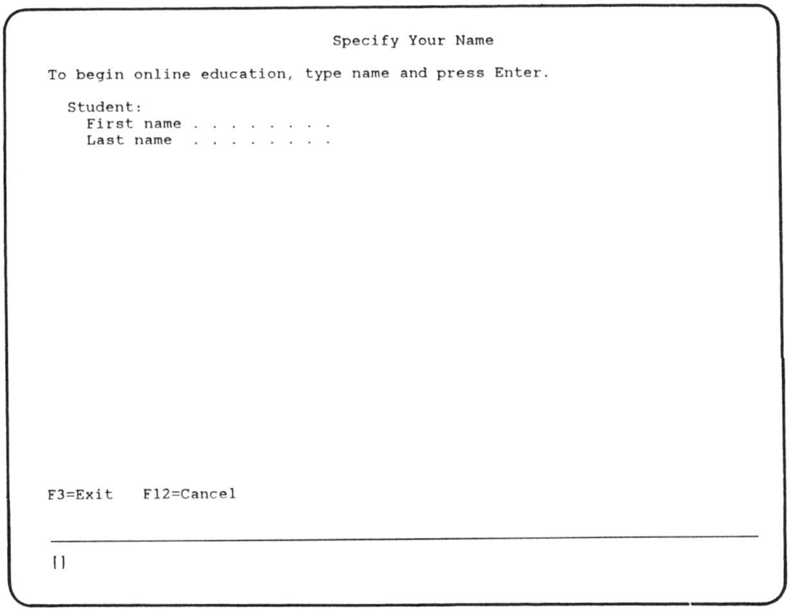

```
                         Specify Your Name
        To begin online education, type name and press Enter.

            Student:
              First name . . . . . . . .
              Last name  . . . . . . . .
















        F3=Exit    F12=Cancel
        _____

        []
```

**Figure 3.18.** Screen used to enroll in AS/400 on-line education.  If this screen appears, enter your name.  If this screen is bypassed, you are already enrolled.

⇒ Press the Tab key.

⇒ Type in your last name.

⇒ Press the Enter key.

You now find yourself at the select course option screen shown in Figure 3.19. This is where you tell the on-line education system what educational information you want to learn. The first module we will take is called "How to Use AS/400 Online Education" and is part of the "Tutorial System Support" course. This module takes about 25 minutes and teaches you how to efficiently get around inside the on-line education system. You can exit the course at any time. To start this course:

⇒ Hit the Tab key five times to position the cursor next to the "Tutorial System Support (TSS)" course.

⇒ Press the 1 key and then press the Enter key.

You are then presented with a list of the modules that comprise the TSS course, as shown in Figure 3.20. Since we want to take the "How to Use AS/400 Online Education" module and that is where the cursor currently is, select that module:

⇒ Press the 1 key and then press the Enter key.

```
                         Select Course

Type option, press Enter.
  1=Select   8=Display description

Option        Course Title
    _         Office Support course
    _         Office Support
    _         Introduction to Data Communications
    _         RPG Programming Course
    _         AS/400 Implementation Course
    _         Tutorial System Support (TSS)




                                                       Bottom
  F3=Exit    F9=Print list   F12=Cancel   F17=Top   F18=Bottom
  _____
  []
```

**Figure 3.19.** Screen used to select from the AS/400 on-line education courses and modules.

```
                      Select Audience Path

  Course title . . . . . . . . . :   Tutorial System Support (TSS)

  Type option, press Enter.
    1=Select   5=Display modules   8=Display description

  Option      Audience Path Title
              How to Use AS/400 Online Education
              All Modules in the Course
              Communications Implementer
              Data Base Administrator
              Data Processing Manager
              Executives
              Office Systems Administrator
              Clerical User (Secretary)
              Office Implementer
              Experienced S/36 System Operator
              Experienced S/38 System Operator
              Programmer/Implementer
              Professional User




                                                        More...
  F3=Exit    F9=Print list   F12=Cancel   F17=Top   F18=Bottom
```

**Figure 3.20.** Screen used to select a module of the TSS course.

You are now presented with the "Select Audience Path" screen shown in Figure 3.20. To start the "How to Use AS/400 Online Education" module,

⇒ Press the 1 key and then press the Enter key.

The system will momentarily present you with a message that tells you to stand by as it loads the course. You are then presented with the introductory screens for "How to Use AS/400 Online Education." Follow the instructions as they appear on the screen and you will have no trouble completing the course. After you complete this course, you are ready to learn more about AS/400 by taking the other modules in the TSS course or any other course of interest.

## THE REAL SOFTWARE—A MODEL

The term *software* is analogous to the term *publication*. Newspapers are a category of publication. Annual reports, novels, and Who's Who directories are some other categories of publications. These different categories fill very different needs. The same situation exists with software. Different categories of software are diverse in function and purpose. We have just explored some special-purpose programs provided with all AS/400 computers. However, these programs do not allow you to perform useful work, which is the reason you bought a computer. The *real software* that allows the user to perform useful work is purchased separately.

The basic categories of real software used in Application Systems can be understood through the simple software model shown in Figure 3.21. There are three

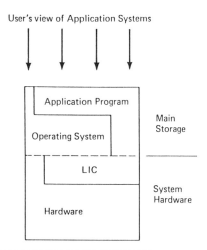

**Figure 3.21.** Conceptual software model of Application Systems' basic software structure. The three layers of the software model work together to perform useful work for the user.

basic categories or software layers commonly used with Application Systems computers: the **application program** layer, the **operating system** layer, and the **Licensed Internal Code (LIC)** layer. While each software layer performs a completely different job, all three work closely together to perform useful work for the user. Although there are some special-purpose programs that don't fit neatly into any of these three categories, the majority of software commonly used to perform business tasks does. Later chapters will focus on the application and operating system layers. For now, let us briefly look at each of the three layers in our software model.

## Application Programs

The top software layer in the software model is the *application program* layer (highlighted in Figure 3.22). The programs in this layer *apply* Application Systems to a specific task (e.g., word processing or accounting) and thus are called *application* programs. They actually perform the task for which the user purchased the computer whereas the other two layers play important support roles.

The *user's view* arrows in the figure indicate that the user usually interacts with the application program layer and less frequently with the operating system. By working closely with the other software layers, the application program processes the various keystrokes made by the user and responds by displaying information on the computer's display or some other output device.

As we see later in the chapter, programs written for System/3X computers can be either directly executed or migrated to Application Systems. This allows Applica-

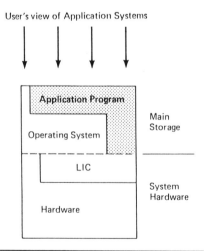

**Figure 3.22.** The application program software layer of the model. The application program defines the particular tasks the computer is performing for the user.

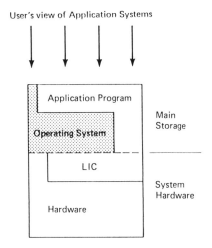

**Figure 3.23.** The Operating System software layer of the model. The operating system provides the environment in which the application program(s) run.

tion Systems users to capitalize on the thousands of application programs available for these popular business systems. There is an application program that can help users with just about anything they wish to do. Some more common functions application programs perform in the business environment are accounting, financial modeling, word processing, database management, electronic mail, and computer graphics. Chapter 4 is devoted to discussing various application programs.

## Operating Systems

The next layer in our software model is called the *operating system* (highlighted in Figure 3.23). The operating system must manage the hardware resources of the computer system and perform tasks under the control of application programs and keyboard commands typed by the user. The application program can rely on the operating system to perform many of the detailed *housekeeping* tasks associated with the internal workings of the computer. Thus, the operating system is said to provide the *environment* in which application programs execute. Operating systems also accept commands directly from the user to do things like copying files and changing passwords.

## LIC Instructions

The third and final layer of software in our software model is called the Licensed Internal Code (LIC) layer (highlighted in Figure 3.24). LIC is a set of highly specialized programs written by the manufacturer of a computer and never tampered with

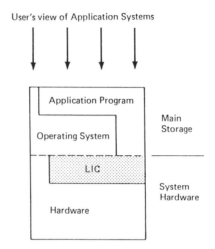

**Figure 3.24.** The LIC software layer of the model. LIC directly controls the hardware elements of the Application Systems and shields application programs and the operating system from hardware details.

by the computer operator or users. The set of LIC instructions in AS/400 computers is embedded deeply within the computer system and is therefore considered to be part of the computing machine itself rather than part of a program running on the machine. Unlike application programs or operating systems, LIC is used only by other programs. That is, LIC never interacts directly with the user or the programmer and exists only to help application programs and the operating system perform their tasks. LIC instructions also help shield application programs from the hardware specifics of computers, allowing for evolutionary product improvements without sacrificing application program compatibility.

It is the particularly rich LIC layer in AS/400 that helps set its architecture apart from those of more conventional computers. The built-in database, single-level storage, object-oriented architecture, and other AS/400 features described in Chapter 1 are all designed into the LIC layer of AS/400, making them *part* of the machine itself. This results in highly efficient, consistent, and easy-to-use implementations of these functions.

## How the AS/400's Software Layers Are Different

One of the basic differences between AS/400 and traditional computer systems can be seen by examining the software layers. Figure 3.25 shows the three software layers of our model (application, operating system, and LIC) in a little more detail. The

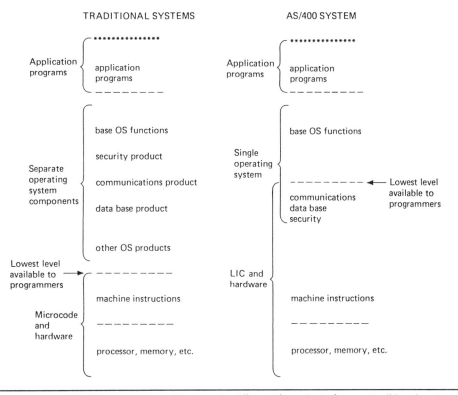

**Figure 3.25.** AS/400's software architecture is different from that of more traditional systems. Implementing more function in the LIC layer and providing a one-piece operating system results in improved efficiency, consistency, and simplicity.

figure shows the traditional software layers side by side with those of the AS/400. The first thing to notice is the difference between where the various software functions reside in the layers. In the traditional system, functions such as security, database, and communications reside in the operating system layer, which is usually made up of a collection of separately purchased operating system products. With this traditional approach, each operating system product must be installed and maintained separately. This is why a highly skilled programmer called a **systems programmer** is needed to support this kind of system.

With the AS/400 approach, much of the basic database, security, and other functions are built into the LIC layer. Because LIC implementations are in general more efficient by nature of their *"closeness"* to the hardware, overall system performance is improved. The operating system for the AS/400 (OS/400) provides all its functions in a single product. This eliminates the need for the operator to install, tailor, and manage the multiple operating system components in traditional operating systems. The price you pay for this simplicity is that you get (and pay for) all OS/400 functions whether you need them or not, whereas the user can select only the traditional operating system components he needs.

Another basic difference lies in the way a programmer "sees" the systems. With the traditional system, system functions such as database management or security reside in the operating system and therefore can be modified by a systems programmer. This gives the systems programmer more flexibility in customizing the computer system at the expense of more complexity.

With the AS/400, you gain ease of use and efficiency at the price of some flexibility. For example, since the database functions are built into the LIC instructions, they cannot be modified. If programmers want to make a change in the way the database is managed, they simply cannot. In a traditional system environment, the database functions are part of the operating system and so they can be modified by a highly trained systems programmer.

## How the Layers Work Together

To better understand how these three software layers work together to perform tasks for the user, let us quickly trace a typical series of events that might occur when you strike keys during a computer session.

In our example depicted in Figure 3.26, a salesperson is using a word-processing application program to type a memo to a prospective customer. Let us set the stage and then see what the various software layers do.

The word-processing application program has just finished processing the latest set of keystrokes and has instructed the operating system to provide the next set of keystrokes when they are available. In complying with the request, the operating system asks the LIC instructions to provide the next set of keystrokes when available.

Now that the stage is set, let us see what happens as the salesperson types the next line in the letter. When she holds down the Shift key and presses the T key on the keyboard to start the next sentence, the terminal sends the **scan code** corresponding to each key over the twinaxial cable to the workstation controller in the AS/400. The workstation controller receives the scan code and translates it into its intended meaning. Because the workstation controller knows that the shift key has been pressed and not released, the scan code associated with the T is translated into the letter T. Next, the workstation controller stores the T in a buffer area and echoes the T to the workstation, where it appears on the display. Notice that the workstation controller manages this entire transaction independent of the main processor or any of the software layers. This is typical of the multi-processor architecture, which allows the main processor to con-

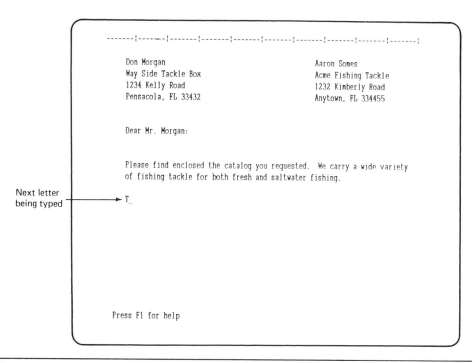

**Figure 3.26.** A salesperson is typing a memo using a word-processing application program. The salesperson has just pressed the T key on the keyboard along with the Shift key.

centrate on the user's application program rather than managing workstation traffic. In fact, the workstation controller will continue to manage all interaction with the salesperson's terminal until she presses the Enter key at the end of the line. The scan code associated with the Enter key signals the workstation controller to interrupt the main processor and notify it that new information is ready for use. Here is where the software layers of our model come into play. First the LIC verifies that all went well in receiving the information, then it notifies the operating system that the information is correct, ready, and waiting for use. The operating system makes the information available to the application program and then reactivates the application program, which was dormant, waiting for the next keystrokes. The application program processes the information as necessary, instructs the operating system to wait for the next keystrokes, and the whole thing starts all over again.

For simplicity, I have glossed over many of the detailed steps that the computer must perform simply to process a series of keystrokes. As complicated as this process may be, computers easily perform these steps in small fractions of a second.

Similar but more complicated cooperation among the three software layers occurs for most functions performed by the computer such as reading or writing a file on a disk and communicating with other computers.

## AS/400 SOFTWARE COMPATIBILITY—WILL S/3X PROGRAMS WORK?

The System/3X computer family is the most widely used business computing system in the world today. As a result, a wide variety of programs have been developed for these computers. The flexibility afforded by virtue of this large and diverse software base allowed System/3X computers to fill many different needs. Of course, this plethora of available programs did not exist when the original System/3X computers were first announced. It took the independent efforts of a great many people over many years to develop the large software base that exists today for System/3X. To capitalize on that software base, software compatibility was a primary objective in the design of AS/400 computers. That is, most programs written for the System/3X family will either run directly on or can be easily migrated to AS/400 computers.

It is important to understand that of the three software layers in our software model, compatibility with programs in the application programs layer is the most important. Why? First, application programs typically represent the primary share of a user's software investment. Being forced to abandon an application program because of incompatibilities may also make the user throw away whatever data and training/experience have accumulated with the application program — both of which can be substantial. Some users have developed custom application programs at considerable cost in development time and money. Incompatibility at the application program level would render these programs virtually useless. Finally, and perhaps most important, application layer compatibility allows Application Systems users access to the thousands of application programs that have been developed for System/3X computers.

What about the operating system and microcode layers? Maintaining compatibility with earlier System/3X operating systems software is not important for several reasons. Operating systems typically represent only a small fraction of the user's software investment. Further, a new operating system is usually necessary to allow the users to have access to the new feature of the computer system not considered by the programmers of the old operating system. Of course the user is automatically supplied with a new LIC layer with every AS/400 system that fully supports the hardware.

### Inside AS/400 Compatibility

To understand AS/400 compatibility you must understand something about the way software is typically written. First, a programmer writes a program's instructions or

**code** using a **programming language** (e.g., COBOL or RPG), which is basically a library of computer instructions from which a programmer may choose to write programs. The list of programming language instructions is called **source code**. To run the program on a computer, the source code instructions must be converted into instructions a computer can understand. This conversion process is called **compiling** the program. When source code is compiled, the result, called **object code**, can be directly executed by the computer hardware.

In addition to programming languages, the programmer can use predefined lists of operating system commands to do things like start programs and present menus. These predefined lists are called **procedures**. With this background, let us look at the way AS/400 provides compatibility with System/3X programs.

Programs written for System/38 computers, in general, are *object-code*-compatible with AS/400 systems. That is, you can take the object code for a program written for a System/38, load it on an AS/400, and run the program. This is possible because of AS/400's **System/38 environment**, which makes the AS/400 system look like a System/38 to the application program. Furthermore, most of the operating system commands used on the System/38 are the same as those used on AS/400. For this reason, System/38 procedures will also run with little or no change.

Programs written for the System/36 are supported on AS/400 through the **System/36 environment**. This is another operating mode of AS/400, one that makes the application program think it is actually running on a System/36. However, because of basic differences between the architectures of the two systems, AS/400 systems are not object-code-compatible with System/36 application programs. A programmer must therefore make some (usually minor) changes in the application program source code, load the System/36 source code on an AS/400, and recompile the source code. The program can then be run under AS/400's System/36 environment. System/36 procedures (i.e., OCL) are also supported in AS/400's System/36 mode, further easing the migration effort. However, if any System/36 assembly language routines are used, they must be rewritten (e.g., converted to a CL procedure). Further, because of the overhead processing associated with the AS/400's System/36 environment, there is a system performance penalty when operating in this mode (see Chapter 1). Chapter 5 further discusses the AS/400 System/3X environments, and Chapter 7 covers migration from System/3X systems to AS/400 in more detail.

## SYSTEMS APPLICATION ARCHITECTURE—THE NEW STANDARD

In today's business world, computers are used in many diverse environments for a wide variety of tasks. To meet these different needs, three major IBM computer system families have evolved: System/390 mainframe computers, AS/400 computers, and Personal System/2 (PS/2). Since there was no single programming standard that covered all of these three computer families, programmers would write programs for a particular computer family. Later, if the user wanted to use the program on a computer from a different family, the program would have to undergo major changes before it could be used.

To provide program compatibility and consistency across the three families of IBM computers, IBM has published a specification called the **Systems Application Architecture (SAA)**. SAA is a set of programming rules that provides a base for the development of application programs that can be used on computers from all three families: System/390, AS/400, and PS/2. SAA is the beginning of a long-term application program strategy much as the **Systems Network Architecture (SNA)** is the long-term communications strategy. As with SNA, the SAA will be expanded over time to meet the needs of users and the overall goal — consistency across the three major IBM computer families.

When a program conforms to the Systems Application Architecture, three nice things happen.

*Program portability:* An application program conforming to the Systems Application Architecture can be easily migrated across family boundaries (e.g., from an AS/400 to a System/390 mainframe) with only minor changes. This allows the user to migrate any application programs to larger (or smaller) computers as business needs change. Further, the same application program can be used on multiple types of computers that may be found in a single business, bringing common function to all users. Another advantage of program portability is that programmers who follow the conventions of the Systems Application Architecture can offer their programs to users of computers in all three families. This gives users a wider variety of programs from which to choose.

*Program interaction:* By following the Systems Application Architecture communications conventions, one Systems Application Architecture program can communicate directly with another Systems Application Architecture program running on a different computer system. The programs in different families of computers in a network can cooperate directly with one another with little or no user assistance. This relieves the user of having to control the interaction between various computer systems and provides for a sophisticated computer environment.

*Standard user interface:* It takes time for a user to learn to use a given application program. Not only must the basic function provided be understood (e.g., spreadsheet and database), but the user must also learn the details of interacting with the user interface of a specific program. This includes function key definitions, how to select a menu item or call up help information, where commands appear on the screen, and so on. The Systems Application Architecture defines standards for these items and many other user interface details. The goal of these user interface standards is to allow for transfer of learning, ease of learning, and ease of use across programs for all three major computer families.

The AS/400 operating system and several programming languages participate in the Systems Application Architecture, providing a base for the development of Systems Application Architecture–conforming application programs for AS/400 computers.

# Application Programs

In the last chapter we saw that three basic software layers in Application Systems cooperate to perform useful work for the user. This chapter concentrates on the top layer of the model—application programs. It is the application program that actually "applies" Application Systems' computational power to a particular business task. Some businesses use application programs designed, written, and sold by other companies. These are called **prewritten** application programs. Other companies choose to design and write their own **custom** application programs or use a combination of prewritten and custom application programs. This chapter looks at both application program alternatives. Some prewritten application programs for AS/400 are discussed. By no means does this chapter provide a complete consumers' guide to all prewritten application software for AS/400. Comprehensive coverage of the many business application program products available today would fill many books, each of which would be obsolete by the time it was published. This chapter helps the reader to make more informed purchasing decisions and gives examples of the kinds of things available from prewritten application programs. In the last part of the chapter, we briefly look at the custom software alternative.

## CAN PREWRITTEN PROGRAMS FIT THE BILL?

Today's prewritten application programs range from simple programs that concentrate on a very specific task to powerful and very complex groups of programs designed to work together. They perform a myriad of functions as diverse as the environments in which computers are found today. There are many prewritten application programs that are useful in most business environments (for example, word processing and accounting). These are known as **cross-industry** application programs because they are not specific to any particular industry segment. Other prewritten applications address the specialized needs of a particular industry (e.g.,

154

manufacturing or utilities). These are called **industry-specific** application programs. Let us examine some examples of each.

## CROSS-INDUSTRY APPLICATION PROGRAMS

Examples of popular available prewritten application programs that help fill the needs of many different types of businesses include the following AS/400 programs:

- OfficeVision/400
- Query/400
- Business Graphics Utility
- ImagePlus
- Facsimile Support/400
- CallPath/400

## OfficeVision/400

There are many time-consuming and labor-intensive activities involved in simply conducting business in a typical office environment—for example, generating/distributing documents, sending/reading notes, and scheduling/attending meetings. The **OfficeVision/400** (5738-WP1) application program for AS/400 systems is designed to streamline these types of activities, improving the overall operation of the office and thus of the business in general. OfficeVision/400 is part of IBM's OfficeVision family, which consists of office productivity products conforming to IBM's Systems Application Architecture (SAA). Before we get into OfficeVision/400 specifics, let's take a look at IBM's overall OfficeVision strategy.

By selecting various OfficeVision products, users can address office needs using any combination of three main IBM product families: PS/2, AS/400, or System/390. In the PS/2 environment, you can use OfficeVision/2 on a Local Area Network consisting of many PS/2s and other types of computers. In the AS/400 environment, you can use OfficeVision/400 and the same workstations used for any AS/400 applications. In the System/390 environment, you would select the OfficeVision family product for the operating system you are using and the same workstations used for any System/390 application program.

Figure 4.1 shows an example of a simple OfficeVision/400 environment. The AS/400 system is running the OfficeVision/400 and display stations, printers, and PS/2s are attached. Any user of any display station or PS/2 can access the functions offered by OfficeVision/400.

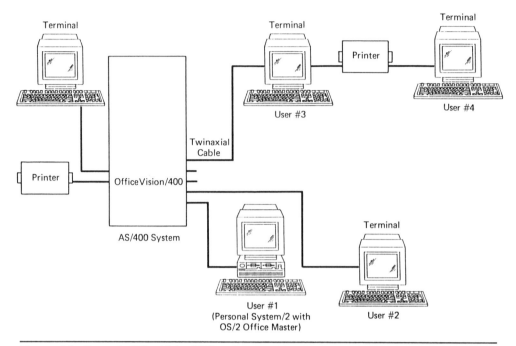

**Figure 4.1.** Example OfficeVision/400 environment.

The first thing a user sees when starting to use OfficeVision/400 is the main menu shown in Figure 4.2. The various functions provided by OfficeVision/400 can all be accessed by selecting the appropriate series of menu options. This menu-driven approach makes OfficeVision/400 easier to use. In addition, OfficeVision/400 provides **on-line help** at almost any point in the program. On pressing the Help key, the user is presented with additional information to clarify what should be done next.

For more experienced OfficeVision/400 word-processing users, the menus can be bypassed by entering commands at the bottom of the screen. This allows the more experienced user to go more quickly to the desired function within OfficeVision/400. Although OfficeVision/400 will not run on an AS/Entry, many similar functions are provided by the DisplayWrite/36 and Personal Services/36 products on an AS/Entry system. Now let us look at the types of functions provided by OfficeVision/400.

## Calendar Management

Meetings, appointments, and the like are basic to the day-to-day operations of most businesses. The calendar functions of OfficeVision/400 provide a tool to ease the scheduling of such events. This is basically an electronic version of a personal

```
                        OfficeVision/400
                                           System:    REBC06
     Select one of the following:
          1. Calendars                        Time:     2:16
          2. Mail
          3. Send message                  April           1992
          4. Send note                     S  M  T  W  T  F  S
          5. Documents and folders                  1  2  3  4
          6. Word processing               5  6  7  8  9 10 11
          7. Directories/distribution lists  12 13 14 15 16 17 18
          8. Decision support              19 20 21 22 23 24 25
          9. Administration                26 27 28 29 30

         90. Sign off                      New Mail

                                      Bottom
          Press ATTN to suspend a selected option.
          Selection




     F3=Exit     F12=Cancel         F19=Display messages
     © COPYRIGHT IBM CORP. 1985, 1991.
```

**Figure 4.2.** OfficeVision/400 main menu. OfficeVision/400 functions can be accessed through menus or commands.

appointment book that does for time management what word processing and electronic mail do for business correspondence.

Each user has a personal calendar to schedule daily activities. To schedule an appointment, simply enter the time, location, subject, and any notes concerning the event being scheduled. You can also elect to have the computer system automatically remind you with an alarm 15 minutes before the event. Entries can be classified as tentative if they are subject to change, or personal where privacy is necessary.

The real power of the calendar function of OfficeVision/400 is its ability to manage many calendars together. If you authorize it, other users can look at your calendar to see if you are available, on a business trip, meeting with a client, and so forth. This reduces the need to walk to the next office to discuss schedules, which causes interruptions and reduces office productivity. Users can be selectively limited to just viewing your calendar or they can be authorized to change your calendar if needed. Through the **group scheduling** capabilities of OfficeVision/400 calendars, a user (e.g., a secretary) can schedule a group meeting with a single operation. Office-Vision/400 will automatically add the meeting to the calendars of all attendees. Alternately, group scheduling allows a user to view up to 10 calendars at once for coordinating purposes and to avoid conflicts with previously scheduled events. Sep-

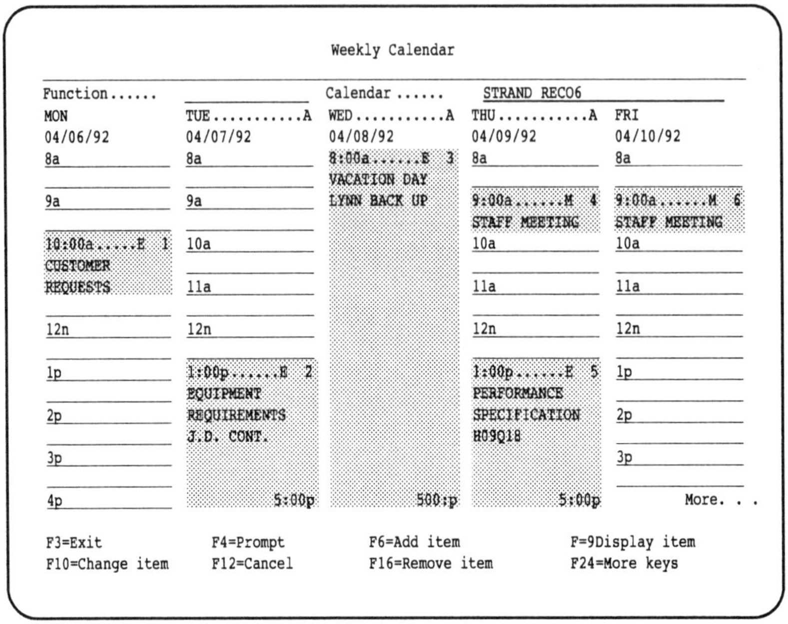

```
                              Weekly Calendar

  Function......     _____      Calendar ......   STRAND RECO6    _____
  MON                TUE..........A WED..........A   THU..........A  FRI
  04/06/92           04/07/92       04/08/92         04/09/92        04/10/92
  8a                 8a             8:00a......E  3  8a              8a
                                    VACATION DAY
  9a                 9a             LYNN BACK UP     9:00a......M  4  9:00a......M  6
                                                     STAFF MEETING   STAFF MEETING
  10:00a.....E  1    10a                             10a             10a
  CUSTOMER
  REQUESTS           11a                             11a             11a

  12n                12n                             12n             12n

  1p                 1:00p......E  2                 1:00p......E  5  1p
                     EQUIPMENT                       PERFORMANCE
  2p                 REQUIREMENTS                    SPECIFICATION   2p
                     J.D. CONT.                      H09Q18
  3p                                                                 3p

  4p                            5:00p        500:p            5:00p     More. . .

  F3=Exit            F4=Prompt      F6=Add item      F=9Display item
  F10=Change item    F12=Cancel     F16=Remove item  F24=More keys
```

**Figure 4.3.** Screen from OfficeVision/400's calendar function.

arate calendars can also be created to manage meeting rooms, equipment, and so on. Because all authorized users have access to these calendars, everyone can check the status and schedule the resources without leaving his or her desk. Finally, programs can be scheduled to automatically run at a specified time using OfficeVision/400's calendar functions. Figure 4.3 shows a screen from the OfficeVision/400 calendar function.

## Electronic Mail

In addition to verbal communications, business is conducted through various written communications, ranging from a hand-delivered note to a colleague down the hall to complex documents express-mailed across global distances. The *mail* functions within OfficeVision/400 allow the same basic things, improved through the speed of electronic communications. With OfficeVision/400, the user can send and receive three types of mail: **messages, notes**, and **documents**. *Messages* consist of a few short lines of text (fewer than 256 characters) that you can immediately send to any other user. They are used for very informal communications such as a simple telephone message or anything you might jot down on a piece of paper and leave on someone's desk. Figure 4.4 shows an example of an OfficeVision/400 message.

```
                           Send Message

  Type message.
     Todd, I need your report today on the sales results for the last quarter.
  Debbie



  Type distribution list and/or addressees, press F10 to send.
     Distribution list..........  _____  _____   F4 for list

  -----Addresses-----
  User ID    Address    Description
  TJS        RCHTOWN
  ADMIN      LOCAL
  _____     _____
  _____     _____
  _____     _____
  _____     _____
  _____     _____

                                                         More. . .
  F3=Exit     F4=Prompt     F5=Refresh   F9=Attach memo slip    F10=Send
  F12=Cancel  F13=Change defaults    F18=Sort by user id   F19=Display messages
```

**Figure 4.4.** Screen used to send an electronic message to another user.

A *note* is more like an internal company memo, providing a basic format and more detailed information. Notes are very useful in eliminating the "telephone tag" commonly found in companies in which the principals are often out or in which time zone differences between offices get in the way.

Finally, OfficeVision/400 documents can be thought of as formal correspondence or comprehensive reports. They are typically generated by a word-processing program (like the text-processing program provided as part of OfficeVision/400).

Notes, messages, and documents can all be sent at electronic speeds to any user or group of users known to the system. These can be users attached to the same AS/400 system as you or on a distant computer system attached through a communications network. Further, you can send the mail to one user, a list of users, or a predefined distribution list. For those not on the system, mail can be automatically printed and placed into the traditional mail system. When electronic mail is received, the user can store, print, reply to, or forward the mail with a few simple keystrokes. When mail is sent, it can be defined as an item requiring action, labeled "high priority" or "personal," or can have attached "memo slips" with additional comments. If authorized, you can work with someone else's electronic mail. This may be helpful when filling in for someone who is out on vacation, for example. A mail log is automatically kept by the system, providing a history of all mail activity.

## Document Management

OfficeVision/400 provides a document library function that allows you to manage the large number of documents typically associated with the office environment. Documents are stored in AS/400 systems in a **document library**. Conceptually, this can be thought of as a filing cabinet within the AS/400 system. As with a filing cabinet, documents in the document library are usually stored in folders with other related documents. OfficeVision/400's library/folder approach to document management allows you to work with documents by name, description, revision date, and type. The AS/400 security system limits document access to those authorized by the document author. Figure 4.5 shows the way you work with documents within a folder. You can also search the document library for documents according to document description, owner, subject, or words within the document itself. In fact, you can search the complete text of all the documents in the library for particular words or phrases. These documents can reside on the user's AS/400 system or a remote system. Figure 4.6 shows a screen used to search for documents by searching for words or phrases contained within the text of a document.

```
                       Work with Documents in Folders

      Folder ..... STRAND
      POSITION TO .......  _____     Starting characters

      Type Options (and Document), press enter.
          1=Create      2=Revise     3=Copy       4=Delete       5=View
          6=Print       7=Rename     8=Details    9=Print options  10=Send
          11=Spell      12=File remote 13=Paginate  14=Authority

      Opt Document      Document Description         Revised    Type

       __   _____
       __   LETTER        Practice Letter             04/08/92   RFTAS400




                                                                  Bottom
      F3=Exit     F4=Prompt    F5=Refresh    F10=Search for document
      F11=Display names only   F12=Cancel    F13=End search    F24=More keys
```

**Figure 4.5.** OfficeVision/400 documents are organized into folders conceptually like those in filing cabinets.

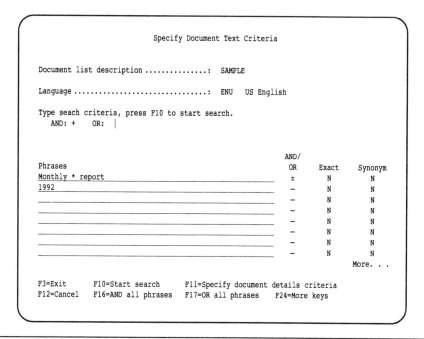

```
                    Specify Document Text Criteria


        Document list description ..............:   SAMPLE

        Language ..............................:   ENU   US English

        Type seach criteria, press F10 to start search.
           AND: +    OR:  |


                                                      AND/
        Phrases                                        OR    Exact    Synonym
        Monthly * report                               ±      N         N
        1992                                           -      N         N
        _____       -      N         N
        _____       -      N         N
        _____       -      N         N
        _____       -      N         N
        _____       -      N         N
        _____       -      N         N
                                                                    More. . .


        F3=Exit      F10=Start search      F11=Specify document details criteria
        F12=Cancel   F16=AND all phrases   F17=OR all phrases    F24=More keys
```

**Figure 4.6.** Screen used to search for a document by specifying words to look for within the text of the document.

## Word Processing

The word-processing functions within OfficeVision/400 allow the user to create documents. Figure 4.7 shows the screen used to create documents. The user types documents using the keyboard in much the same way as with a typewriter. Since the document is temporarily stored in memory, it can be easily modified. Whereas the electronic mail functions within OfficeVision/400 allow for the creation of simple notes and messages, the word-processing area of OfficeVision/400 provides a full-function document creation facility.

The basic capabilities of OfficeVision/400 word processing include changing, inserting, moving, copying, and deleting text. Text can be underlined, highlighted, and centered on a page. A document can be searched for key words or phrases, allowing you to quickly get to the right spot in a long document. Global changes to a document can be performed with a single command, and support for subscript and superscript text is provided. For longer documents, OfficeVision/400's word processing can generate a table of contents and an index and can handle footnotes. With the addition of the Language Dictionaries/400 program (5738-DCT), various proofreading capabilities can automatically check for spelling errors against multiple dic-

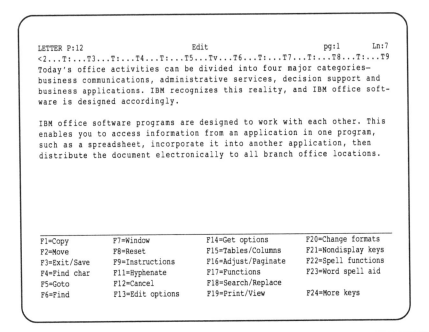

```
LETTER P:12                        Edit                    pg:1      Ln:7
<2...T:...T3...T:...T4...T:...T5...Tv...T6...T:...T7...T:...T8...T:...T9
Today's office activities can be divided into four major categories—
business communications, administrative services, decision support and
business applications. IBM recognizes this reality, and IBM office soft-
ware is designed accordingly.

IBM office software programs are designed to work with each other. This
enables you to access information from an application in one program,
such as a spreadsheet, incorporate it into another application, then
distribute the document electronically to all branch office locations.




F1=Copy          F7=Window          F14=Get options      F20=Change formats
F2=Move          F8=Reset           F15=Tables/Columns    F21=Nondisplay keys
F3=Exit/Save     F9=Instructions    F16=Adjust/Paginate   F22=Spell functions
F4=Find char     F11=Hyphenate      F17=Functions         F23=Word spell aid
F5=Goto          F12=Cancel         F18=Search/Replace
F6=Find          F13=Edit options   F19=Print/View        F24=More keys
```

**Figure 4.7.** Screen used to create documents in OfficeVision/400's word-processing function.

tionaries and make corrections. These dictionaries can be general, user-defined, or specialized (e.g., foreign language, medical, and legal). To improve understandability, the reading grade-level analysis allows you to select proper terminology based on the intended reader's education. As in other areas of OfficeVision/400, contextual help text is provided by pressing the help key. However, **hypertext links** are also provided in the OfficeVision/400 word-processing help text. With hypertext links, key words within the help text are highlighted, indicating that more help text (related to that key word) is available. This allows the user to more easily make his/her way through the help text and find the needed information. For those who wish to use WordPerfect for the AS/400, OfficeVision allows you to completely replace the OfficeVision word processing function with WordPerfect for the AS/400.

It is often desirable to embed information, graphics, or images into documents to improve appearance, completeness, and understandability. OfficeVision/400's word processing allows you to embed columnar tables of information that may result from a database file query, for example. Simple mathematical calculation can be performed on data in a document without having to leave the word-processing function. Furthermore, graphics (for example, those created by the Business Graphics Utility) can be embedded into documents to provide line graphs, bar charts, and the like. Finally, images imported from other computer systems can be embedded into documents. Images are computer-captured photographs that look like newspaper-quality photographs. Although OfficeVision/400 has no facilities to generate such images, they can be imported from other computer systems such as a Personal System/2–based publishing system.

Once a document is created, it can be stored in the document library, printed, or sent through the OfficeVision/400 electronic mail system described earlier in this chapter.

## Directory Management

Three types of directories can be maintained through OfficeVision/400: **personal directories, distribution lists**, and the **system directory**. Personal directories provide a free-form method of dealing with structured information. Things such as a telephone directory or an office supply inventory can be managed through a personal directory. First, the user defines the type and format of information to be displayed. Then the information must be entered into the system. From then on, the information can be maintained, searched, printed, or otherwise manipulated as with any computer database. For example, you can look up a person's phone number by specifying the exact name, a partial name, or other search criteria. Figure 4.8 shows an example of a telephone directory using personal directories.

```
                      Specify Personal Directory Criteria

   Type choice, press Enter

   Personal directory...............:   EXAMPLEDIR        Name, F4 for List

   Description......................:   IBM-Supplied Example Telephone Directory

   Type search criteria, press Enter.
        Last name ..........    _____   Blank=All
        First name .........    _____     Blank=All
        Street address ......   _____ Blank=All
        Postal code ........    _____         Blank=All
        Area code ..........    ____             Blank=All
        Phone number ........   _____       Blank=All




   F3=Exit       F4=Prompt         F5=Refresh          F6=Add entries
   F11=Change entries    F12=Cancel      F13=More tasks     F19=Display messages
```

**Figure 4.8.** Example of a personal phone directory using the OfficeVision/400 directory function.

Distribution lists are used to send an electronic mail item (note, document, etc.) to a predefined list of users with one operation. A typical distribution list might be a list of department members, all managers, the whole office, all secretaries, and so on. Through this area of OfficeVision/400, distribution lists can be created, maintained, or printed.

Finally, the system directory contains a list of all system users along with pertinent information such as mailing address and information indicating whether the users are local, remote, or indirect. Local users usually reside in the same building as the AS/400 and are attached directly to the computer system. Remote users are typically located at a distance from the AS/400 system and are attached via communications lines. Indirect users are those who do not use the computer system but receive OfficeVision/400 electronic mail in printed form rather than through the system. The system directory helps with the administration of OfficeVision/400 users. In a network of AS/400 systems running OfficeVision/400 (all running V2R1.1 of OS/400 or later), the system directory of one AS/400 can be **shadowed** on all other AS/400 systems. That is, users of one system can send electronic mail to users of another system. The users can look up each other's electronic mail address with facilities in OfficeVision/400. If the system directory of one AS/400 system is changed (e.g., the user's electronic mail address), all other AS/400 systems in the network will be updated to reflect the change. This reduces the administrative effort associated with a network of AS/400 systems.

## Bridging to Other Functions

In addition to the functions that are built into OfficeVision/400, the capability to bring in additional functions is included. The OfficeVision/400 main menu has an item called *decision support* (as shown in Figure 4.2) that provides a path to some separately purchased program products like Query/400 and the Business Graphics Utility. Providing access to these products through the OfficeVision/400 main menu makes for simpler operation. Further, another OfficeVision/400 menu item can be displayed to offer functions defined by programmers employed by the business owning the computer system. Again, providing access to these customized functions through a single main menu improves ease of use.

Finally, OfficeVision/400 provides an application programming interface that allows other programs to interact directly with OfficeVision/400. This type of program-to-program interaction allows a programmer to add custom programs that cooperate with OfficeVision/400 while shielding the user from any complexities of this interaction.

## Query/400

To manage a business is to make many decisions based on the information available. Since computer systems manage the information of the business, it makes sense that the computer system should provide the management information necessary to make good business decisions. We have already discussed the way vast amounts of business information are organized in AS/400 database files. The problem, however, is that too much information can be as bad as not enough. **Query/400** (5738-QU1) is an application program designed to help summarize and sift through the business information in AS/400 databases. You can start Query/400 through the OfficeVision/400 menu, appropriate function keys, or by issuing a command on any AS/400 command line.

Figure 4.9 shows the Query/400 main menu. To get the information you want from an AS/400 database, in the form you want it, you must use a **query**. A query provides the *blueprint* specifying which information will be retrieved from the database and how it will be presented to the user. Figure 4.10 shows the results of a

```
QUERY                          Query

Select one of the following:

  1. Work with queries
  2. Run an existing query
  3. Delete a query

 20. Files
 21. Office tasks




Selection or command
==>_____
_____
_____
F3-Exit        F4-Prompt      F12-Previous
_____
[]
```

**Figure 4.9.** Main menu of the Query/400 application program.

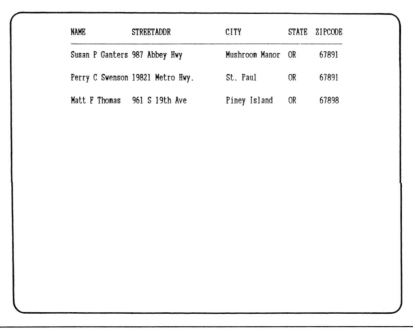

| NAME | STREETADDR | CITY | STATE | ZIPCODE |
|---|---|---|---|---|
| Susan P Ganters | 987 Abbey Hwy | Mushroom Manor | OR | 67891 |
| Perry C Swenson | 19821 Metro Hwy. | St. Paul | OR | 67891 |
| Matt F Thomas | 961 S 19th Ave | Piney Island | OR | 67898 |

**Figure 4.10.** Report resulting from a user query to a telephone directory data base.

query to a telephone directory database. Users can create their own query by answering a series of questions presented on the screen. Since no programming experience is required for this, users' dependency on programmers is reduced, allowing the computer system to become a more flexible tool. However, users do need to learn some simple steps to create a query. Depending on their motivation and sophistication, they may or may not wish to create their own queries. If need be, a programmer can create a library of commonly used queries for users. Once the query is defined, it can be saved in the system, allowing any authorized user to generate the report at any time by issuing a single command. The results of a query can be displayed on a terminal's display, printed on a printer, or saved in a new database file. The information can be merged into documents using OfficeVision/400 or the DisplayWrite 4 word-processing program used on Personal System/2 computers.

Query/400 can be used on any AS/400 database defined using the interactive data definition utility (IDDU), data description specification (DDS), or structured query language (SQL), all discussed in the next chapter. There is also a version of *Query* available for the AS/Entry, called **Query/36**.

## AS/400 Business Graphics Utility

Humans have always drawn images to present and interpret information. Images are native to humans and thus are both enjoyable and powerful communication devices. The greater the amount of information to be conveyed, the greater the need for graphic representations. It is therefore not surprising that business relies heavily on images to convey information to customers, employees, management, and so on. With the increased use of computers, it is also not surprising that computer-generated images (called *computer graphics*) are common in today's business environment.

The **AS/400 Business Graphics Utility (BGU)** (5738-DS1) provides Application System users with a tool to construct a computer image. BGU provides straightforward menus and contextual on-line help text. This, along with the exercises and tutorials provided in the *BGU User's Guide*, allows nonprogrammers to create and use computer graphics.

This is how you create graphics with BGU. First, through a series of menus (or commands for more experienced users), you define the appearance and format of the desired image. Here you tell BGU the type of image you wish to construct. You can choose from pie graphs, bar graphs, line graphs, surface graphs, histograms, Venn diagrams, or text charts. Other things you can control include font style, size, color, and position.

Once you define the format and appearance of the graphic image, you are ready to input the data into the graph. You can provide the data by specifying a database file containing the data or by keying in the data from a keyboard. After the data have been placed into the graph format by either means, BGU can display the image in black and white or color on a graphic workstation such as a PS/2. Because data are input separately from designing the graph format, the same BGU graph format can be used over and over again with different versions of the data. The chart management facility of BGU allows you to manage (copy, rename, etc.) your BGU graphics library. The data can be modified and then immediately regraphed to perform a *what-if* type of analysis.

Images can also be printed on a plotter or graphics printer (e.g., a 4224 printer) or stored on the system using the **Graphics Data Format (GDF)**. As a GDF file, the image can be integrated into OfficeVision/400 documents and business application programs, and be used by other GDF-compatible computer systems (e.g., System/390).

Although there were BGU versions for the System/36 and System/38 computers, AS/400 BGU has been enhanced in the areas of GDF support, database input, number of chart types and fonts, and so forth. Most of the graphic images created with System/36 BGU can be migrated to AS/400 BGU through available migration aids. However, some System/36 BGU graphic images cannot easily be migrated (e.g., graph format and chart members). System/38 BGU graphics should easily migrate to AS/400 BGU through available migration aids.

### ImagePlus/400

While computers have become the preferred way of collecting, managing, and distributing information in business, there is still a lot of paper circulating in today's offices. This is due to the fact that a lot of the information needed to support daily business operations does not lend itself to being encoded in traditional computer systems. Examples of such information are signed documents, photographs, and documents that contain both text and drawings. Because of this hard-to-manage information, many highly computerized businesses still have to resort to the manual methods of doing business that have been with us since before the advent of computers. They must still deal with rows of filing cabinets, overflowing in-baskets, envelopes, stamps, mail delays, wastebaskets, couriers, and folders. Often, handling this hard-to-manage information creates bottlenecks in an office's productivity and can significantly delay the entire business cycle. Fairly recent advances in computer performance and optical storage technology have resulted in products, such as IBM's ImagePlus Systems, to handle this hard-to-manage information.

ImagePlus is a family of hardware and software products designed to capture, store, and manipulate **images**. An image is basically an electronic photograph of a document that is stored inside a computer. Virtually any type of document can be easily captured inside a computer system as an image. ImagePlus facilitates the office changeover from a paper system to an electronic image system. That is, ImagePlus does for hard-to-manage documents what word processing did for standard letters and reports.

To understand the concepts, let's trace some hard-to-manage documents through a hypothetical insurance company using ImagePlus. For the purposes of our example, we will process a claim made by Mr. Lowrey (a customer) for the repair of damage caused by a recent hurricane. Figure 4.11 shows the ImagePlus system used by our insurance company to process claims.

First, the insurance company's mail room receives three estimates from various contractors for the repair of Mr. Lowrey's home. Since these are signed estimates with handwritten notes and include photographs of the damage, they fall into the category of hard-to-manage documents. They are first sent to the operator of the **scan** workstation so that an image of each estimate document can be created in the computer. The scan workstation consists of a Personal System/2 running the PS/2 Image-Plus Workstation Program, an 8508 Monochrome Display, and a 3118 scanner (a

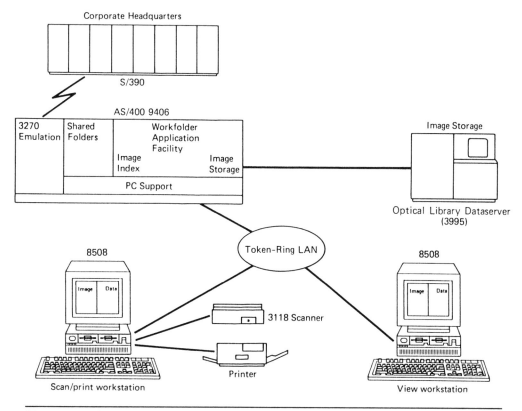

**Figure 4.11.** Example ImagePlus environment.

printer may be added so that the workstation can double as a print workstation, as shown in the figure). The scanner is similar to a copy machine, but rather than producing a duplicate image on another sheet of paper, the scanner electronically produces a duplicate image in the PS/2s memory. The extra-wide 8508 Monochrome Display allows the user to view an image on one side of the screen and enter textual information (e.g., name, address, phone number, account number, and date case was opened) on the other. Once the image is in the PS/2, the image it is compressed to conserve valuable disk space. The images are then sent to the AS/400 via PC Support over the Token-Ring Network (or through an Ethernet attachment), using the communications capabilities of PC Support, and are stored in a shared folder on an AS/400 disk unit. Then the ImagePlus Workfolder Application Facility/400 (5733-055), which is specially written to use the facilities of the ImagePlus system, takes over. The Workfolder Application Facility utilizes the AS/400's built-in database functions to index the stored images. This indexing associates the images with Mr. Lowrey's account number and other pertinent information to facilitate the quick retrieval of the images. That is, all information related to Mr. Lowrey's claim is linked together inside the computer system, in an electronic workfolder, which is called a **case**. Another thing the Workfolder Application Facility does is to place a copy of the images on the 3995 Optical Library Dataserver shown in Figure 4.11 and described in Chapter 2.

In our example, the Workfolder Application Facility allows the claims supervisor to prioritize Mr. Lowrey's case with the other active cases and assign the case to a claims processor manning a **view** workstation. Like the scan workstation, the view workstation is based on a Personal System/2, the PS/2 ImagePlus Workstation, and the 8508 Monochrome Display. The 8508 will allow the claims processor to view an image on one side of the screen and the associated textual information (e.g., name, address, phone number, account number, and date case was opened) on the other. There is no need for a scanner or a printer at the view workstation. The claims processor manning the view workstation can now easily view all of the information associated with Mr. Lowrey's case. During the processing of Mr. Lowrey's claim, the claims processor can take actions such as: suspend the case while waiting for additional information, suspend the case for a specified number of days, or complete the processing and close the case. Since the information about Mr. Lowrey's case is all in order, the claims processor completes the necessary processing and closes the case. Selected information about Mr. Lowrey's case is sent to the System/390 computer located at corporate headquarters. For now, the images pertaining to Mr. Lowrey's case are removed from the AS/400's fixed disk, freeing space for other active cases, but the 3995 Optical Library Data server will keep a permanent record on optical disk for audit purposes. Later, if some of Mr. Lowrey's case images are needed, they can be recalled from the 3995 Optical Library Data server. They can be displayed on a view workstation as before or they can be sent to a **print** workstation if hard copies are required — for external correspondence, for example.

This is one simple example of an ImagePlus environment. A very important point about the whole ImagePlus System's architecture is that it is designed to accommodate other application programs. That is, any programmer can write an application program that uses image capture, manipulation, storage, indexing, and printing functions provided by the application programming interfaces (API), found in the Workfolder Application Facility, to accommodate many different business environments. For example, a real estate office can capture photographs of the exterior and interior of the houses that are for sale and store them in an ImagePlus system. Then, via computer images, a real estate agent can essentially "walk" prospective buyers through the house before they ever leave the real estate office, saving everyone a lot of time. And this is just the beginning. Image processing is in its infancy; it will clearly play a role of increasing importance in businesses of the 1990s and beyond.

## Facsimile Support/400

Facsimile Support/400 (5798-RYC) is a program for AS/400 systems that, in conjunction with PS/2s and other programs, provides basic support for sending and receiving facsimiles (faxing). Figure 4.12 shows a simple setup that can be used to send and receive faxes at a company named Atole Enterprises. In our example setup, a PS/2 equipped with a Fax Concentrator Adapter/A is attached to a standard telephone line (or more than one). The PS/2 is used to control the communications between the AS/400 and any of the millions of fax machines in the world that con-

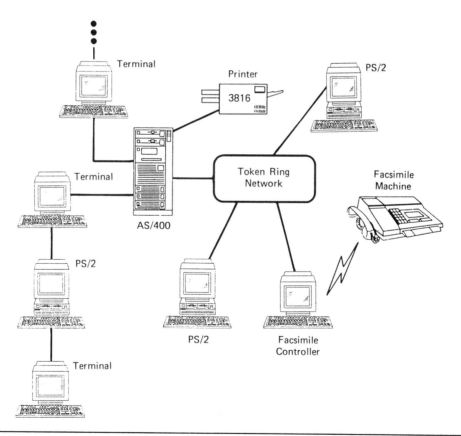

**Figure 4.12.** Facsimile Support/400 allows fax machines to be used as remote printers and scanners for the AS/400 system.

form to the industry standard **Group 3 Facsimile Service**. The PS/2 is attached to the AS/400 via a Token-Ring Network. The other PS/2s and terminals are general-purpose AS/400 workstations attached to the AS/400 via that same Token-Ring Network. With this setup, all of the other fax machines in the world appear to be a printer to the AS/400 system. So anything that an Atole user could print, that user can now send to any fax machine — with a cover sheet generated by Facsimile Support/400. Alternately, the Atole user could request that the AS/400 system automatically send the fax after business hours, when the phone charges are less expensive.

When someone sends Atole a fax, it is received over the phone lines by the PS/2 with the Fax Concentrator Adapter/A. It is then transferred to the AS/400, where it can be stored in a document folder, displayed on a graphics-capable workstation, or printed on any printer supporting the compressed image function of Advanced Function Printing (e.g., a 3816 printer).

In addition to providing this basic fax support, Command Language (CL) commands can be embedded in programs to allow programmers to incorporate fax functions in their application programs.

## CallPath/400

CallPath/400 (5738-CP2) is a programmers' tool for the AS/400 that allows a programmer to write applications that coordinate a business's telephone system with application programs. For example, application programs can be written to automatically sequence through and dial a list of potential customers, making the telemarketing staff more productive. In another example, a CallPath/400 application program could be written to identify a caller by phone number (using the Calling Line Identification service offered by the phone company) and automatically pull up that customer's information to the operator's display. If the call needs to be transferred to another extension, the user can simultaneously transfer the telephone call along with the screen of customer information to the telephone and workstation of the other employee with a few keystrokes.

It is important to understand that CallPath/400 by itself cannot perform these functions. CallPath/400 is a program that is basically an extension to the operating system to make it easier to write application programs that interact with telephone equipment. For this reason, CallPath/400 is really an **enabler** rather than an application program. An enabler is a program that provides services to application programs to make the programmer's life easier and to provide an insulation layer to help maintain application program compatibility as hardware and software evolve. That is, CallPath/400 is a tool for the programmer who wishes to write an application program that conforms to IBM's CallPath Services Architecture. This architecture is IBM's stated long-term direction for coordinating application programs and telephone equipment.

## INDUSTRY-SPECIFIC APPLICATION PROGRAMS

The cross-industry application programs discussed to this point are of a highly general nature, able to fill the common needs found in even the most diverse business environments. They were designed to be as general as possible to cover the largest market possible—sort of the "all things to all people" approach. For example, the OfficeVision/400 Office application program might be used to fill the needs of a department store in one instance and a legal office in the next.

In most cases, a business also has some needs that are more specialized to its particular industry. Therefore, another type of prewritten application program, called an **industry-specific** application program, may be desirable. As the term *industry-specific* implies, this type of application program is specially designed to address the needs of a well-defined business type. A real estate office has application program needs that differ from those of a dental practice. Each would benefit by an appropriate prewritten yet highly specialized industry-specific application program. Many software companies have put a great deal of effort into developing industry-specific programs for the System/3X computers. Since AS/400 systems can run many of these programs as well as those specially written for the AS/400, highly specific business/professional environments can be addressed.

There are industry-specific applications designed for manufacturing companies, insurance companies, real estate offices, medical practices, construction companies, law practices, churches, and so on. These programs are often **modular**, meaning that they are really several different programs designed to work closely together. Each program or *module* can be used individually or share information with the others. Modular programs allow you to select only the modules you need, reducing costs for those not needing "the works."

An example of a modular, industry-specific application program is IBM's **Manufacturing Accounting and Production Information Control System/Data Base (MAPICS/DB)**. MAPICS/DB is designed to meet a wide variety of needs for manufacturing (e.g., a furniture manufacturer) and process companies (e.g., a gasoline refiner). It consists of 17 separate programs or modules, each providing specific functions. They can be broken down into three areas:

- Order processing and accounting
- Advanced manufacturing
- Process

The order processing and accounting modules of MAPICS/DB meet basic business needs in the areas of general ledger, accounts payable, accounts receivable, order entry, purchasing, and so on. Many of these modules are really very general in nature, allowing them to fit very well in manufacturing or nonmanufacturing companies.

The advanced manufacturing MAPICS/DB modules focus on the manufacturing flow through the plant. They help manage the bill-of-materials of products, monitor in-process inventory, balance work center loads, track labor, cost jobs, and schedule production. These modules are designed specifically for manufacturers and would be of little use to a legal office, for example.

Finally, the process MAPICS/DB modules fill the very specialized needs of the process companies. This includes dealing with recipes, batch quantities, yield calculations, and batch/lot tracking.

In addition to the basic MAPICS/DB modules, other companies have produced companion programs that work with MAPICS/DB to provide additional functions. These types of "add-on" program offerings are very common when dealing with the more popular industry-specific application programs.

MAPICS/DB is just one example of an industry-specific application program. Hundreds of software companies have written thousands of industry-specific application programs for Application Systems, and new application programs are appearing almost daily. Before considering custom software, discussed next, industry-specific software should be carefully considered.

## CUSTOM APPLICATION PROGRAMS

Prewritten application programs fit many needs. They are relatively inexpensive, flexible, and convenient tools. In some cases, however, users may find that the fit of their application program needs to be that of a tight glove. This is especially true in environments where the Application Systems are needed to perform highly unusual and specific tasks or where there is a need to conform to existing company procedures. In these cases, it may be better to develop **custom** application programs written to the user's exact specifications.

Custom application programs are designed and written by programmers employed by the company or by consultants contracted just for that purpose. In either case, the basic development steps are usually the same. First, a software specification is developed that describes what each program does. Then a preliminary version of the program is written that demonstrates the function that will eventually be in the final program. This preliminary version is evaluated by the user and the specification is altered to reflect any needed changes. Last, the final program and user manuals are written and put in place at the user's location. Typically, user training will be provided by the developer and any problems will be ironed out. Once the user accepts the program, the software has to be supported; users will need a place to go when they have questions not addressed by the manuals. Support also includes making necessary changes to the application program, as the changing business environment will often require. This kind of ongoing support is critical to the success of any computer automation project.

Most of the time, custom application program development is initially more expensive and time-consuming than the prewritten application program approach. In many environments, however, this additional expense and time can be recovered by the increased productivity that can result from custom applications that precisely fit the needs of the environment. An additional benefit of custom application programs is their ability to change as a company changes. Getting major modifications to prewritten application programs may be difficult or impossible in some cases. The AS/400 functions and programming tools provide a very productive software development environment.

The basic architecture of AS/400 systems makes for a very productive program development environment. The built-in database and single-level storage provide high-level structures and consistency. According to IBM, this, along with the programming tools available for AS/400, can increase programmer productivity about 3 to 1 over that of the System/36. Custom application programs used with System/36 and System/38 computers can be run on AS/400 through the use of the appropriate migration tools. Chapter 5 discusses some of the programmer productivity and migration tools used with AS/400.

# 5

# Operating Systems

$\mathsf{F}$ew areas in information processing create more confusion and apprehension than the operating system. This chapter helps remove some of the mystery associated with the operating systems used with Application Systems. The reader will become familiar with operating system topics such as interactive processing and multi-user capabilities and how these concepts apply to the business environment.

## INTRODUCTION TO OPERATING SYSTEM CONCEPTS

The operating system provides the necessary interface that allows the user and application programs to interact with AS/400 computers. The user can interact directly with the operating system's user interface to manage files on a disk, start application programs, print files, and so on. The operating system also performs tasks directly under the control of application programs without any user assistance. The application program initiates tasks by directly interacting with the operating system through the **application program interface (API)**. This is simply a set of operating system commands that can be issued directly by the application program. The API simplifies the job of the application programmer, since it is not necessary to become involved with the details of hardware interaction. Further, when an application uses the API, it is shielded from changes in the computer hardware as new computers are developed. The operating system can be changed to support new computer hardware while preserving the API unchanged, allowing application programs to run on the new computer.

To understand the job of the operating system, it is necessary to understand a few basic concepts:

- Batch versus interactive processing
- Multi-User
- Multi-Application

**176**

## Batch versus Interactive Processing

To understand the concepts of **batch processing** and **interactive processing**, consider an analogy between the postal service and the telephone. If you wish to ask a distant friend some questions, you can either write a letter or phone. With the first option you gather all your thoughts, put them on paper, and put the letter in a mailbox. A few days later (assuming your friend is responsive) you go to your mailbox and get the responses to your questions in the form of a document. This is analogous to batch processing with a computer: You request the computer to answer some question(s) or perform some task(s). Some time later (from minutes to days) you can go to the printer and get the computer's responses in the form of a report. In the early days of computing, batch processing was the only alternative for computer interaction. You would submit your request (called a **batch job**) to the computer by placing a stack of computer punch cards (see Figure 5.1) in an electromechanical device called a *card reader*. The computer would read the cards, perform the requested task(s), and respond by generating a computer printout. Today, batch processing still has its place, but the batch jobs are usually submitted by typing commands into a computer terminal rather than by using punched cards. However, some card readers are still in use today on some older computer systems.

Moving back to our analogy, at times you cannot simply write down your list of questions in a letter because some of the questions will depend on answers to one or more initial questions. In this case, you either have to send several letters back and forth or call your friend to discuss the questions. Calling is preferable if you need an answer to your question in a hurry. Having a dialogue with your friend over the phone would be analogous to interactive processing on a computer. With interactive processing, you have a dialogue with the computer system from a terminal: You

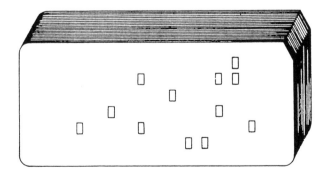

**Figure 5.1.** Earlier computer systems used stacks of paper cards to input programs and data. The information was encoded on the cards by punching hole patterns.

type in questions or requests and the computer immediately responds. The primary advantage of interactive processing is that the user gets an immediate response, which is required in many business applications (e.g., airline reservations and a retail checkout lane). Interactive processing was developed after batch processing and is now widely used in most business environments.

Some business applications of computers use a combination of batch and interactive processing. For example, a payroll clerk might type information from time cards into a computer terminal in a dialogue style (interactive processing). Once all time cards are entered and verified to be correct, the clerk may issue a command to the terminal that tells the computer to print all checks (a batch job). The clerk would later get the checks from the printer.

Application Systems operating systems support both batch and interactive processing.

## What Is Multi-User?

A computer is said to be a **multi-user** computer system if the hardware and software enable a single computer system to be shared by two or more users simultaneously. For contrast, Personal System/2s and Personal Computers are examples of computer systems primarily designed to interact with one user at a time and thus are called **single-user** computer systems.

With a multi-user computer system, there are from two to many hundreds of computer terminals attached to a single computer. Each terminal provides its user with a "window" into the computer system and allows the user to perform tasks independent of all other users. Although the single computer system is being used simultaneously by many users, users are usually unaware of the activities of other users and seem to have their own computer system. However, a user may see the computer "slow down" (increase response time) as more and more users sign on to the computer and start doing work.

There are several advantages of a multi-user over a single-user computer system. First, since the computer system hardware and programs can be simultaneously shared by many users, no one has to stand in line waiting for a "turn on the computer." Everyone (assuming enough terminals are attached) has access to the computer whenever needed to do a job. Other advantages offered by a multi-user system are in the areas of security, accounting, backup/recovery, and the like. Chapter 7 discusses the pros and cons of multi-user systems versus single-user systems and local area networks.

As seen later in the chapter, the operating systems used with Application Systems support a full multi-user environment.

## What Is Multi-Application?

Many people confuse multi-application with the term *multi-user*, which refers to the ability to have a single computer system shared among two or more users simultaneously.

**Multi-application** (also called **multi-tasking**) means the ability, provided by some operating systems, to switch between two or more independent application programs from a single workstation. The opposite of multi-application is **single-application**, which means that the computer user must finish using one program before another can be started. The operating systems for all Application Systems support a multi-application environment, as is seen later in this chapter. In an office environment workers are often interrupted in the middle of one task to perform another. This makes the multi-application capability of operating systems particularly useful in that it allows the user to easily switch back and forth between several simultaneously resident application programs as interruptions occur.

## OPERATING SYSTEM PRODUCTS

Application Systems use one of two operating systems. The AS/Entry computers use the IBM **System Support Program (SSP)** originally developed for System/36 computers. All models of the AS/400 systems exclusively use the IBM **Operating System/400 (OS/400)**. This section provides an overview of both operating systems and then looks more closely at OS/400.

## SSP—An Executive Overview

The System Support Program, commonly called SSP, was the operating system originally offered for IBM System/36 computers. Because of the popularity of that computer family, SSP has become widely used in the business community. As a result, many application programs were developed for SSP and the System/36 by many different software companies.

As the System/36 computers evolved, SSP was revised to support the enhancements in the computer hardware. Although each new version of SSP provided additional functions, compatibility with earlier application programs was maintained.

SSP is the operating system used on the AS/Entry systems and provides full compatibility with earlier System/36 computers. It consists of a set of programs designed to perform many diverse hardware "housekeeping" tasks under the control of either the computer user or an application program. Tasks performed by SSP

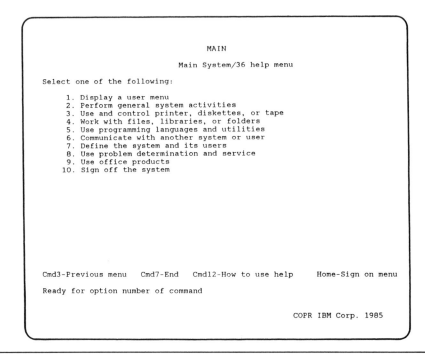

```
                              MAIN
                       Main System/36 help menu

          Select one of the following:

                1. Display a user menu
                2. Perform general system activities
                3. Use and control printer, diskettes, or tape
                4. Work with files, libraries, or folders
                5. Use programming languages and utilities
                6. Communicate with another system or user
                7. Define the system and its users
                8. Use problem determination and service
                9. Use office products
               10. Sign off the system




          Cmd3-Previous menu   Cmd7-End   Cmd12-How to use help      Home-Sign on menu

          Ready for option number of command

                                                       COPR IBM Corp. 1985
```

**Figure 5.2.** The main help menu presented by the SSP operating system used on the AS/Entry.

include managing multiple users, providing security, managing the flow of batch and interactive jobs through the system, sending information to a printer, and so forth.

After users sign on to an AS/Entry, they can see SSP's main help menu, shown in Figure 5.2. From this menu, the user has two methods of initiating SSP tasks. More experienced users will issue SSP commands (called operation control language or OCL) at the SSP command line. OCL allows quick access to all SSP functions. Groups of OCL statements can be stored as a **procedure** and thereby executed by a single command. Less experienced users can step through a series of menus to perform operating system tasks. Although this method is not as fast as using OCL commands, it prompts the user at every step, making it easier for novices. These menus, along with on-line (computer-based) help text, reduce the number of publications needed to operate the system. SSP contains over 2000 screens of on-line help text similar to that shown in Figure 5.3. If users get stuck while performing some operating system task, they can press the Help key. SSP's help facility then presents users with textual information concerning the operation in question.

In addition to performing tasks under direct control of the user, SSP can perform tasks under direct control of an application program. A user can issue SSP commands through keyboard entries. Application programs issue SSP commands

```
How to Use Help                Introduction

This tutorial describes how to use the help support provided with the system.
It is divided into the selections listed below.  Select the option number for
the item you wish to display and press the Enter key.  From the first display
shown you can view the next display by pressing the Roll Up key.  To view a
previous page in this tutorial, press the Roll Down key.  To use the Roll
keys, you must press and hold down one of the shift keys, and then press one
of the Roll keys.

Select one of the following:
     1.  The command and function keys you can use.
     2.  How to use help menus
     3.  How to use help procedure and control command displays


Option:


Cmd3-Return to previous menu   Cmd7-End tutorial
                                              COPR. IBM Corp. 1983
```

**Figure 5.3.** Example of SSP's help text, presented in response to pressing the Help key.

through the SSP application program interface (API). This is a defined protocol for passing information and requests directly between the application program and SSP with no user interaction required.

It is the job of the operating system to provide for communications. SSP comes standard with the basic communications facilities to support remote workstations. Separately ordered extensions to SSP, such as the **SSP Communications Feature** and the **3270 Device Emulation Feature**, add communications functions like asynchronous communications support and communications with S/390 computers. Other optional SSP add-ons include the **Tape Support Feature** and the **System/36 Utilities**. The Tape Support Feature allows a tape backup device to be attached. The System/36 Utilities is a package of programs primarily designed to aid the programmer in writing application programs.

## OS/400—An Executive Overview

Operating System/400 (5738-SS1), commonly called OS/400, is a multi-user operating system exclusively used with all AS/400 computer systems. It works closely with the LIC instructions in AS/400 systems to implement the database, security, single-level storage, and so on that are basic to AS/400 architecture. OS/400 represents a divergence from the more traditional operating systems used with the earlier System/3X computers. Like SSP, OS/400 is a set of programs that perform housekeeping tasks based on requests from both users and application programs. Any AS/400 user can load and switch between multiple batch or interactive tasks, each protected from disruption by other tasks or users. Unlike SSP, however, OS/400 participates in the Systems Application Architecture (SAA) described in Chapter 3. SAA is an overall strategy that defines standards in the areas of user interfaces, application program interfaces, and communications methods. It is intended to provide consistency (resulting in improved ease of use) and compatibility across IBM's major product families: System/390, AS/400, and Personal System/2. OS/400 provides a platform for the development of new application programs consistent with the Systems Application Architecture. For example, OS/400 along with the PC Support extension to OS/400 provides the first step in supporting the distributed relational database as defined by the Systems Application Architecture.

Although OS/400 offers the user complex and sophisticated features, many things have been done to make OS/400 easier to use. One of the most significant enhancements is the incorporation of the **Operational Assistant**. Based on many of the ease-of-use functions of the System/36, the Operational Assistant is a new set of menus and functions for OS/400 that masks many of the OS/400 concepts users have found confusing. The Operational Assistant helps the user do things like work with printer output, work with batch jobs, and work with electronic messages. Figure 5.4 shows the main menu presented by OS/400's Operational Assistant. Originally, the Operational Assistant was an optional extension to OS/400, but it is now provided as standard and has become the default user interface for OS/400.

To initiate OS/400 tasks, the user can either type in a command or step through a series of menus and prompts. Novice or infrequent users will appreciate the menu structure as it guides them through any OS/400 function. More experienced users will likely use the commands that provide results more quickly than stepping through the menus.

Other OS/400 items that directly address ease of use include automatic configuration of devices and the table-driven customization. Extensive help and on-line (computer-based) documentation is provided to reduce the need to go to reference manuals when the user needs more information. On-line education is built into OS/400, allowing users to learn how to use the system while sitting in front of their terminal. Chapter 3 provided a hands-on session with OS/400's help and on-line education facilities.

In addition to performing tasks under direct control of the user, OS/400 can perform tasks under direct control of an application program. Application programs

```
ASSIST                 AS/400 Operational Assistant (TM) Menu
                                            System:   S1010272

To select one of the following, type its number below and press Enter:

         1. Work with printer output
         2. Work with jobs
         3. Work with messages
         4. Send messages
         5. Change your Password

        10. Manage your system, users, and devices
        11. Customize your system, users, and devices

        75. Documentation and problem handling

        80. Temporary sign-off

Type a menu option below
===>

F1=Help    F3=Exit    F9=Command line       F12=Cancel

_____
[ ]
```

**Figure 5.4.** Main menu presented by the Operational Assistant component of OS/400.

issue OS/400 commands through the OS/400. This is a defined protocol for passing information directly between the application program and OS/400 with no user interaction required. Often, OS/400 subsequently calls on the routines of the LIC instructions to affect the desired action. This interaction between the different software layers was discussed in Chapter 3. OS/400 provides multiple application programming interfaces to maintain compatibility with programs written for System/36, System/38, and of course AS/400. The AS/400 application programming interface provides some new capabilities not found in earlier operating systems, such as the structured query language method of dealing with databases.

As we saw in Chapter 3, OS/400 provides on-line education facilities and on-line help to assist users during interaction with the operating system. If a user gets stuck on some operating system screen, pressing the Help key causes some help text to appear on the screen, as seen in Chapter 3. The particular help text shown depends on where the cursor was on the screen when the Help key was pressed; that is, the text will address the particular item at which the cursor was positioned. This is called **contextual** help.

Extensive database and communications support allows AS/400 to manage large amounts of information and participate in many communications configurations. Available application development tools improve the productivity of programmers for those writing their own custom application programs.

For current users of System/36 or System/38 systems, the OS/400 System/36 and System/38 Modes (along with the migration aids) ease the migration to AS/400 systems.

## A CLOSER LOOK AT OS/400

The previous section provided an overview of OS/400. Even though OS/400 is fairly easy to use, it has many complex features and functions. A complete description of these features would require a separate book. However, the remainder of this chapter looks briefly at some of the most important topics:

- Database support
- Communications support
- Systems management features
- Application development facilities
- System/3X compatibility

## Database Support

A database provides a tool used to organize large quantities of similarly structured information in a computer system. Examples of information commonly found in databases are telephone directories, inventories, and personnel records. OS/400 works together with the LIC instructions in AS/400 computers to provide a "built-in" relational database. The fact that the AS/400 database is designed into the basic functions of AS/400 computers sets them apart from more conventional computers. We discussed the basic characteristics of the AS/400 database in Chapter 1. In this section, we look at some features of OS/400 that allow you to use AS/400's database functions.

The first step in creating a database of information is to define the database structure you desire. This structure, usually designed by a programmer, defines the format in which the information will be stored. Figure 5.5 shows the example telephone directory database structure introduced in Chapter 1. In defining the structure, things like the length, name, and type of data (for example, numbers or textual characters) of each field are specified. In our example database structure, the first field, which is the name field, is 30 characters long and holds alphanumeric characters.

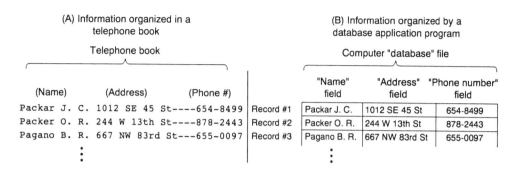

**Figure 5.5.** Example data base structure used in a telephone directory data base.

With AS/400, this structure information is defined within the built-in database itself rather than within a program. This externally described structure can then be used by any application program(s) on the system. This greatly reduces the effort involved in writing or modifying application programs that use the database information.

The database **structure** is typically defined by a programmer and determines exactly what kind of information will be stored in the database. The database structure can be defined through the data description specifications (DDS) or the interactive data definition utility (IDDU) functions provided as standard with OS/400. Either of these approaches provides a central repository of structure related information containing things like field names, field lengths, and data types. This information is very useful to programmers when writing application programs that use information in databases. A third way to define a database structure is through the separately purchased SAA Structured Query Language/400 (5738-ST1) program. SAA Structured Query Language/400 (SAA SQL/400) allows for the use of the **Structured Query Language (SQL)**. SQL is an industry-standard set of commands for creating, accessing, and manipulating relational databases. It can be thought of as an extension to the OS/400 programming interface that allows a programmer to include SQL commands in an application program. Once these programs (including SQL statements) are compiled, they can then be executed on an AS/400 system whether it has the SAA SQL/400 program or not. Recent changes to SAA SQL (i.e., SAA SQL Version 2) have made several enhancements to the original SQL product for the AS/400 (called SQL/400 Version 1). First, the speed at which SQL statements are executed has been improved. For users (not necessarily programmers) who perform SQL queries to AS/400 databases, there is an improved user interface included with SAA SQL/400 Version 2 called the **SQL/400 Query Manager**.

The SQL language is part of IBM's Systems Application Architecture (SAA) and is supported on larger IBM System/390 computers as well as on Personal System/2s. This means that SAA-conforming application programs can use SAA SQL/400 functions while at the same time maintaining the ability to more easily migrate among System/390, AS/400, and PS/2 computers. For programmers, SAA SQL/400 has an **SAA Common Programming Interface (CPI)** that is designed to make applications written for the AS/400 more portable to other SAA systems (e.g., PS/2 with OS/2 or S/390 computers). This is a step toward the goal of the Systems Application Architecture: application program compatibility across the major IBM product families. This new SAA CPI also makes it easier to access databases on other SAA systems over communications networks (i.e., better support for **distributed databases**).

After the database structure is defined, data are typically input through application programs designed for that purpose. Products like the Data File Utility provide the programmer with a tool to help develop simple application programs necessary to load a database structure with information.

After the database is loaded with information, the user can manipulate the data with SQL, DFU, Query/400, or application programs written for that purpose. We just discussed SQL and DFU, which provide the user with interactive data access and the programmer with extended tools for writing database application programs. Query/400, covered in the last chapter, allows the user to generate custom database reports (i.e., database queries) without the help of a programmer. With the **Distributed Data Management (DDM)** functions of OS/400, the user need not know where the database resides; that is, if the needed database resides on a different AS/400 located elsewhere in the communications network, DDM will automatically get the information for the user. While DDM has always allowed distributed database activity with remote AS/400 systems, there was no support for interacting with any SAA-compatible databases on other SAA computer systems (e.g., IBM's ES/9000 line of computers). Recent enhancements in the DDM function of (OS/400) include the first step in support of the System Application Architecture (SAA) defined **Distributed Relational Database (DRDA)**. The current DDM support for DRDA is called the **remote unit of work**. This allows an AS/400 application program to include SAA-compatible SQL statements that interact with data residing on another SAA-compatible database on a distant computer system. That is, the user now has access to the data stored on other computer systems that comply with IBM's System Application Architecture (e.g., an IBM ES/9000 computer system with an SQL/DS database). However, this first step into the realm of distributed SAA databases does not allow the user to interact with multiple remote SAA databases during a single database transaction — a function IBM intends to provide in a future release.

Using application programs (prewritten or custom) to access and manipulate information in an AS/400 database, businesses can combine all of the methods of accessing information to provide an environment that is tailored to their particular needs. These application programs may, unbeknownst to the users, employ one or more of the previously discussed database access methods, depending on the specific need. Using the CICS/400 (5738-DFH) extension to OS/400, programmers can run CICS application programs (COBOL) on an AS/400 and access data on the AS/400 or some other computer (e.g., an S/390 or OS/2 computer) running CICS. Application programs that use CICS are very common in the IBM S/390 user community. CICS/400 allows programmers to migrate S/390-based CICS application programs to the AS/400 or use their CICS experience to write new CICS application programs specifically for the AS/400. The communications functions provided by the CICS environment provide another way for AS/400 programmers to write/migrate application programs that give users access to information stored in the AS/400 and other computer systems.

Many of these different methods and tools for creating, loading, and accessing AS/400 files and databases were carried over from the System/36 and System/38 product lines. Some of these different methods and tools provide functions highly redundant with others. This was done intentionally to provide application program compatibility with the System/36 and System/38. Providing all these different methods for managing AS/400 databases makes it easier to migrate System/3X application programs to AS/400. This helps preserve the significant investment made by businesses in application programs, user training, data accumulation, and so on. At the same time, improved database tools (e.g., SQL/400 and CICS/400) not available with System/3X computers are provided for AS/400. A single program can use any combination of old (System/3X) functions and new AS/400 functions. This allows maximum flexibility for new database application programs and added capabilities when modifying System/3X application programs that have been migrated to AS/400. Further, different application programs can simultaneously use different methods to access the same database files without interfering with one another.

Although OS/400 provides the programmer/user with many ways to "get at" database information, there are other functions necessary to make a complete database management system. In a typical database environment, many different users are constantly making changes to the information in the database. These changes are called database **transactions**. To maintain the accuracy or **data integrity** of the information in the database at all times, OS/400 plays the roll of a traffic director. First, OS/400 prevents two people from simultaneously updating the same information. Without this protection, the integrity of the database is at risk. For example, two travel agents making a reservation for their respective customers simultaneously call up the same seat in an airliner. Both reservationists see the seat as available. The first reservationist reserves the seat for Mr. Jones and posts that change to the database. The second reservationist, who still sees the seat as available, reserves the seat for Ms. Smith and posts this change to the database, overwriting Mr. Jones's reservation. Neither reservationist knows that an error has been introduced! That is a data integrity problem. Although this may seem to be an unlikely series of events, if it can happen it will, particularly in very active database environments in which many thousands of transactions are generated every hour. OS/400 prevents two people from updating the same database information. This is called **record level locking**. Two other functions of OS/400 are **commitment control** and **journaling**. Commitment control is a facility that allows an application program to be designed so that a user must complete all changes related to a database transaction before the transaction is permanently reflected in the database. This helps ensure the data integrity of the database in the event of a system failure in the middle of a transaction. It also allows a transaction to be canceled in process if the user feels the transaction is erroneous.

Journaling is a task performed by OS/400 in which every database transaction, in addition to changing the database, is stored in a separate file of transactions. This journaling works in conjunction with normal backup procedures to allow for recovery of database information in the event of information loss — for example, if the information in an AS/400 database becomes corrupted through a user error or hardware failure. The recovery process would involve loading a previously made backup tape and restoring the database through a simple restore command. However, none of the database transactions made since the backup tape was made would be reflected in the newly restored database. Thus, the database has been recovered only to the point at which the last backup copy was made. Thousands of transactions may have been made since the last backup, and these will have to be reapplied to the restored database. This is where journaling comes in. Because all transactions performed since the last backup are stored in the separate journal area, these transactions can be automatically applied to the newly restored database to bring it to the point immediately before it was corrupted. Without journaling, every transaction performed since the last backup would have to be manually reentered, which can be a very time-consuming process. There are other more subtle improvements made with OS/400 Version 2 and the AS/400 Licensed Internal Code (LIC). For example, deleted database records are now automatically reused, eliminating the need to execute the reorganize physical file command to recover unused disk storage space, and support is provided for **variable length fields** — a new data type for the AS/400.

## Communications Support

Communications facilities included in OS/400 allow a properly equipped AS/400 computer to communicate with a variety of different computing equipment in a variety of ways. First, OS/400 provides support for remote workstations, allowing terminals and printers to be located far away (e.g., across the country) from the AS/400 computer system itself. This allows remote offices to perform all the functions available to those users located in the same building as the AS/400. Further, OS/400 provides the programming support for communications with other computer systems (both IBM and non-IBM) such as System/390, Personal System/2, System/3X, and other AS/400s. In any case, there are different communications protocols that can be used as discussed in Chapter 1. OS/400 includes support for the following protocols:

- Async
- Bisync
- SDLC
- X.25
- IEEE 802.5 (IBM Token-Ring Networks)
- IEEE 802.3 (Ethernet Networks)
- ISO 9314 (FDDI networks)
- IDLC (for ISDN networks)

Chapter 6 provides some hardware and software configurations for various communications networks. For now, it is just necessary to understand that OS/400 comes with the programming required to support these different types of communications environments.

With the addition of some optional OS/400 extensions, AS/400 systems can also participate in other communications environments defined by the **Open Systems Interconnect (OSI)** international standards organization. These OS/400 extension products include **OSI Communications Subsystem/400** (5738-OS1)**, OSI Message Services/400** (5738-MS1), and **OSI File Services/400** (5738-FS1). OSI Communications Subsystem/400 provides the basic communications support necessary for AS/400 systems to communicate with other OSI-compatible systems (i.e., both IBM and non-IBM computer systems). OSI Message Services/400 builds on the capability provided in OSI Communications Subsystem/400 allowing AS/400 systems to exchange electronic mail with other OSI-compatible computers using the X.400 OSI standard (Message Handling Systems or MHSs). Finally, OSI File Services/400 allows AS/400 systems to manage and exchange files with other OSI-compatible computer systems via the ISO FTAM international standard. By conforming to international standards, the OSI communications extensions to OS/400 allow AS/400 systems to communicate with other types of computer systems (i.e., IBM and non-IBM) that conform to the OSI standards. Another extension to OS/400 called AS/400 TCP/IP Communications Utilities (5738-TC1) allows AS/400 systems to participate in communications networks that use the Transmission Control Protocol/Internet Protocol (TCP/IP). TCP/IP is commonly used over a LAN (e.g., Ethernet) in which computer systems (e.g., UNIX-based systems) of different brands communicate with one another. The IBM TCP/IP Server Support/400 product (5798-RWY) gives clients access to AS/400 database files and folder files via Sun Microsystems' Network File System (NFS) commonly used in TCP/IP environments.

Having AS/400 systems participate in a communications network is one thing, but managing that communications network is something else. Network management tasks include things like problem determination, problem tracking, making network configuration changes, and distributing necessary changes. The network management functions needed vary depending on the type of communications network involved. For example, in a simple Token-Ring Network, OS/400 can automatically notify the network operator of any problems that develop in the token-ring adapter or cable and record the error to help in problem determination. In more complex communications environments, OS/400 has other functions that help manage the communications network. For example, suppose an AS/400 in Pittsburgh is part of a network managed from a central System/390 computer located in San Francisco. The network operator in San Francisco uses a System/390 program called **NetView** to manage the entire network. Now a problem develops in the communications link between the AS/400 in Pittsburgh and the System/390 in San Francisco. OS/400 automatically notifies the network operator in San Francisco that a network problem has been detected. This is done through an **alert** message that is automatically sent by OS/400 to the computer in San Francisco. Once an alert notifies the network operator of the problem, several OS/400 functions help identify and correct the problem. First, the **Distributed Host Command Facility (DHCF)** allows the network operator to interact with the AS/400 as if the System/390 terminal in San Francisco was actually a remote AS/400 workstation in Pittsburgh. Using another OS/400 network management feature called the **Link Problem Determination Aid (LPDA)**, the network operator can also issue network commands to test the health of network elements (e.g., modems). Once the cause of the problem is determined, the necessary fix can be put in place. If a change to some AS/400 programming is necessary, OS/400's **Distributed Systems Node Executive (DSNX)** provides a way to distribute and install new programs or changes directly from San Francisco. Alternately, to exchange files between the S/390 host (running MVS/ESA) in San Francisco and the AS/400 in Pittsburgh, the **NetView File Transfer Program** (5730-082) can be used. Thus, the San Francisco–based network operator can use her expertise to analyze and fix the problem without having to travel to Pittsburgh. This kind of network management environment makes for speedy problem determination and correction resulting in less system down time.

Other products that are central to supporting networks of multiple AS/400 systems are IBM OMEGAMON/400 and **SAA SystemView System Manager/400**

(5738-SM1). These products allow a central AS/400 system (with or without the help of a S/390 and NetView) to manage a network of AS/400 systems and their associated PS/2s. SAA SystemView System Manager/400 and IBM OMEGA-MON/400 are discussed under "Systems Management" later in this chapter.

In our example network, the System/390 user was able to access the remote AS/400 system from the System/390 terminal. In the same way, an AS/400 user can access a remote System/390 from the AS/400 workstation. This is possible because OS/400 can make an AS/400 workstation act like or **Emulate** the 3270-type display used with the larger System/390 computers. This **3270 emulation** capability allows the local user of an AS/400 computer attached to a System/390 to interact with the System/390 as if his computer were a 3270-type device. Conversely, OS/400 allows remote 3270 terminals to access programs and data on the AS/400 system as if they were AS/400 workstations.

OS/400 supports IBM's Systems Network Architecture (SNA). This is a published set of rules governing various aspects of computer communications from protocols (e.g., SDLC) to document formats (e.g., Document Content Architecture [DCA]) and electronic mail (e.g., SNA Distribution Services [SNADS]). It is SNA that provides the common ground on which different types of computer equipment can efficiently exchange information. OS/400's **Advanced Peer-to-Peer Network (APPN)** architecture, originally developed on the earlier IBM S/36 computers, has now been adopted as part of SNA. Further, APPN support in OS/400 Version 2 has been expanded (APPN end-node support) to allow more direct interaction with traditional SNA networks. The **DDM** function of OS/400 allows an AS/400 user to access data on a remote AS/400 as if the data were located on the local AS/400 system. With distributed data management, the user need not know which computer system has the needed data. DDM will find it. Still other communications functions provided with OS/400 include the **Display Station Passthru (DSPT)** and **Object Distribution**. DSPT allows a user of one system to sign on to some other computer in the communications network as if the two systems were directly attached. This allows one workstation to access any computer system in the network. The Object Distribution facility of OS/400 makes sending information or programs to remote locations much simpler. A common use for this facility is to distribute application programs developed at a central site to remote computers.

Introduced with OS/400 Version 2 is an **SAA Common Programming Interface**. This allows AS/400 programmers to develop application programs that conform to IBM's System Application Architecture. Since IBM's SAA-compliant computer systems (i.e., PS/2, AS/400, and S/390) are also converging to the SAA Common Programming Interface, portability of AS/400 applications written to the SAA Common Programming Interface is improved. That is, application programs written to the SAA Common Programming Interface provided in OS/400 Version 2 should be able to be more easily modified to run on IBM's other SAA systems (e.g., an S/390-based ES/9000 computer).

In addition to those functions provided as standard with OS/400, there are many separately purchased programs that add other communications capabilities. **AS/400 PC Support** (5738-PC1) is a program that allows Personal System/2s (or Personal Computers) to cooperate with AS/400. In the simplest form of this cooperation, PC Support allows a properly equipped PS/2 to be used as a workstation for AS/400 — that is, the PC Support allows a PS/2 to emulate an AS/400 terminal or printer. In fact, a single PS/2 can appear to be up to five different devices (or **sessions**) to an AS/400. This allows users to define their PS/2 as an AS/400 terminal (session #1), their PS/2 printer as an AS/400 printer (session #2), and still have three sessions left over. Some of these other sessions might be used to sign on to another AS/400 system as a separate workstation, for example. Although the PS/2 is emulating AS/400 workstations, it still keeps its ability to run PS/2 programs. To simplify things for the user, PC Support provides the menu. From this menu, the user can access programs residing on either the AS/400 or the PS/2. The user need not be concerned about whether the program runs on the AS/400 or the PS/2, thus improving ease of use.

PC Support also provides for the free exchange of information between the PS/2 and the AS/400 system. Since the PS/2 has some computing power of its own, it is called an **intelligent workstation** and can do things that a normal ("dumb") workstation cannot. For example, information in AS/400 databases can be brought down to the PS/2 and manipulated using a spreadsheet program. Further, a document created on the PS/2 can be transferred up to the AS/400 system and manipulated by OfficeVision/400 text processing or sent through OfficeVision/400's electronic mail system. Finally, the AS/400's disk storage can be used as an extension to the PS/2's disk storage through the use of **shared folders**. Shared folders are areas of disk storage that can be accessed by any authorized AS/400 user. Through these shared folders, the AS/400 can be the central storage element in a network of PS/2s and AS/400 users, allowing any authorized user access to the information. In the same way that information can be shared, printers and communications links can also be shared. For example, through PC Support's **virtual printer** functions, a PS/2 user can automatically send documents to AS/400 printers and vice versa. Since PC Support uses an advanced communications technique called **Advanced Program-to-Program Communications** (**APPC**), the functions available to PS/2 users are the same regardless of the communications method being used. The users get the same benefits from PC Support whether they are local workstations (twinaxial attached), remote workstations (through a 5494), or attached via a Token-Ring Network.

So PC Support allows the user to perform the needed functions on the system best suited for the job while hiding many of the complexities of this dual environment from the user. One enhancement introduced with PC Support Version 2 is that more PS/2 memory can be made available for DOS application programs by implementing the **extended memory** technique, which shifts some of the PC Support program into memory above the critical 640-KB memory area. Another improvement in PC Support Version 2 gives programmers more tools (more APIs) to develop cooperative processing application programs for both the AS/400 and for PS/2s. More about computer processing in a minute.

The central administration functions of PC Support make it easier to perform systems management tasks (e.g., update the software on a group of PS/2s) on any PS/2 in the network from the AS/400 system. PC Support can be used with PS/2s running either the DOS operating system (with or without Windows 3.0) or the OS/2 operating system. Another enhancement to PC Support provides a call-level interface for PS/2-based application programs that allows a PS/2 program to send SQL statements, which are then executed on the AS/400 system. That is, a PS/2 program can now be written to directly manipulate data stored on an AS/400, allowing for a closer cooperation between the PS/2 and the AS/400. Further, PC Support can now coexist with Novell NetWare® LAN client functions in the same workstation. This means that a single workstation can concurrently access information on both an AS/400 (using PC Support) and on Novell servers (with the Novell NetWare software).

When an AS/400 provides some resource to a PS/2 (e.g., disk storage, information, or printers), the AS/400 is said to be a **server** for the PS/2 and the PS/2 is called a **client.** This is the origin of the term **client/server computing.** The disk and printer sharing provided by PC Support is a simple form of client/server computing commonly in use today. Another form of client/server computing that is becoming more commonplace uses a PS/2 to present the AS/400 user with an enhanced (graphical) user interface commonly found in PS/2 environments. One example of this client/server environment is provided by adding the RUMBA/400 (RPQ 5799-PLT) add-on to PC Support. RUMBA/400 together with PC Support allows AS/400 users (using a PS/2 with either OS/2 or DOS/Windows) to interact with existing AS/400 application programs via a graphical user interface (i.e., windows, button bars, and so on.). Users interacting with AS/400 application programs via Apple Macintosh computers get a graphical user interface via the Macintosh Emulator product.

While disk/printer sharing and enhanced user interfaces are very useful, these are simple implementations of the powerful client/server model. A more advanced example of client/server computing would be a network on which multiple servers — each managing a different database — reside along with a pool of clients who use the data. With the proper application programs on the servers and the clients, the users of such an environment would be able to access the data on any database located anywhere in the network. The client application programs would provide an easy-to-use graphical user interface and allow the user to specify the information he or she wanted to see in human terms. The client application program would then communicate over the network to the application programs running on one or more servers, to collect the needed data. Finally, the client would present the information in the form most useful for that user. The interaction between the client application program and the server application program(s) would be performed without the users even knowing that it had occurred. The level of client/server computing, also called **cooperative processing**, makes for a very flexible computing environment and can more fully utilize the strengths of various computers in a network. The industry standards and programming tools necessary to build these types of client/server application programs are available today and becoming more pervasive. The Application Programming Interfaces (APIs) provided in PC Support allow for the development of OS/2, DOS/Windows, and AS/400 application programs that directly interact with one another. Further, the AS/400 Client Series of application development tools is comprised of tools designed to build client/server application programs that use OS/2, DOS/Windows, and Apple Macintosh computers as clients and the AS/400 as a server. Client/server computing, still in its infancy, will have a role of growing importance over the next few years.

The AS/400 Communications Utilities (5738-CM1) program product complements the communications function of OS/400 for interacting with System/390 computers. This set of programs augments OS/400 communications functions in the area of interchanging electronic mail and files with various System/390 computer environments over an SNA communications network. For example, AS/400 Communications Utilities allows AS/400 Office users to exchange information with users of the **OfficeVision/VM** and **OfficeVision/MVS**. These programs run on the System/390, providing those users with functions like those of OfficeVision/400 (for example, electronic mail and calendaring). The other basic function provided by AS/400 Communications Utilities is called **Remote Job Entry Facility (RJE)**. RJE allows an AS/400 system to emulate an RJE workstation used to submit batch jobs to or receive output from System/390 computers.

## Systems Management

With any computer system, various tasks must be performed in support of the computer system itself by someone trained to be the system's **operator**. These tasks include such things as authorizing new users, making backup copies of the information kept on disk storage, keeping track of the physical assets, documenting and resolving system problems, installing software upgrades, identifying and resolving communications network problems, monitoring performance/capacity, planning for future computing needs, and more. These tasks necessary to support the day-to-day operation of a computer system are collectively called **systems management** tasks.

Some of today's computing environments are fairly simple, involving one computer system and a handful of users. Others are enormously complex, involving many computer systems of varying types, worldwide communications networks, multiple application programs, hundreds or thousands of workstations and users, modems, printers, and so on. In smaller environments, there is typically not a large data processing staff available to perform the systems management tasks. In fact, systems management is often performed by clerical staff with little or no experience in systems management. In this environment, the simpler systems management is, the better.

As the complexity and size of a computing environment increases, so does the effort (read "cost") of managing that computing environment. When you consider the amount of activity going on at blazing speeds, the amount of equipment, and the number of people involved, you can begin to understand how systems management responsibilities can quickly overwhelm even the most astute data processing personnel.

It is well known that both simple and complex environments can benefit from automated tools (i.e., still more computer programs) to help with systems management. Many software companies (both IBM and others) have already delivered systems management tools for the AS/400 that help streamline systems management tasks. However, since the tools were usually developed independently by various software companies, they usually don't cooperate with one another. Thus, the same information may have to be entered into two different tools, and users must learn a new user interface with every new tool.

To bring more order to the realm of systems management tools, IBM has defined a framework called **SystemView** that is designed to improve the efficiency and reduce the cost associated with systems management activities. The SystemView strategy is to publish a framework or "blueprint" to guide the development of a cooperative family of integrated systems management tools. By publishing the SystemView framework, IBM has basically encouraged the many different companies to modify their systems management tools or to create new systems management tools that follow the SystemView framework.

What does the user get by using a set of SystemView-compliant systems management tools? Let's find out by looking at the SystemView framework depicted in Figure 5.6.

There are three basic elements in the SystemView framework: the **End-Use Dimension**, the **Data Dimension**, and the **Application Dimension**. The End-Use Dimension addresses the need for a consistent user interface for all systems management tools. It defines the appearance and behavior that all SystemView tools should present to the user. Having a consistent user interface will reduce the training requirements for the users, since the concepts and techniques learned on the first SystemView tool will be automatically transferable to any other SystemView tools.

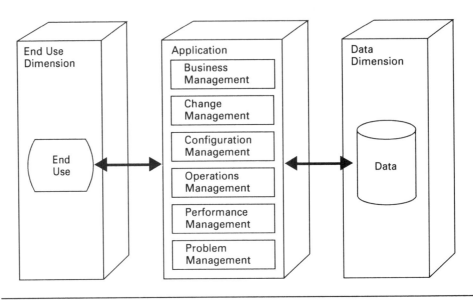

**Figure 5.6.** The SystemView Framework.

The user interface specified by the SystemView End-Use Dimension complies with the Common User Access (CUA) user interface defined in the Systems Application Architecture (SAA) and is further specified by the "SAA SystemView End-Use Dimension Consistency Guide."

The Data Dimension of SystemView defines the information types and formats that will be shared by all SystemView-compliant tools and provides facilities to access that data in a consistent way. Having to enter the same data more than once into the independent data structures of systems management tools wastes time and provides more opportunity for data inconsistency. By providing a common set of shared data, the SystemView allows for data to be entered one time and then to be used by many different systems management tools as necessary.

Finally, the Application Dimension of SystemView defines six different types of systems management tools. These six different types of systems management tools or **disciplines** include the following:

> **Business management**, which allows users to track physical assets and manage the finance and accounting associated with a computer system(s)
>
> **Change management**, which allows the systems management personnel to plan, implement, and track changes made to the computer system(s)
>
> **Configuration management**, which helps in documenting, planning, and modifying the configuration (physical and logical relationships between components) of the elements comprising the computer system(s)

**Operations management**, which helps devise/maintain the policies and procedures used to efficiently process a business's workload with the computer system(s)

**Performance management**, which helps define, monitor, and plan the level of performance users should expect from the computer system

**Problem management**, which helps plan how computer-related problems are prevented, detected, tracked, and resolved.

With this understanding of IBM's SystemView framework, let's see how the AS/400 plays in the SystemView structure. Figure 5.7 shows where OS/400 and some example extensions to OS/400 fit into the Application Dimension of the SystemView Framework. As shown in the bottom half of the figure, many functions provided as standard in OS/400 can be mapped into the SystemView Framework. For example, as users can begin to use the AS/400 system, the disk storage will begin to accumulate business information often vital to the day-to-day operations of the business. This information becomes an asset to the business and should be pro-

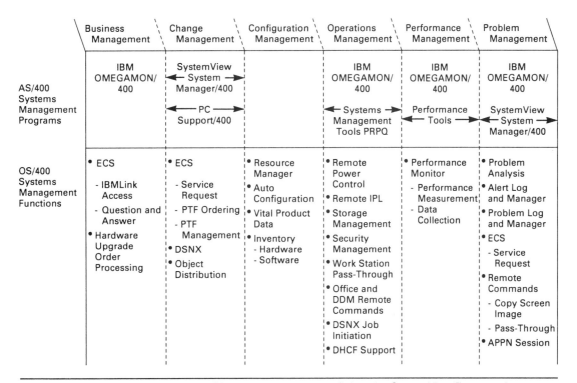

**Figure 5.7.** How OS/400 and other AS/400 system programs fit into the SystemView Framework.

tected as such. OS/400 provides several functions that allow the system's operator to protect against loss of information from user errors, hardware failures, intentional corruptions, and so forth. First, the system's operator can make backup copies of the information on disk storage to magnetic tape. With OS/400 Version 2 Release 2, these backup copies can be made while users are actively using the systems. This feature is called "**save while active**." Before the "save while active" function was provided, the systems operator had to regularly reserve a block of time and dedicate the AS/400 system to backup operations, making it unavailable to the users. Now the backup operations can occur while users are still performing useful work.

If the information on the AS/400 disk storage is lost, the backup tapes can be used to **restore** the AS/400 disk storage to the state at which the last backup was made. With the additional journal function of OS/400 described in the "Database Support" section of this chapter, all transactions subsequent to the backup but prior to the failure can be posted to the restored information. This typically completes the recovery procedure, and the information on the AS/400 system is restored to the point just before the failure occurred. Another recovery function in OS/400 used to guard against disk unit failures is known as **checksum**. With the checksum approach, a mathematical formula is used to store redundant information on disk storage in addition to the business information. If one of the disk units fails, the redundant information on the remaining disk units can be used to automatically regenerate the lost information on the replacement fixed disk. Checksum provides a way, at the cost of increased disk storage requirements and an additional load on the computer, to avoid having to do a restore from backups in the event of a disk unit failure. The backup/restore/journaling and checksum methods of protecting and recovering information reside in the "Operations" discipline of the SystemView Framework. Since AS/400 is designed for office environments in which technical skills are usually limited, these systems management tasks and others (like collecting information about system problems, backing up user libraries, enrollment of users, and automatic cleanup of the system messages/job logs) can be accomplished through the Operational Assistant user interface introduced in Chapter 3. The Operational Assistant simplifies the interaction between the system's operator and OS/400 through additional menus and functions.

In addition to the functions provided as standard with OS/400, there are other systems management tools available as optional OS/400 extensions or application programs. For example, a large company may have one AS/400 system at the headquarters location and multiple AS/400 systems distributed to other locations throughout the country or around the world. Rather than provide AS/400 and OS/400 personnel at each of the locations, it is often desirable to have a centralized staff of experts that can support all of the AS/400 systems throughout the company — a central help desk. That help desk can then coordinate all outside resources (e.g., IBM's customer support structure or an application software company's support system) as the single point of contact for the whole company. The **SAA SystemView System Manager/400** (5738-SM1) extension to OS/400 provides facilities to support centralized systems management. Formerly called the Systems Management Utility, SAA SystemView System Manager/400 allows a central AS/400 system/site/staff to perform systems management tasks for a network of remote AS/400 systems. Specifically, it addresses two disciplines of systems management: change management and problem management. In the area of change management, it allows the staff to apply and track changes made to the AS/400 system(s). These changes might be Program Temporary Fixes (PTFs) that correct known problems or installing a whole new version of OS/400. The updates can be sent electronically to the remote AS/400 systems over existing APPN or traditional SNA networks.

In the area of problem management, the System Manager/400 provides a way for the staff to maintain an electronic problem log. As users or the AS/400 system itself (through Alerts) report a problem, that problem can be automatically noted in the electronic problem log. These problems can be prioritized, and notes can be kept on the activities associated with each problem. If IBM's customer service needs to get involved, the problem, with all of its notes, can be sent electronically to IBM's support network. If the central support site has an S/390 computer system, SAA SystemView System Manager/400 can cooperate with the S/390 and allow all support activity to be performed from that system.

The IBM SAA SystemView OMEGAMON/400 product (5738-ES1) also provides tools helpful in managing a single AS/400 system or a network of AS/400 systems. The base IBM OMEGAMON/400 product allows you to monitor various operational parameters within the AS/400(s). When you set thresholds on the monitored parameters, OMEGAMON/400 will notify you of any out-of-limits conditions that arise. By adding the optional IBM SAA SystemView OMEGAMON Services Automated Facilities/400 product to IBM OMEGAMON/400, you can set up groups of actions that will be taken automatically when an out-of-limits condition is detected. Another add-on product to IBM OMEGAMON/400 is IBM SAA SystemView OMEGAMON Services OMEGAVIEW/400. OMEGAVIEW/400 allows you to create a graphical representation of your monitored conditions on a personal computer running OS/2. For example, you could graphically depict a nationwide network of AS/400 systems on the personal computer's screen. When an out-of-limits condition occurred, a red triangle with an exclamation point would appear. By double clicking on the triangle with your mouse, more detailed information about the problem would be presented. While the IBM OMEGAMON/400 product fits into some of the same SystemView disciplines as System Manager/400, it provides different systems management functions within those disciplines.

Another product that fits in the SystemView framework is the IBM AS/400 Performance Tools (5783-PT1). This menu-driven program gives access to system load information automatically logged by the system. With these tools, you can "tune" the performance of the system and project future performance requirements. The tool provides performance reports that can be as high-level or as detailed as needed. System utilization, response time, and number of transactions are statistically treated. The expert-systems-based "advisor" function introduced with AS/400 Performance Tools Version 2 assists the system manager in interpreting performance analyses and often recommends specific actions. AS/400 Performance Tools help the system manager determine where the system is and where it is going in terms of capacity and performance. For smaller systems or those not requiring the function of AS/400 Performance Tools, the Performance Tools Subset/400 (5798-RYP) provides basic performance planning tools. Also, the Performance Investigator/400 (PRPQ #5799-PRG) runs on a PS/2 under DOS/Windows and graphs in real time (15-second samples) items like CPU utilization, response time, and so on. One PS/2 can monitor up to 16 AS/400 systems.

## Application Development

Many businesses find that writing their own custom application programs is the best method of solving business problems through computers. To this end, the basic architecture of AS/400 has been optimized to make writing and maintaining custom application programs as easy as possible. The database built into all AS/400s is one example of this. The ability to create databases that do not reside in any one program (externally described data) and to create different logical views of the same physical data is a major benefit to programmer productivity. This is particularly true when the need comes to modify or add programs that use the database information in a different way. Single-level storage and the concept of objects help the programmer by automatically managing the complexities of memory sizes, disk storage paging, and file sizes. Programmers can therefore spend their time making the application program more powerful or easier to use instead of managing internal computer logistics.

The programmer has several **programming languages** from which to choose, including:

- AS/400 PL/1
- AS/400 Pascal
- SAA AD/Cycle RPG/400
- ILE RPG/400

- AS/400 BASIC
- SAA AD/Cycle COBOL/400
- SAA C/400
- ILE C/400
- RM/COBOL-85
- SAA FORTRAN/400

These commonly used programming languages can be thought of as the library of instructions from which a programmer constructs a program. The language selected depends on the requirements of the application program and the skills of the programmer(s). The "ILE" languages conform to the AS/400's **Integrated Language Environment (ILE)**. The ILE environment is an architecture designed to increase programmer productivity by allowing the binding of modules into a single program, even if the modules were written in different ILE languages.

In addition to these traditional programming languages, OS/400 provides another language called **Command Language (CL)** for performing operating system tasks. CL can be used to issue a single operating system request or to create complex programs that present the user with menus and initiate other application programs. Designed in OS/400 are functions that allow the application programmer to participate in the **Document Interchange Architecture (DIA)**. This set of rules published by IBM allows for the smooth flow of electronic documents through different types of computers and programs. Other OS/400 features make it easier for the programmer to provide on-line help text and use graphics (i.e., GDDM support), making the application program easier to understand and use.

To further augment tools available to the programmer, the separately purchased **IBM AS/400 Application Development Tools (ADT)** package is available. This programmer tool kit is based on programmer tools available with earlier System/3X computers and consists of the following:

*Program Development Manager:* This program provides all the elements of ADT assembled into one integrated programming environment. It allows the programmer to work with lists of items being developed. Rather than copying each item individually, the Program Development Manager allows you to perform the copy with one operation. It provides convenience that improves productivity and makes for a more pleasant programming environment. For those familiar with the **Programmer and Operator Productivity (POP)** environment on the System/36, this is the same type of thing with a few enhancements.

*Source Entry Utility (SEU):* This tool can be thought of as a specialized "word processor" for programmers that is used to write application programs. It provides a **full-screen** editor, which means that you can work an entire page of text at a time. It provides the basic capabilities of copying, deleting, and moving text (programming statements) as well as some automatic **syntax** or grammar checking. A "search" function allows you to automatically locate particular statements in a program. The split-screen function allows you to simultaneously view two different areas of a program or two separate programs for purposes of comparison. Many of the commands used with SEU are similar to those used in Development Support Utilities and Source Entry Utility programs of System/3X computers.

*Screen Design Aid (SDA):* This program allows the application programmer to interactively design, create, and maintain the user interface of a program—that is, the actual images seen by the user of an application program can be generated through the SDA. This tool saves the programmer considerable time that would otherwise have to be spent programming all screen images from scratch. Since SDA is interactive, the programmer can easily change the screen being designed (e.g., different color and fields) and immediately see the results of the change. Once a screen image is completed, it can be printed for use in program documentation.

*Data File Utility (DFU):* This utility program is primarily intended to help a programmer write simple database management programs. Typical programs in this area include data entry (filling up a database with information), retrieving information (inquiry), or making necessary changes to a database (file maintenance). Although OS/400 itself provides a way to perform these tasks, DFU and user-written applications programs make these tasks easier for the user.

*Advanced Printer Functions (APF):* This tool provides a potpourri of special printing functions—things like the printing of **optical character recognition (OCR)** characters that can be read by machines and **bar code labels** read by scanners. APF also lets you generate bar graphs and define your own print styles and special symbols.

In addition to the Application Development Tools, there are other separately purchased tools for the AS/400 programmer. Among these are the Application Program Driver (5730-095), Application Dictionary Services/400 (5733-080), Advanced Function Printing Utilities/400 (5738-AF1), WindowTool/400 (5798-RYF), SAA Structured Query Language (5738-ST1), Business Graphics Utility (5738-DS1), and Query/400 (5731-QU1).

The Application Program Driver (5738-PD1) is yet another tool for programmers that provides many of the services commonly needed by application programs (e.g., menu design, fastpath support around menus, and security). Further, the Application Program Driver can provide a single menu interface to all application programs. This makes for a consistent user interface for users who need access to more than one application program.

Application Dictionary Services/400 builds a directory of data and programs residing on the AS/400 system. It is used by the programmer to keep an inventory of the data and program items stored on the system and can be used to evaluate the impact of a proposed change to an application program.

The Advanced Function Printing Utilities/400 extension to OS/400, not to be confused with the "Advanced Printer Functions" just discussed, provides a means to combine text, image, and graphics into a document. This document can then be printed on any AS/400 printer that supports the Intelligent Printer Data Stream (IPDS) format (e.g., the 3816 Page Printer). Advanced Function Printing, also supported by other IBM computer systems, is commonly used for such things as generating forms that are then merged with the appropriate text and printed. In this example, the utilities provide an alternative to purchasing and loading preprinted forms into your printer. With Advanced Function Printing, the form is interactively generated and stored in the computer system. Then, as needed, data can be merged with the form image and printed. Another use for Advanced Function Printing is in merging a company logo (or any image) on letterhead with the text of the letter — again eliminating the need to purchase and load letterhead.

WindowTool/400 is a tool used to build a text-based windows user interface for existing AS/400 application programs on nonintelligent terminals (Figure 5.8). With

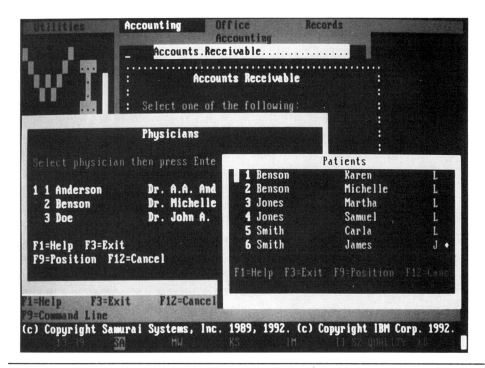

**Figure 5.8.** User interface created by WindowTool/400 on a text-only, nonintelligent workstation.

WindowTool/400 systems, operators and programmers can subdivide the screen into boxes (called *windows*) and provide user interface items like pull-down windows, pop-up menus, action bars, and so on. Although no graphics is supported with WindowTool/400, the user interface provided on nonintelligent text-only workstations with WindowTool/400 is a step towards the graphical user interface that has become so popular on intelligent workstations (e.g., Windows™ and OS/2 presentation manager on a PS/2). Alternately, application programs can be written to some enhanced OS/400 application programming interfaces (**DDS Windows support**) to provide the best user interface available to the user. That is, a user with a personal computer or InfoWindow II workstation will automatically be presented an enhanced user interface with pop-up windows, scroll bars, and so on. A user of a workstation that doesn't support the enhanced user interface functions of OS/400 will be presented a standard user interface (e.g., a simple menu). The programmer simply writes the application programming using the DDS Windows application program interfaces. The OS/400 and associated hardware automatically tailor the user interface for each user's workstation based on its capabilities. RUMBA/400, mentioned earlier, recognizes and works with application programs that use the new DDS Windows application programming interfaces.

SAA Structured Query Language (SQL), Business Graphics Utility (BGU), and Query/400 were all mentioned in Chapter 4. SQL provides the programmer with additional commands that can be embedded in application programs to efficiently manipulate database information. BGU is a programmer's tool for creating computer-generated graphics. Although users with no programming experience can use BGU interactively to create their own graphs, the programming interface provided by BGU gives the application programmer convenient access to graphics functions. Finally, Query can be used by the programmer to define database reports that can be executed by the user. Once the query has been defined, the AS/400 system need not have the Query/400 program to simply execute the query. Again, although the user can often use Query without the assistance of a programmer, a programmer can also take advantage of Query when writing application programs.

Once the programs have been written using AS/400 programming tools, they must be tested for correctness and any problems must be diagnosed and fixed. OS/400 provides an **interactive debug facility** for this purpose. This facility allows the programmer to closely control and monitor the new or modified application program as it is executing on the AS/400. Because one of the most frustrating tasks for the programmer can be debugging the program (finding and fixing programming errors), this facility is very important.

The only thing constant is change. So even when an application program is completely tested and put into productive use, there will be a need to make changes as the business environment changes and to fix newly discovered program errors that were not caught during testing. This activity is called supporting or **maintaining** the application program. In addition to AS/400's externally described database design, there are some tools that help with this maintenance. OS/400's **cross-reference facility** and **data dictionary** support provide the programmer with the means to determine which application programs use what database information. With this information, the programmers can assess the impact of a proposed change to an application program or database. The data dictionary support also provides a single place to go for information concerning database field names, data types, and the like.

The built-in features of AS/400 and OS/400 along with additional tools (i.e., Application Development Tools, SQL, etc.) make for productive application program development and maintenance. However, there are other AS/400 programming tools for those wishing to implement the more structured **Computer Aided Software Engineering (CASE)** methodology. CASE is a structure and methodology for managing and executing application development projects from inception of the project through ongoing software maintenance activities. IBM's strategy or framework for CASE is called **AD/Cycle**. AD/Cycle is not a product, but rather a Systems Application Architecture–based framework for CASE. Some AD/Cycle development tools currently exist for the AS/400 but not yet enough to completely fill out the AD/Cycle Framework. Some tools were developed by IBM, and some were developed by other software companies (e.g., Synon Corporation and Easel). It is IBM's intention to develop and offer more AS/Cycle tools and to encourage other software companies to develop more AD/Cycle tools.

Figure 5.9 shows the AD/Cycle Framework. Near the top of the figure, the custom application program development cycle is depicted from "Defining User Requirements" through the "Production and Maintenance" phases. The elements of the AD/Cycle Framework are shown in the figure as shaded boxes. At the very top of the figure, the **Cross–Life Cycle Tools** component of AD/Cycle is shown. This component consists of the set of tools used throughout the development process. It includes tools that do things like set/monitor the project schedule/resources (project management), define/enforce consistent development practices to be followed by the programming staff (process management), help create the documents associated with the project and the resulting products (documentation tools), and so on.

The other types of tools defined in the AD/Cycle Framework are those that are used to actually perform the custom application development process itself. Before we go into the different types of tools used to actually perform the development process, let's glance at the all-important Application Development Platform component underlying the AD/Cycle Framework (shown near the bottom of the figure). This element is the heart of the AD/Cycle Framework. The Application Development Platform component of AD/Cycle is a set of services and rules that defines the AD/Cycle Framework in detail. The AD/Cycle services and rules, when adhered to

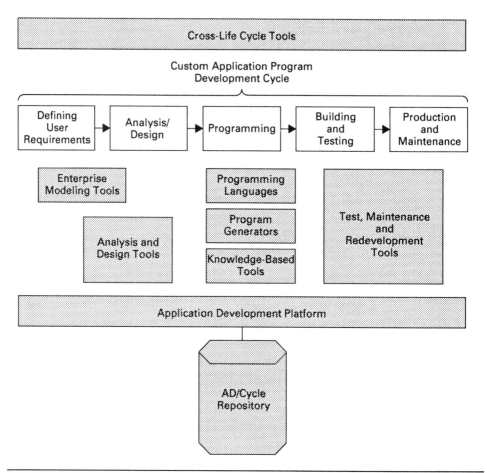

**Figure 5.9.** The AD/Cycle Framework.

by developers of programming tools, allow for the integration of many different programming tools designed and written by many independent software companies. That is, IBM has published the AD/Cycle specifications to encourage other companies to write programming tools that conform to the AD/Cycle Framework. This is how the AD/Cycle Framework can allow the programming tools from many different companies to work together, sharing information and reducing the duplication of effort/information. It is through the Application Development Platform component of AD/Cycle that all other programming tools have access to the central body of information, called the **AD/Cycle Repository**, shown at the bottom of the figure. With the information stored in this central repository, any programming tool written to the AD/Cycle Framework can have access to or store any appropriate information about the development process or application program of interest. This AD/Cycle Repository also reduces the redundant information often generated by programming tools not designed to work together. Reducing redundant information helps improve productivity and reduce the opportunities to introduce errors into the application development process. The SAA AD/Cycle Application Development Manager/400 (5738-LM1) is an AS/400 program product that implements the Application Development Platform of AD/Cycle in an AS/400 system. It gives the application programmers access to a shared library of programming objects and prevents one programmer from overwriting an object updated by another programmer. It also provides a structure through which an application programmer must traverse as he/she develops an application program. Version control and software configuration management functions are also provided.

Now let's look at the types of tools used to perform the actual program development as defined in the AD/Cycle Framework. The first set of tools shown in the figure are called the **enterprise modeling tools**. These tools are used to create, validate, and maintain a software model of the business processes that will be automated by the custom application programs being developed. Enterprise modeling tools provide a structured way to look at the processes an enterprise performs, the information those processes use, and the policies and practices that control the processes. By modeling the enterprise with these tools, the development team and the eventual users can define and document a single set of requirements for the application program development project. It is paramount to a successful application program development project that all parties clearly understand the requirements to be met at the beginning of the project.

The **analysis and design tools** allow the project team to develop the specifications for the application programs that support the requirements defined with the enterprise modeling tools. The first phase of analysis and design is to analyze the requirements and define the functions, user interface, and reports for the application programs to be developed (i.e., the **functional design**). Tools used during the functional design often help the project team build a **prototype**, which is used to validate the user interface and reports that will be generated by the final application program. The second phase of this process involves identifying the data elements the application programs will need and defining a model of the way data to be used by the application programs will be organized within the system (i.e., the **data design**).

Several different tools in the AD/Cycle Framework are used during the "Produce" phase of the development project. **Programming languages** are used by the programmers to actually write the application programs. Among the programming languages supported by the SAA-compliant AD/Cycle Framework are C, COBOL, FORTRAN, RPG, and various procedure languages (e.g., REXX). Each different language has its own set of strengths and weaknesses. It is the job of the project team to decide which language(s) will be used for a specific application program. Also residing in the Programming Languages component of AD/Cycle and used during the Produce and Build/Text phases are the tools used to enter, compile, and debug a program. The IBM SAA AD/Cycle CoOperative Development Environment/400 (CODE/400 – 5733-073) provides AD/Cycle-compliant tools for this. CODE/400 uses a combination of tools residing on both a PS/2 (running OS/2) and the AS/400 that are designed to cooperate with one another. These tools include debugging tools and a language-sensitive editor that can detect syntax errors for that language and provide direct access to reference information related to the selected programming language.

**Program generators** are one level above programming languages in that they automatically generate programs defined by the project team. In some cases, they can be used to increase programmer productivity by allowing project team members to define a task at a very high level and allow the generator to automatically write the necessary program. For example, Synon Corporation has developed a family of program generators that work within the AD/Cycle Framework.

Finally, **knowledge-based tools** support the development of a class of custom application programs that employ expert system techniques for solving problems. **Expert systems** are application programs that attempt to capture the knowledge of a human expert and then draw conclusions on any presented information based on that expert knowledge. While expert systems are not the answer to all application program needs, they can be very effective in addressing many business needs. Two examples of knowledge-based tools are the IBM KnowledgeTool/400 (5798-RYE) and the Neural Network Utility/400 (5798-RYB). KnowledgeTool/400 is a tool used by programmers to write application programs that use rule-based expert system technology. These application programs are designed to capture the expertise of humans in a set of rules later used by the application program to make decisions and recommendations on any new data provided. For example, a rule-based expert system application program for the medical profession might try to diagnose an illness based on a set of symptoms entered into a computer system. The Neural Network Utility/400 takes a different approach. Rather than having the expert and programmer develop a set of rules, the Neural Network Utility/400 will analyze a set of existing information in order to identify and classify patterns in the information. For example, if a bank has a database containing information about loan applicants and their subsequent payment records, the Neural Network Utility/400 can be employed to look for patterns in the information and identify characteristics that tend to indicate that the party will pay off a loan on schedule. During this analysis phase, the neural network is said to be **training on the data**. Once the neural network is trained, it can then look at the information collected from new loan applicants and help management determine the risk associated with each applicant based on history.

In the next phase of the application program development project, "Production and Maintenance," the **test, maintenance**, and **redevelopment** tools are introduced. Build tools are used to "assemble" all the pieces of the application program(s) (e.g., object code modules, subroutine libraries, etc.) into a working system. Test tools help the programmers simulate inputs to the application program and monitor outputs. Tests can be defined and then run during initial testing and rerun later to validate any changes made to the application program after it is in use. Maintenance tools include things to increase the productivity of the programmers when they correct errors or implement changes in the application program while it is in use. An example of a maintenance tool is an "impact analysis tool," which allows programmers to assess the amount of effort needed to implement a requested change before the change is started. This allows the level of effort required for the change to be measured against the value of the change in order to help prioritize work. Redevelopment tools are also designed to help increase the productivity of the data processing organization in maintaining application programs over time. One type of redevelopment tool, for example, allows a programmer to examine the components of an application program, store that information in the central repository, and then restructure the application program without changing its function. Others allow a programmer to understand how various application programs are interrelated.

Over the past few decades, application programs have grown enormously in complexity and size — a trend that shows no sign of abating. Old methods of application development are not effectively meeting the challenges posed by contemporary application development. AD/Cycle is IBM's strategy to address the needs of custom application development for the SAA environment. The AD/Cycle Framework set of rules and services is designed to allow a programmer to choose from a wide variety of (AD/Cycle-compliant) programming tools developed by many different software companies and integrate them into a coherent and efficient application development environment.

## System/3X Compatibility

To preserve most of the System/3X user's current investment in application programs, OS/400 provides a way to use most existing System/3X application programs on an AS/400. OS/400 and related products allow most programs written for a System/36 or System/38 to be migrated with little or no change to an AS/400. OS/400 supports this capability by providing multiple programming interfaces as shown in Figure 5.10. First is the **AS/400 native** programming interface. This provides support for new functions like the Structured Query Language. The System/38 programming interface provides a high level of compatibility with System/38 application programs. Because AS/400 was based on the same basic architecture as the System/38, the two are naturally very compatible and there is little system performance

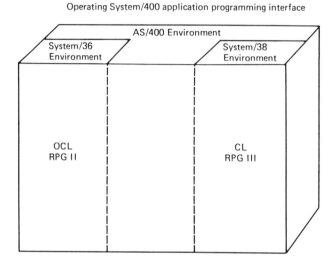

Operating System/400 application programming interface

**Figure 5.10.** The three basic elements of the OS/400 application programming interface provide a high level of compatibility with application programs written for System/3X computers.

impact to operating in OS/400's System/38 environment. OS/400 is automatically switched into the System/38 environment when a System/38 program is executed. OS/400's System/38 environment can also be activated through CL.

The System/36 programming interface of OS/400 is not as clean a fit as that for the System/38, but it still provides a migration path for most System/36 application programs. OS/400's System/36 environment interprets the OCL used with the System/36 and can execute RPG II and COBOL application programs after they are adapted to the AS/400 environment. Since applications originally written for the System/36 don't take advantage of the AS/400 architecture, the performance of the AS/400 is reduced when executing in the System/36 environment. With the System/36 and System/38 environments of the AS/400, programs for the S/36 and S/38 can be developed on an AS/400. However, they must be compiled on the S/36 or S/38 before they can be used on those systems.

Two tools are available to help migrate System/3X application programs to AS/400: the **AS/400 System/38 Migration Aid** and the **OS/400 System/36 Migration Aid**. These tools run on their respective System/3X systems and provide the programmer with a way to analyze data, libraries, files, and programs that are to be migrated to AS/400. Chapter 7 discusses migration from System/3X to AS/400 in more detail.

# 6

# Application Systems Communications

As/400's standard functions plus the many communications options and supporting software provide users with flexibility when configuring AS/400 for various communications environments. This flexibility, however, can also cause confusion when trying to determine which options and programs are needed for a particular environment. This chapter will help guide you through the jungle of business communications available through Application Systems.

Chapter 2 looked at some communications hardware for Application Systems and Chapter 5 looked at communications software support in OS/400. In this chapter, we examine some of the most popular communications environments and provide example configurations for each.

## COMPUTER COMMUNICATIONS IN THE OFFICE—AN INTRODUCTION

Just as a woodworker cherishes a solid block of mahogany, businesspeople cherish accurate, timely, and manageable information. If one activity is most crucial to a business of any size, it is the act of communicating this information to the proper decision maker. Based on the information available to the decision maker, important choices are made that can have far-reaching effects on the success of the business. Improve communications in a business and you are likely to improve productivity and profitability. Ironically, as a business grows, it becomes more important and more difficult to maintain efficient, accurate communications—the very thing that facilitated business growth in the first place. Communications difficulties grow geometrically with the size of the business.

Today's businesses are quickly finding that computers are a communications tool unequaled in significance since Bell invented the telephone. Computers are already commonplace in the business environment, and now there is an increasing emphasis on computer communications. This communication can occur between two computers or among a group of computers in a communications network. This allows business information to move at electronic speeds. Further, communication allows users at remote locations access to vital business information on a distant computer.

AS/400 computers represent a powerful communications tool. All provide some standard communications features to facilitate getting computer support through Electronic Customer Support. As was seen in Chapter 2, there is also a full complement of communications options and peripherals, which with the associated software allow AS/400 to participate in many different communications environments.

## WHAT IS SNA?

In earlier times, computers were like islands, each performing very specific tasks independent of any other computer. As computer systems became more and more popular, they grew in number and also spread over wide geographic distances. Then, almost as an afterthought, it became desirable to attach remote users to computers as well as to link distant computer systems. This led to specialized communications hardware and programming that limited the flexibility of both the communications configurations and the communications functions available. Businesses were constantly faced with massive programming changes and incompatible hardware elements when trying to grow or adapt to new requirements. For this reason, in 1974 IBM introduced a set of communications conventions called the **Systems Network Architecture (SNA)**. This set of published communications standards provided a direction for the evolution of flexible, cost-effective communications. SNA was a set of standards that IBM committed to support as a strategic direction for future products. It defined communications protocols, hardware specifications, and programming conventions that made for coherent growth of communications facilities. Since 1974, IBM and many other companies have provided computer hardware and programming products that conform to SNA, and SNA is now a widely accepted direction for computer communications in the business environment. Further, SNA itself has been expanded and updated in an evolutionary way to meet the changing and growing needs of business environments. All Application Systems support SNA communications. Since SNA is still IBM's strategic direction for communications, investments in SNA hardware and software will be protected over time.

## ELECTRONIC CUSTOMER SUPPORT COMMUNICATIONS

AS/400 systems (except the 9402 Model F02) come standard with the communications equipment necessary to participate in Electronic Customer Support. This is a link to IBM or other support providers that allows you to obtain answers to technical questions, report problems, receive Program Temporary Fixes (PTFs), and the like. The services provided by Electronic Customer Support are discussed further in Chapter 7. In this chapter, we look at the communications configuration used to participate in Electronic Customer Support. Although you need not be a communications expert to use Electronic Customer Support, understanding the basic communications link available to you will remove the mystery.

Figure 6.1 shows the AS/400 communications link to Electronic Customer Support. Every AS/400 system (except the 9402 Model F02) comes standard with the 232/V.24 adapter used to communicate over a switched telephone line. The 232/V.24 adapter provides the electrical interface and handles the communications protocol used with Electronic Customer Support. A Modem adapts the computer information into electrical signals suitable for telephone line transmission. OS/400 comes standard with the necessary functions to manage the telephone communications link.

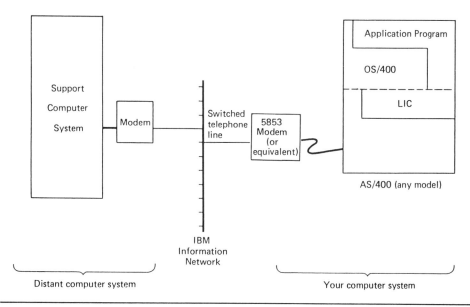

**Figure 6.1.** Communications configuration used for Electronic Customer Support.

When Electronic Customer Support is desired, the user instructs OS/400 to place a toll-free call to the **IBM Information Network**. This is a nationwide communications network that provides many services, including connections to the appropriate Electronic Customer Support computer system. The user is then linked to Electronic Customer Support and can perform the desired tasks.

For simplicity, the rest of the communications configurations provided in this chapter do not show the Electronic Customer Support communications link. The reader should understand that all communications configurations shown are in addition to the Electronic Customer Support link that is provided with most AS/400 systems.

## REMOTE WORKSTATIONS

Often those who need access to Application Systems are not conveniently located at the same location as the computer system. In these cases, Application Systems' communications can be employed to provide access to distant or **remote** users. The way to provide computer access to remote users is to provide them with workstations (terminals and printers) attached to Application Systems over telephone lines. Figure 6.2 shows an example of how remote workstations can be attached to an AS/400 (9404). As with local users, the remote users are provided with workstations including terminals and printers. The remote workstations are attached to the 5494 Remote Workstation Controller. This device helps manage the traffic between the remote workstations and the AS/400. It provides the same services to remote workstations as the Twinaxial Workstation Controller (Chapter 2) provides for locally attached workstations. The telephone line in our example is a **leased line**, meaning that it provides a continuous connection between the remote site and the AS/400. The modems at each end of the telephone line handle the electronic details associated with sending and receiving information over the telephone line. The 7861 Modems were chosen because they allow for communications at up to 19,200 bits/second on leased telephone lines.

Any of the workstations discussed in Chapter 2 can be remotely attached in this fashion. In our example, we have 3486 and 3487 terminals, a PS/2, and 4234 and 4230 printers. Except for the 4230 printer, all these workstations are attached directly to the 5494 Remote Control Unit with twinaxial cable. To illustrate how the printer port provided on the 3487 (and 3486) display can be used, the 4230 printer is cabled directly to the printer port on the 3487 display. With this type of arrangement, the 4230 is still under direct control of the remote AS/400. It is simply another way of cabling the printer, one that may be more convenient, depending on the user's environment. The PS/2 workstation is equipped with the **System 36/38 Workstation Emulation Adapter**. This provides the electrical interface necessary to attach the PS/2 to the twinaxial cable used with Application Systems. AS/400's **PC Support**

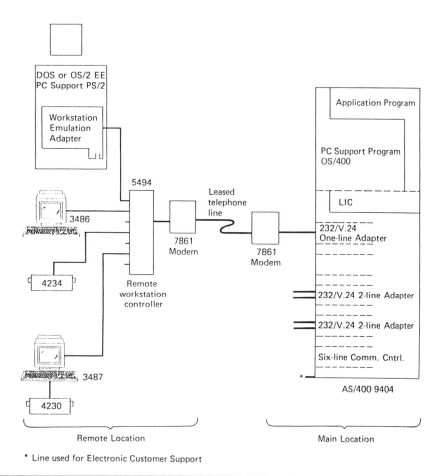

**Figure 6.2.** Remote workstations can be attached to an Application System through Remote Workstation Controllers.

program provides the programming for both the PS/2 (running DOS, Windows, or OS/2) and the AS/400 that allows the PS/2 to act like an Application Systems workstation. (Note that the AS/Entry's version of the PC Support program does not provide the PS/2 with this programming. For this reason, the **Enhanced 5250 Emulation Program** would be necessary for System/36 interaction.) In this configuration, the PS/2 has access to the information, disk storage, printers, and so on, of the AS/400 (i.e., the AS/400 is a server for the PS/2 client). Alternately, specially written application programs residing on the PS/2 and AS/400 can directly interact (cooperative processing), allowing for a highly flexible computing environment. Client/server computing and cooperative processing were introduced in Chapter 5.

On the AS/400 side, OS/400 provides the necessary communications functions to support the remote workstations as if they were locally attached — that is, the application program need not be specially written to support the remote workstations. In fact, the application program cannot tell the difference between local and remote users. In our example, we have provided five separate communications lines that can be used to attach remote workstations from five different locations. Larger AS/400 systems can support up to 64 lines. This allows a single AS/400 to serve the needs of users at many different remote locations.

We achieved the first line by installing a 232/V.24 Adapter, which is supported by the Multi-Function I/O Processor provided as standard with all AS/400 systems (except the 9402 Model F02). The remaining four lines were provided by installing a Six-Line Communications Controller and 2 EIA-232/V.24 Two-Line Adapters.

## DISTRIBUTED COMPUTER COMMUNICATIONS

In some cases, the computing needs of a business can be met with a single computer system. This is particularly true for smaller businesses or businesses in which most computer needs are at a single location. In many cases, however, the needs of a business may be best satisfied by using multiple computer systems. Instead of providing remote users with remote workstations, as discussed in the previous section, you may provide remote users with their own small computer system. For example, a retail chain may want a computer system at each retail location as well as a computer system at headquarters (Figure 6.3). As shown, all computer systems are joined through a communications network that allows them to easily move information (for example, daily cash register receipts) from place to place as necessary. This is called a **distributed computer network**.

When you place or **distribute** the computer systems at the site (where they are needed), several nice things happen. First, since all users are locally attached to their respective computer system, they often enjoy improved system performance (reduced response time) as compared with remotely attached workstations that are slowed down by communications line limitations. Further, the distributed computer system can consolidate communications. This is particularly true at larger remote locations, which may need a large number of communications lines to support all the remote workstations. With a distributed computing approach, remote users would be locally attached to their distributed system, which could then communicate summary information to other computers through a single communications line. In some cases, it may be an advantage to provide the remote location with some control over the distributed system. They may have unique requirements that can be met by an available prewritten application program. They could then acquire the program and get the support of the software firm in meeting their unique needs, all without

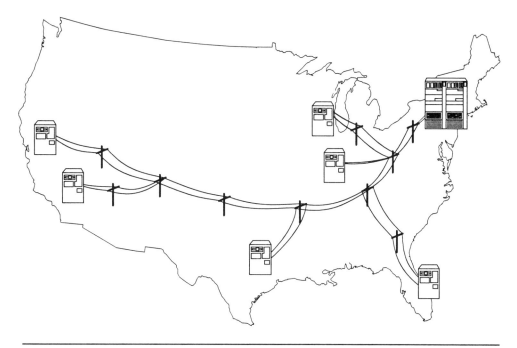

**Figure 6.3.** Example of a distributed network for a retail chain headquartered in New York City.

becoming computer experts or blindly relying on the headquarters computer staff. This makes the remote location more productive while reducing the workload at headquarters.

The disadvantage is that a large distributed computer network is often more difficult to manage than a single computer system. However, since Application Systems were designed for a distributed environment, there are system management and network management tools that ease this task. As discussed in Chapter 5, OS/400, IBM OMEGAMON/400, and SAA SystemView System Manager/400 provide some of these tools. When a distributed network is to be managed by a System/370 or System/390 computer system, IBM's NetView products provide some other useful functions. Now let us look at some example communications environments in which Application Systems participate in a distributed computing environment.

## AS/400 Distributed Network

Multiple AS/400 systems can be attached together through communications lines to create a distributed computer network. An example distributed network of this type might consist of five small AS/400s (e.g., 9404 F10s), each distributed to a remote

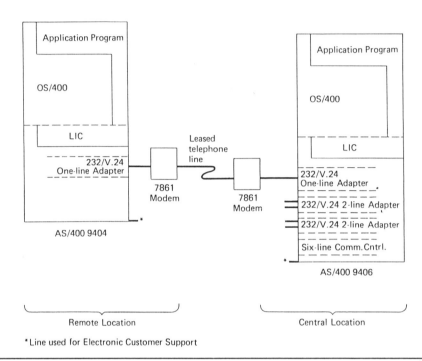

**Figure 6.4.** Configuration used for attaching distant AS/400 systems together.

location, and a larger AS/400 (e.g., a 9406 F90) at the business's headquarters. Figure 6.4 is an example of AS/400 hardware and software configurations for one of the remote locations and the headquarters location. The remote location configuration (9404 F10) would be duplicated for every remote location. Further, the AS/400 at each end would be equipped with the appropriate local workstations to support the users at the respective locations. These are not shown to prevent confusion with options needed to support the communications link.

The 9404 used at the remote location is equipped with an EIA 232/V.24 One-Line Adapter that provides one communications line (in addition to the standard communications line used for Electronic Customer Support). This adapter is supported by the multi-function I/O processor provided as standard equipment with all 9404 systems. Since the remote AS/400 system need communicate only with the central AS/400 system, this is the only adapter needed. The 7861 Modem allows for communications at 19,200 bits/second over leased telephone lines. OS/400 has the communications functions necessary to manage the communications link.

At the central location, the larger AS/400 is in constant communication with all remote locations. It collects the summary information needed by headquarters to consolidate all remote location activity. In our example, one communications line is used for each remote location. This means the central AS/400 must have at least five communications lines (in addition to that used for Electronic Customer Support). To meet this need, an EIA 232/V.24 One-Line Adapter is first added. This adapter works with the multi-function I/O processor provided as standard with all AS/400 systems. Next, a Six-Line Communications Controller and two associated EIA 232/V.24 Two-Line Adapters are added. Thus, the AS/400 system now has five communications lines (in addition to the one used for Electronic Customer Support). One 7861 Modem is required at the central site for each communications line, making a total of five (one is shown).

With our example communications configuration and appropriate application programs, there are several different ways in which the distributed AS/400 systems can work together. In the simplest form, the distributed computing environment could use OS/400's **Distributed Data Management (DDM)** support, which allows a user of a remote AS/400 to query a database on the central AS/400 or any other AS/400 in the network. The user need not even know that the database needed is located on another computer system. The DDM function of OS/400 will automatically locate, retrieve, and present the information to the user, reducing the complexity of the system from the user's viewpoint. Alternately, a user of one system may actually want to sign on and directly interact with one of the other systems in the network. Another OS/400 function, called **Display Station Passthru (DSPT)**, supports this type of interaction by allowing a user to sign on and interact with any other AS/400 in the distributed network as if the user were directly attached to that system.

More sophisticated cooperative processing between the central and remote AS/400 systems is also possible and becoming more prevalent. OS/400 functions such as Advanced Program-to-Program Communications (APPC) and Advanced Peer-to-Peer Networking (APPN), along with OS/400 extensions such as PC Support and SAA Structured Query Language/400, let programmers write application programs that can efficiently delegate processing tasks and share information among the various AS/400 systems in a network. APPC is a communications convention that allows a program on one AS/400 system to initiate actions on a remote computer system (e.g., start a program or perform a database query) without any assistance from the user.

APPN is a networking scheme that manages the logistics necessary for one AS/400 in the network to know details (location, communications links, available application programs and data, etc.) about all of the other AS/400 systems in that network. APPN also dynamically selects the most appropriate communications link (if more than one is available) based on things like cost, line speed, and security level. IBM's Systems Network Architecture (SNA) has adopted APPN as a strategic networking scheme, making it important in other environments (i.e., PS/2 and S/390 communications networks). Since OS/400 supports the SNA, documents can be freely exchanged between nodes using SNA's Distribution Services (SNADS) conventions. This provides a coherent electronic mail environment in which users need not concern themselves about who is where in the network. Further, any AS/400 file can be sent from any node to any other node on the network. This can be useful for distributing program or data updates from a single point in the network. Further discussion of these OS/400 communications functions can be found in Chapter 5.

Often, the central location provides technical support to all remote locations. This support includes troubleshooting network communications problems and distributing new software and software updates. Through the Electronic Customer Support, the central site can also provide its own technical question/answer database. This database can contain any type of company-related information from operating procedures to technical information about a custom application program. Thus, any user anywhere in the distributed network can look up questions and the corresponding answers without playing telephone tag or waiting for the headquarters staff to respond. If a question is not covered in the database, it can be submitted to the headquarters staff. Once the staff responds with an answer, it is added to the database so that it is available the next time that question is asked. As covered in Chapter 5, SAA SystemView System Manager/400 provides functions that allow the central support site to manage changes to the AS/400 systems in the network and the problems that are reported.

## AS/400 and System/390 Distributed Network

In some cases, it is desirable to distribute Application Systems while having a System/390 (or a System/370) computer system at the central or headquarters location. The larger System/390 computers can provide much more computational resource than even the largest AS/400 system in the areas of performance, capacity, peripherals, and the like. The central location may need the kind of muscle provided by a System/390 computer. In other cases, the central location may already have a System/390 computer system and wish to distribute a mid-size computer system to a remote location or departments within the business to better meet user needs. In any case, AS/400 systems can exist in a distributed computer network consisting of AS/400 systems and System/390 computers. Figure 6.5 shows an example of an AS/400 9406 configuration that can be used to communicate with a System/390 computer. Since the 9406 comes standard with an extra 232/V.24 communications line, no options are needed inside the AS/400 system. The 7861 Modem can allow the computers to communicate at 19,200 bits/second over leased telephone lines.

OS/400 on the AS/400 side is designed to work closely with the System/390's operating systems and the NetView network management program at the central site. Together, these programs provide network management support for the Distributed

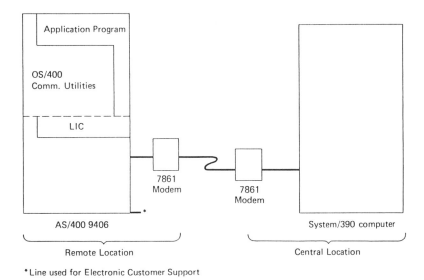

**Figure 6.5.** Example of a communications configuration used to attach an AS/400 to an S/390 computer.

Host Command Facility and the Link Problem Determination Aid, which lets the System/390 operator remotely troubleshoot network problems. If a System/390 user is responsible for supporting the network, it is possible to use the System/390 network management tools discussed in Chapter 5 — such as alert messages that notify the network manager of hardware problems and the Distributed Host Command Facility, which allows the network manager's S/390 workstation to act like an AS/400 workstation for troubleshooting purposes. By adding an AS/400 system at the central site, SAA SystemView System Manager/400 could also be used to help track changes and problems in remote AS/400 systems.

Conversely, the AS/400 users can sign on and directly interact with the System/390 from their AS/400 workstation (5250-type workstation) as if they were using a System/390 workstation (i.e., a 3270-type workstation). Thus, the users of either system have access to any system in the network if the system's security allows it. This is made possible by OS/400's **3270 Device Emulation** support. This allows an AS/400 workstation to emulate or "act like" a 3270 workstation. The AS/400 Communications Utilities discussed in Chapter 5 allow an AS/400 user to transfer files with and submit batch jobs to the System/390 through its **Remote Job Entry Facility (RJE)**. This also allows AS/400 Office users to exchange electronic mail with System/390's Office Vision users. The System/390 also supports the SNADS, DDM, and APPC protocols just discussed providing electronic mail, distributed database interaction, and direct program-to-program interaction.

These communication functions, along with others discussed in Chapter 5, allow AS/400s and System/390s to cooperate in a distributed computer network. The Systems Application Architecture provides a framework with which application programs developed on either system (say, the System/390) can be migrated to the other (the AS/400). Our example shows only one simple method of attaching an AS/400 to a System/390 computer. With the Systems Network Architecture (SNA) support of OS/400, the proliferation of high-speed digital networks, and the adoption of Advanced Peer-to-Peer Networking by SNA, many other alternatives for S/390–AS/400 distributed network communications are possible.

## AS/400 AND LOCAL AREA NETWORKS

We have just seen how a group of computers can communicate with one another over great distances. In some business environments, however, there is a need to provide communications links among multiple computer systems, all of which are located at the same place. For example, just as we provided remote locations with a distributed computer system in the last section, it may be desirable to provide a department or functional area of a business with its own **departmental computer system**. This provides workers in that functional area with more control and flexibility to apply the computer system in a way that best meets their needs. Since the departmental system represents additional computing power, it can help reduce the workload on the central computer system while also providing the local department with reduced response times. A business may also have a local collection of computer systems from several different manufacturers that need to communicate with one another.

In any case, **Local Area Networks (LANs)** provide one way for a local group of computers (such as those located in the same building or on the same campus) to communicate very efficiently. Because of distance limitations and legal right-of-way issues, however, this communications link cannot by itself be used between distant computers (e.g., computers across town from each other) — all participating computers must be in the same location. While distant LANs can be linked together with more traditional communications lines, the computer systems on any one LAN must be in the same building or on the same campus. This distance limitation is the price you pay for getting the high speeds associated with LANs.

### AS/400 and the Token-Ring Network

The **Token-Ring Network** is an IBM-developed LAN able to move information at speeds from 4 to 16 Mb/second. Figure 6.6 shows the basic architecture of the

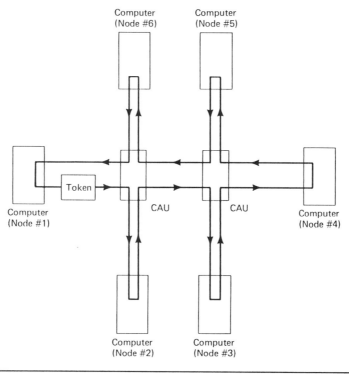

**Figure 6.6.** The basic structure of a Token-Ring Network.

Token-Ring Network. Each computer that participates in the network is called a network **node** and can share information, programs, and computer equipment with other nodes in the network. The nodes of the network are arranged in a "ring" pattern, thus giving the network its name. The twisted pair (two-wire) cable used in the network is connected to the computer's Token-Ring Adapter at one end and to the **8230 Controller Access Unit (CAU)** at the other. The CAU is the device, typically located in a wiring closet, that actually makes the electrical connections between the cables to each node in the network. One CAU supports the attachment of up to eighty nodes. A modular jack is used to attach each network node to the CAU, which lets nodes be quickly added to or removed from the network. The CAU can automatically bypass any powered-off or failing nodes by detecting their inactivity. Multiple CAUs can be cabled together using the same twisted pair cable to allow more nodes in the network. With the proper cable components, a single Token-Ring Network can contain up to 260 nodes over several kilometers. Multiple Token-Ring Networks can be linked together by a bridge, allowing still more network nodes to communicate with one another. Information is transferred over the network at either

4 or 16 Mb/ second (depending on which version of the network is installed) using the "Token Passing" communications protocol. This protocol, as discussed in Chapter 2, sends messages around the ring from node to node in a circular fashion.

With this understanding of the Token-Ring Network, we now examine three example Token-Ring Networks. It should be understood that variations and combinations of the following examples are also possible, allowing flexibility in meeting specific needs.

### Token-Ring: AS/400 and PS/2s

Figure 6.7 shows a small Token-Ring Network consisting of several PS/2s (the clients) and an AS/400 (the server). The AS/400 is also in communication with a remote site that is not part of the local area network.

First, let us focus on the Token-Ring Network. In this example, the AS/400 acts as a server to the PS/2s in the network. You may recall from Chapter 5 that a server is a network node that provides some resource to the other network nodes. The AS/400, through the AS/400 PC Support program, provides disk storage (thus the AS/400 is a **file server**) and printers (thus the AS/400 is a **print server**) for use by the other network nodes. PC Support also provides the necessary programming to allow a PS/2 to act like or **emulate** an AS/400 workstation. Anything you can do from a standard AS/400 terminal, you can do from any of the PS/2s in the network (and more, as we will see).

AS/400 fixed disk space is made available to the other nodes through the **shared folder** function of AS/400 PC Support. Just as a folder in a filing cabinet is used to store related information, a fixed disk "folder" is a designated area on the AS/400 fixed disk that can store related computer information. A folder can hold information and programs directly usable by a PS/2 in the network or it can contain documents understandable by both the AS/400 and the PS/2s. A shared folder is an AS/400 disk storage area that can be simultaneously accessed by any authorized network node. This is desirable because different computer users in an office often need access to the same information for different reasons. Although all users have access to the information they need, the shared folder concept simplifies systems management and data backup, and improves security by providing one centralized source for the information.

Through PC Support, the AS/400 printers can also be shared among any authorized users in the network. This capability is called **virtual printers**. With this feature of PC Support, a PS/2 can be set up to automatically redirect all of its printer output to a printer attached to the AS/400. Thus a PS/2 user on the network can use any high-speed, high-quality printer(s) attached to the AS/400 system. The AS/400 will receive and hold the print output in a temporary holding area in disk storage called the **print queue**. This frees the PS/2 user to go on to the next task rather than

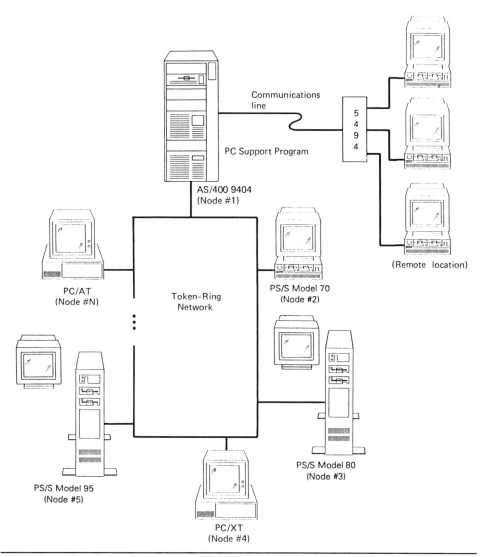

**Figure 6.7.** Token-Ring Network consisting of an AS/400 server and multiple PS/2s.

waiting for the printer to finish. When the printer becomes available, the information stored in the print queue will automatically be printed.

Another capability of AS/400 PC Support is to allow the PS/2s in the network to freely transfer information in and out of AS/400 databases. Unlike the shared folder used to exchange AS/400-type documents, this transfer facility allows a PS/2 user to extract information directly from AS/400 databases using record selection criteria, sorting options, and other database-related functions. With this capability, the PS/2 user can manually request specific information from the AS/400, work with it using PS/2 application programs (e.g., a spreadsheet program), and then send it back to the AS/400 if desired. The PC Support program handles the detailed interaction between the PS/2 and the AS/400, including the translation between AS/400's information format (EBCDIC) and PS/2's information format (ASCII). PC Support also provides the necessary application programming interfaces (APIs) to allow a programmer to write application programs that directly query AS/400 databases and then process the information on the PS/2 as necessary. Since the application program gets the needed AS/400 data automatically, the user need not know where the information is located. In these environments, the AS/400 is acting as a **data server** in the network.

As we saw in Chapter 5, PC support can also be used to implement a cooperative processing environment in which the functions necessary to perform the needed tasks are divided as appropriate between application programs on the AS/400 and application programs running on the PS/2s.

Other functions in PC Support include the ability to send simple text messages between network nodes and provide an Organizer–user interface. PC Support's **Organizer** is a menu structure that allows the PS/2 user to initiate all programs and functions through a coherent user interface. The user need not be concerned with which system (AS/400 or PS/2) is actually running the program; the programs and information needed are accessed simply by selecting menu items.

In our example, the AS/400 is attached to PS/2s at a remote site through a communications line separate from the Token-Ring Network. This is to illustrate that AS/400 PC Support is designed to provide the same functions to any PS/2 regardless of the type of communications link. The PS/2s at the remote site can do everything that the local PS/2s on the Token-Ring Network can. In effect, the remote PS/2s attached via a communications line are part of the same network as the local PS/2s on the Token-Ring.

What about using PS/2s as Token-Ring Network servers rather than AS/400? Many of the functions previously described can also be done by using a properly equipped PS/2 as a server rather than an AS/400. A PS/2 as a server allows you to share disk storage and printers and send messages in much the same way as previously discussed. In fact, a PS/2 server often provides better performance if all you need is to share fixed disk space with other network nodes. This is because of the more complex programs (longer code paths) used in AS/400 systems and ever-increasing PS/2 disk storage speeds. Also, PS/2s are less expensive than AS/400 systems.

On the other hand, an AS/400 server can provide things that a PS/2 server cannot. First, AS/400 can run the more advanced business applications used by System/3X and those specially written for AS/400. Programs written for the AS/400 can utilize the built-in database, single-level storage, object level security, and all the other inherent characteristics of the AS/400 discussed in this book. So some of the considerations in selecting a server include whether or not you want to use the additional capabilities, storage capacities, peripherals, and application programs offered by AS/400. A PS/2 server cannot offer those. Also, because AS/400 PC Support also provides remote PS/2s with the same capabilities as those on the Token-Ring Network, long-distance communication requirements are met in a consistent fashion with an AS/400 server. Choose the server based on your needs as identified today and those projected for the future.

## Token-Ring: AS/400 and AS/400

In some environments, multiple AS/400 systems may be located close enough together to allow them to communicate using the Token-Ring Network. This may be the case in a distributed computing environment in which each of several departments in a single building has its own AS/400 system. When communication distances make it possible, the Token-Ring Network is the preferred method of attaching AS/400s together because of the high speed (up to 16 Mb/second) with which information is transferred. Figure 6.8 shows a Token-Ring Network consisting of three AS/400 systems. Each AS/400 system is in a different department within the same building, and each has its own terminals and printers attached via twinaxial cable. The three AS/400 systems are then attached via the twisted pair cable used in the Token-Ring Network.

Communications functions of OS/400 (discussed in Chapter 5) are supported over Token-Ring Network connections. This means that systems attached in this manner can cooperate in much the same way as discussed in the section on AS/400 Distributed Network (DSPT, DDM, client/server, etc.). The chief advantage of the Token-Ring Network attachment of multiple AS/400s is the speed at which information can flow between systems.

## Token-Ring: AS/400 and S/390

IBM's larger System/390 computer family members (for example, 9390, 3090) can also participate in a Token-Ring Network. This may be desirable if the main computer system is an S/390 and the business wishes to distribute computing power to other departments through AS/400 systems. The AS/400 cannot match the computing power of the larger System/390 computer systems, making them more desirable for more computer-intensive environments. The AS/400, however, is designed to be located in an office environment and operated by less experienced personnel. For this reason, the AS/400 may be the desired computer for distributing computing capability to other departments within a business.

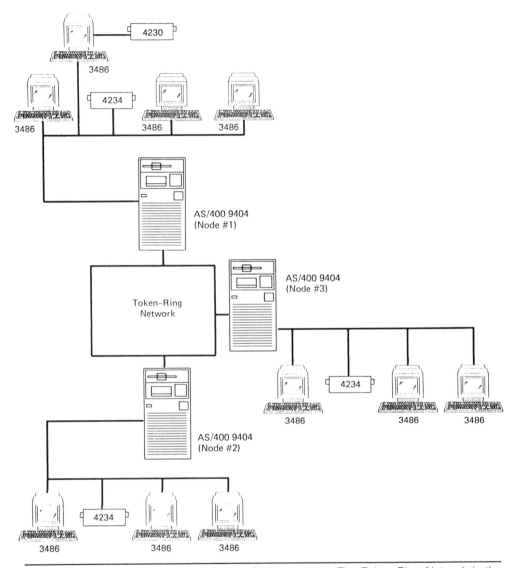

**Figure 6.8.** Token-Ring Network of three AS/400 systems. The Token-Ring Network is the preferred method for attaching local AS/400 systems together.

In Figure 6.9, we have added two PS/2s and a System/390 computer to the Token-Ring Network discussed earlier. The first thing to understand about this configuration is that the PS/2s can do everything described in the earlier section, "Token-Ring: AS/400 and PS/2s." Similarly, direct AS/400 users can do the things described in the previous section, "Token-Ring: AS/400 and AS/400." The new

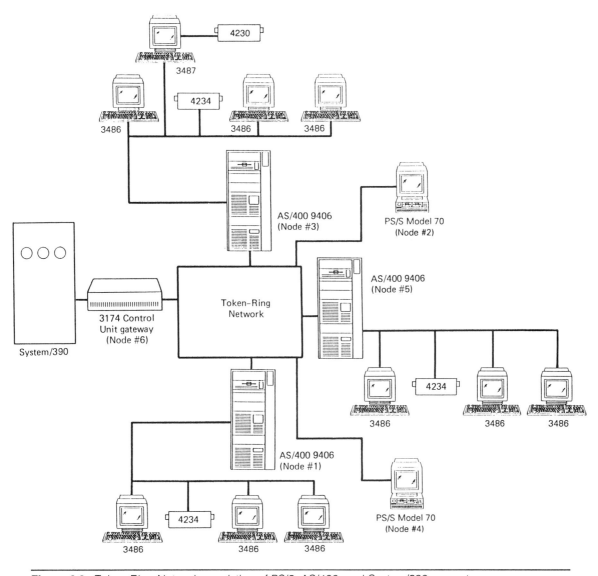

**Figure 6.9.** Token-Ring Network consisting of PS/2, AS/400, and System/390 computers.

news is that the other network nodes can now interact with the System/390 computer as well.

Communications functions of OS/400 (discussed in Chapter 5) are supported over the Token-Ring Network. Again, the chief advantage of the Token-Ring Network is its information transfer speed.

With the proper System/390 and PS/2 programming, the PS/2s can use S/390 printers and fixed disk space. With the **APPC/PC** program for the PS/2s, properly written PS/2 application programs can interact directly with S/390 and AS/400 programs as well. With the continued growth of SNA and SAA, Token-Ring Network communications between various computer systems will become more commonplace and powerful over time.

### An AS/400 Configuration for Token-Ring Networks

Now that you understand why an AS/400 might be attached to a Token-Ring Network, let us see what it takes. Figure 6.10 shows an example of an AS/400 configuration that can participate in a Token-Ring Network. The AS/400 is equipped with the 16/4 Mbps Token-Ring Adapter, which performs the detailed electrical communications tasks necessary to send information to other nodes in the network.

OS/400 provides the basic communications support necessary for communications over the Token-Ring Network. If PS/2s and PCs are part of the network, the AS/400 PC Support program was included to allow the AS/400 to act as a server and otherwise interact with the PS/2s. If S/390 computers are in the Token-Ring Network, the AS/400 Communications Utilities discussed in Chapter 5 provide improved electronic mail and information transfer between AS/400 and System/390.

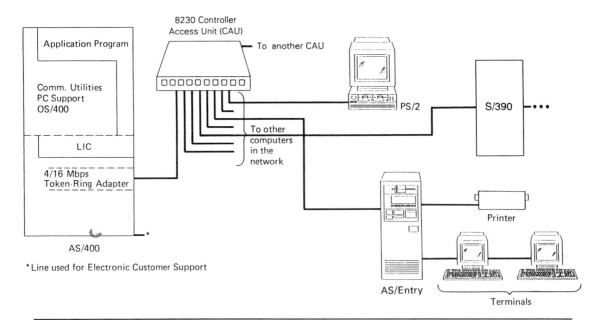

**Figure 6.10.** Example of an AS/400 configuration used to participate in a Token-Ring Network.

## AS/400 and the Ethernet LAN

**Ethernet** is a type of local area network in widespread use today. The Ethernet LAN is widely supported by many different computer manufacturers, which is why it is commonly found in "open systems" environments where many different types and brands of computers communicate with one another.

Figure 6.11 shows the basic architecture of an Ethernet LAN. Each computer is attached as a tap-off of a common cable or information **bus**. For this reason, Ethernet is called a **bus-wired** network. Information is transferred over the Ethernet network at a rate of 10 million bits/second (10 Mbps).

An Ethernet LAN is basically a party line on which all nodes can transmit messages for all nodes to hear. Every node has equal access to the cable and can send a message at any time without warning. When one node transmits a message, it is received by all nodes. Each node then examines the address contained in the message to see if the message is intended for that node. If not, the message is discarded.

To ensure that information is sent around the Ethernet network in an orderly and reliable way, there is a protocol that each node follows when transmitting messages. This protocol is called *Carrier Sense Multiple Access/Collision Detect* (CSMA/CD). Its name is a mouthful, but really it's a quite simple protocol. In fact, we follow this protocol in our everyday telephone conversations. Here, too, only one person can speak at a time or neither is clearly understood. One party waits for the other to finish before beginning to speak. Thus the phone line only carries one party's voice at a time and the message is clear. This is the "CSMA" part of CSMA/CD. The "CD" part of the protocol handles the times when two nodes start

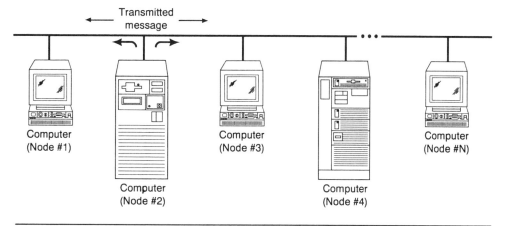

**Figure 6.11.** The basic structure of an Ethernet local area network.

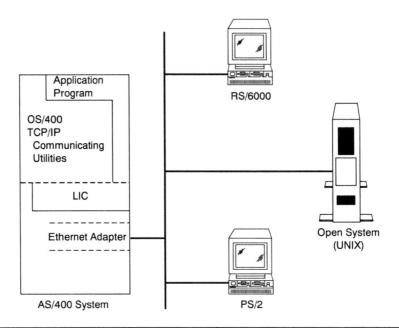

**Figure 6.12.** Example of an AS/400 configuration suitable for an Ethernet local area network.

transmissions simultaneously. To understand this part of the protocol, think of what you do during a telephone conversation when you begin talking at the same time as the other party. Typically, you both stop talking and begin again a second or two later, hoping that this time one of you begins sooner than the other. This is exactly analogous to the situation with CSMA/CD. If two (or more) nodes begin transmitting a message at the same time, the messages "collide" on the network. The nodes monitor for such a collision, and when one is detected, all nodes stop transmitting and begin again after a pause of random length. Usually, one node will begin its retransmission before the other, thus gaining control of the network.

Figure 6.12 shows an example of a small Ethernet LAN consisting of different computer systems including one AS/400, one IBM RISC System/6000 computer, one PS/2 (Personal System/2), and a Unix based computer—which could be any brand as long as TCP/IP communications are supported over the Ethernet LAN. The Ethernet LAN Adapter allows the AS/400 to physically connect to the Ethernet cable. The TCP/IP Communications Utilities provide the support for the TCP/IP protocol commonly used over Ethernet Networks.

# 7

# Application Systems and Your Business

An important first step in bringing Advanced Business Systems, or any, computers into your business environment is planning. Largely depending on how well you plan, introducing new computer resource(s) can be like pouring either water or gasoline on a fire. Many readers will already have a significant number of computers in their business and will add Application Systems to their computer arsenal, whereas others will be bringing Application Systems in as their first business computer. In either case, the information in this chapter should help you understand how to introduce Advanced Business Systems computers into your particular environment. The chapter starts by discussing what you should consider when looking at Application Systems versus PS/2s versus Local Area Networks. Then it covers software selection. followed by some specific Application Systems hardware configurations appropriate for small, medium, and large businesses. In addition, the following topics will be discussed:

- Business decisions
- Implementation management
- Physical planning
- Training
- Ergonomics
- Security
- Technical support
- Service
- Migrating from System/3X to AS/400 systems

This chapter is not a complete guide to introducing Advanced Business Systems into any business, but it does provide a starting point for developing your plan and discussing some important issues.

## WHAT ARE MY BUSINESS COMPUTING NEEDS?

Many businesses today use some type of computer system(s) to help run their business. These businesses must constantly evaluate whether their current system is good enough. Those businesses still using manual methods must determine whether automating their business might help. This book certainly cannot answer the question for you, but it can provide a starting point. Whether your business has millions of dollars worth of computer systems or none at all, the way to begin answering these questions is to forget about computer hardware and software and look very closely at your business. Too often, businesses buy computer systems and then look for problems to solve. A properly managed computer project should start by careful consideration of the collective business needs of all functional areas within the business. Independently attacking specific business problems can often result in a "dead-end" computer solution that provides no coherent growth strategy for the future. From the very start, key people from all business areas should be collected into a project team. Since all business areas will be involved, the top management of the business must consistently demonstrate a commitment to the project. Without top management involvement, disagreements among the peer business areas are slow to be resolved and the sense of priority is diminished. Lack of consistent top management commitment at either the investigation or implementation phases of a computer project is a common cause of unsuccessful projects, which can be quite expensive.

The project team should start by reviewing the overall goals of the business (or segment of a larger business) over the next few years. In some cases, these goals will be well known, but in others a great deal of soul-searching will be necessary. These goals should be as specific as possible and should include any business strategies in place to achieve these goals.

After the business goals are clearly defined, the project team should look closely at the current day-to-day operations of the business as it is and document the movement of information through the entire organization. Only after the information flow is understood can the team candidly discuss what is good and what is bad about the current way of doing business. Work to identify the sources of problems rather than focusing on symptoms. Understand the interaction between the various areas of the business. Consider the flow of information from one group to another as you trace the business cycle. Chances are, not every problem that you will uncover can be solved through a computer. For example, a computerized inventory tracking system will not solve inventory problems if just anyone can casually walk into the inventory storeroom and walk out with what he or she needs with no controls. Computers are only a tool for effectively managing a business. They will not manage your business for you.

Only after you have examined your current operation with a critical eye can you begin to see if a computer solution makes sense for your business. In the case of small businesses, this type of analysis can be done in a matter of weeks or even days. With larger businesses, it can span months or even years and is typically done on an ongoing basis. Some businesses choose to do the analysis on their own. If you want assistance with solving business problems with computers, there are plenty of places to turn, including consultants and computer manufacturers.

## WHEN SHOULD I CONSIDER APPLICATION SYSTEMS?

When looking for ways to meet business computing needs, there is a seemingly endless series of questions. Before we get into how to select an Advanced Business Systems to meet your needs, let us pause and glance at some other alternatives.

## What about Personal System/2?

Although this book is about IBM's mid-size computer systems, to make good buying decisions it is important to understand how these differ from IBM's Personal Systems/2 (PS/2) family. The first difference between Application Systems and PS/2 computers is that PS/2s were primarily designed to be used by one person at a time (single-user) and Application Systems were designed to be simultaneously shared by many users (multi-user). Although there are some environments in which PS/2s can be used as small multi-user computers, their hardware and software architectures are primarily geared for single-user computing. Because Application Systems are multi-user computers, multiple PS/2 systems must be purchased to serve an equivalent number of users. Further, since all users of an Application Systems share a single computer, they can share equipment (printers) and information (inventory data). To obtain this sharing of equipment and information, the multiple PS/2s must be networked together through a Local Area Network (LAN). With the LAN, PS/2s can also freely share equipment and information as long as the PS/2 programs were written for the LAN environment. So which is best? The PS/2 LAN versus multi-user system debate still rages, and it is clear both approaches have merit. Here are some things to consider to help make the decision. Multi-user systems are more mature than LANs simply by virtue of having been around longer. Since PS/2s were originally used as independent computers, many of the application programs for PS/2s do not support LAN environments. Application programs for Application Systems are typically more comprehensive and support the multi-user environment. This means that there are more tried-and-true business applications for Application Systems than for PS/2 LANs. Further, multi-user systems were designed to be just that, whereas PS/2 LANs were more of an afterthought. This often means that a fair amount of technical skill is required to support a PS/2 LAN. Things like the number of workstations, technical support level, and systems management activity determine which approach yields the lowest cost. Do not forget to consider the PS/2 LAN with Application Systems as the server as discussed in the Chapter 6 section, "Token-Ring: AS/400 and PS/2s." Many times, this can provide the best of both worlds. Finally, the most important thing to consider is the application program(s) under consideration for each approach, since PS/2s and Application Systems are not software-compatible, and application programs written for one will not run on the other. The approach with the best-fitting application program will normally provide the best results.

## What about RISC System/6000 Computers?

The RISC System/6000 family of computers is IBM's entry into the "open systems" area where international standards take precedence over the proprietary innovations of individual companies. RISC System/6000 computers have a split personality in that they can be used as high-function workstations for a single user or as general-purpose multi-user computer systems in typical business environments. Since the AS/400 has no capability to be used as a high-function workstation for things like computer aided design and technical publishing, the RISC System/6000 family is clearly the pick for those applications.

In the general-purpose multi-user computer system arena, however, there is certainly room for confusion when deciding between the RISC System/6000 and the AS/400 families of computers. To resolve this confusion, let's look at some of the design points of each family. The AS/400 system's architecture includes a built-in relational database. In other words, the AS/400 hardware and operating system have been designed specifically to provide the database function commonly needed in business environments. Most other computer systems (including the RISC System/6000) require separately purchased database programs that sit on top of the operating system to provide users with a relational database. Since the AS/400 system's database is implemented in the hardware and operating system, the performance and elegance of the database implementation is improved. Further, the programmer productivity afforded by the built-in AS/400 database makes it a good system for those writing and maintaining their own business application programs.

Finally, AS/400 systems are leading the way in the implementation of IBM's Systems Application Architecture. All things being equal, if you need to coexist with a network of other IBM systems following SAA, an AS/400 may be indicated. It should be noted, however, that AS/400 computers can also participate in the non-SAA "open systems" environments (the primary target of RISC System/6000 systems) through OS/400's support of the OSI and TCP/IP communications protocol.

While the RISC System/6000 has no built-in database, there are relational database programs available that add this capability to the system. While this added database will add an additional workload on the RISC System/6000, this is only problematic if not considered for when selecting which RISC System/6000 model is needed. For those migrating programs and data from a UNIX multi-user computer system, the migration to an RISC System/6000 will be much more natural than migrating to an AS/400. For those migrating programs and data from System/36 or System/38 computers, the migration to the AS/400 will be much more natural than migrating to a RISC System/6000. If you have a need to coexist with computer systems of many different brands, the "open systems" foundation on which the RISC System/6000 is built will be a plus.

## What about System/390 Computers?

The IBM System/390 (and System/370) computer family is also widely used to fill business needs. Like Application Systems, System/390 computers are multi-user computer systems that allow many users to share the system. There are System/390 computers that offer the same level of computing power as that provided by all but the smallest Application Systems. There are also System/390 computers that provide computational power well beyond even the largest Application Systems. Although System/390 and Application Systems can share information, one cannot run application programs written for the other. So what should you consider when choosing between System/390 computers and Application Systems? Again, the system that can run the application program that best fits your needs has a strong advantage when it comes to making a selection. There are more prewritten business applications for Application Systems than for System/390 computers. In the event you intend to write your own custom application programs from scratch, the programmer productivity features of Application Systems are a strong point. However, it may be that your business has already developed the System/390 application programs you would like to use, in which case the System/390 is desirable. Another reason to select a System/390 approach may be that you need more computing power than is available in the Application Systems family. This may often be the case in a highly technical environment, in which the System/390 architecture is a better fit than that of the Application Systems. One final and important consideration is that System/390 computer operators (not necessarily users) require more data processing experience than is needed by the operator of Application Systems (see Chapter 3).

## CHOOSING THE SOFTWARE

Application Systems computers become a useful business tool only when they are executing the appropriate software. Although there are many ways of generating a strategy for introducing computers, considering software needs before selecting detailed hardware configurations usually makes sense. The hardware requirements, such as memory size and disk storage space, will, in part, be based on the needs of the software selected.

The application programs you select must perform the tasks needed by your end users both today and in the foreseeable future. Chapter 4 has already discussed some application programs commonly used with Application Systems. Selecting the basic type of application program is often fairly simple; for example, an accounting department needs an accounting application program and a secretary needs a word-processing application program. What is more difficult is identifying the specific application program that best fits your particular needs. Is a custom application program preferred or will a prewritten application program be acceptable? If a prewritten application program is desired, exactly which one is the best for your needs? If a custom application program is desired, who should write it and what should it include? The answers to these questions depend largely on the specifics of a given business environment and thus are beyond the scope of this book. However, a few basics remain the same whether you are selecting a program for a multinational corporation or one for a corner fish market. First, you must precisely understand the task(s) you are trying to put on a computer before pursuing any application program alternatives. A thorough knowledge of the task(s) helps you to identify specific requirements your application program must meet. After a detailed understanding of the task(s) is obtained, a search can begin through the many prewritten or off-the-shelf application programs. If you can find an appropriate prewritten application program that fits your needs, you can avoid the expense, delay, and ongoing effort associated with custom software development and maintenance. Good prewritten application programs can be quite flexible. However, since everyone typically has slightly different needs and methods even within a given business function, you can bet that any prewritten application will have some features you do not need and will not have other features you will wish it did. Do not forget to consider the more specialized type of prewritten application program—vertical market applications. Vertical market application programs address a highly specific segment of users such as lawyers, doctors, distributors, and manufacturers.

There are many sources of information about the many prewritten application programs on the market. Of course, computer companies and consultants can help you select particular application programs to fit your needs. There are also many popular computer and trade magazines that periodically conduct extensive reviews of prewritten application programs. These can be excellent and timely sources of information.

For specific or highly specialized needs, prewritten application programs may not be adequate. In this case, custom-developed software may be desirable. Although the development and maintenance of custom software is a long-term commitment that is typically expensive, it may be less costly in the long run to pay for the development of custom software than to settle for a prewritten application program that does not do the job. If you do select the custom software route, an important step is to select the proper developer. Businesses that have their own programming staff can do their own custom program development. If you do not have your own programmers, it will be necessary to seek outside help—that is, an outside software developer. In either case, it is the developer who will have the largest effect on the ultimate success or failure of the custom development activity. The developer's job is not an easy one. In addition to programming expertise, the developer must become an expert in all aspects of your business, must be a good communicator to understand and discuss software requirements, must understand human psychology when defining the user interface for the program, must be a proficient teacher to train the end users on the new program, and, finally, must be dependable and reliable, and therefore available to provide technical support and software maintenance and any needed modifications.

## CHOOSING APPLICATION SYSTEMS HARDWARE

Selecting the proper Application Systems hardware components that will together fit your needs can be confusing. You must select among the Application Systems and their disk configurations, feature cards, peripherals, and so on. Although we cannot possibly cover all needs for all environments in the limited scope of this book, we can examine some business environments—for example, a small business, a medium business, and a large business—and outfit them with the appropriate Application Systems configurations. With the insight provided by outfitting these hypothetical business environments, you will be better prepared to properly select the Application Systems components useful in your environment. Assistance in selecting specific Application Systems configurations is available from IBM or authorized remarketers.

## Small Business Environment—Bob's Gearbox Co.

Our hypothetical small business is a gearbox manufacturer named Bob's Gearbox Co. Bob's has a standard line of gearboxes and also accepts orders for custom gearboxes. It is a private corporation (owned by Bob, of course) and has 32 employees. Bob has been in business five years and has experienced moderate growth. He currently conducts business by noncomputer methods but finds himself needing to streamline his operation as the business grows. Bob is particularly concerned that his profits seem to be shrinking as his sales increase. A study of Bob's business shows that there are two basic causes for this. First, his sales staff often commit to discounted pricing on a gearbox order to capture the business. The trouble is that Bob never really knows what it actually costs him to produce a given gearbox. He uses standard cost estimates to price a customer's order and hopes that the actual cost of building the gearbox is close to this.

The second basic problem uncovered in the study is that Bob's inventory is not well managed. The production department is often hampered by not having the right parts and raw materials in inventory. This often causes slips in the delivery of customer orders that hurt customer satisfaction and fuel heated arguments among the marketing manager, the production manager, and the materials manager. Finger pointing is commonplace. The study also showed that 25 percent of the inventory items in stock are obsolete and will never be used.

In this scenario, it is clear that Bob has outgrown his manual methods of doing business. Bob needs a better way to track the actual costs associated with manufacturing his products. This may uncover the fact that his sales staff often sell gearboxes at or below cost. Bob also needs help tracking his inventory. He needs to know when critical parts are getting low and what parts are slow-moving. The deficiencies in Bob's business can be addressed with the proper computer solution.

Let us examine the Application Systems configuration suitable for Bob's Gearbox. Bob will use the Manufacturing Accounting Production Information Control System (MAPICS/DB) to help gain better control over his business. By selecting the appropriate modules (programs) within the MAPICS/DB family of software, Bob can track manufacturing costs more closely (Production Control and Costing and Product Data Management modules) and better manage his inventory (Inventory Control module). Bob also chooses to take advantage of the computer system to automate the general accounting functions of his business such as payroll, accounts receivable, accounts payable, and general ledger. Bob will also use the Order Entry and Invoicing module to track and bill customer orders. The Cross-Application Support module is required on all systems. Through a questionnaire, this module allows Bob to customize MAPICS/DB for his particular business environment. Further, Cross-Application Support automatically passes information among the various MAPICS/DB modules, making them function as a single system. Based on the requirements of the software and Bob's business transaction volumes, Bob will get the AS/400 9402 shown in Figure 7.1. The AS/400 9402 system was selected for its low cost and the Model F04's ability to be first upgraded to an F06 and then replaced by a larger 9404 AS/400 system. The standard 988MB of disk storage will be expanded to 1976 MB to provide enough storage for the system software, the MAPICS/DB modules, and associated data. The Model F04 system's ability to expand to 3952 MB of disk storage will allow for some expansion as Bob's business grows. Bob will also expand the standard 8 MB of main storage to 16 MB by adding an 8-MB Main Storage option. The optional Battery Power Unit will help prevent disruption of the system by power failures — Bob can do without the extra headache. The 5853 modem will be used to access IBM's Electronic Customer Support network.

To keep costs down, the First Workstation Attachment feature will be used to build an inexpensive operator console for the system. The keyboard is provided with this feature, and an 8508 monochrome display will be used. For the users, four 3486 displays will be provided initially. One display is for the inventory clerk, one is for the purchasing agent, one is for the production department, and one is for Bob so he

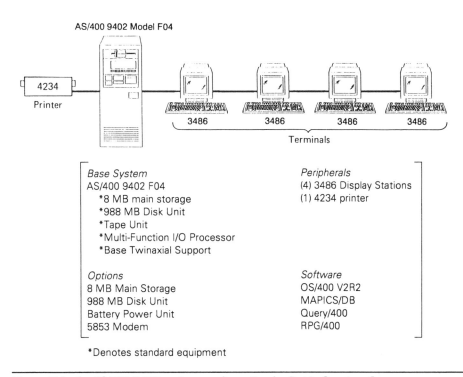

**Figure 7.1.** An AS/400 9402 system configuration for Bob's Gearbox Company.

can get the management information he needs to make intelligent decisions. The 4234 printer will be used to produce the various reports provided by MAPICS/DB. The 1.2-GB Cartridge Tape Unit will allow data stored on disk to be backed up on tape. This will help prevent important business information from getting accidentally lost. Of course, Bob will need the AS/400's operating system OS/400. Bob will also get the Query/400 program so that he can generate customized reports as needed.

## Medium Business Environment—Johnson & Thornbush

Our hypothetical medium business is an advertising agency named Johnson & Thornbush. This company has been in business for 12 years. Their business started with one major account, and today they have 17 active clients. Steve Johnson and Perry Thornbush are both still active in managing the business. The main office has 74 people and is located in Chicago, Illinois. A second office with 7 people is located in Ft. Lauderdale, Florida, to handle several large accounts in the southeast. Almost every person at each location has a PS/2 providing personal productivity tools for things like market analysis, trend analysis, word processing, and financial modeling.

Steve Johnson recently sponsored a company-wide study to find a way to address the business goals of increasing marketing effectiveness and reducing operating costs. The results of the study revealed that the market analysis being done by one PS/2 user would seldom correlate with the market analysis done by another PS/2 user. The cause of the disagreement in information was that there were different versions of the area demographic information residing on the various PS/2 disk units used in the market analysis. Even though one person has responsibility for periodically updating the demographic information and distributing the updates, it seems that eventually different versions of the information emerge, making the market analysis inaccurate. Further, as the company's market coverage grows, the demographic information is growing in size and becoming impractical to distribute via diskettes. It is apparent that more sophisticated data management and analysis techniques will become necessary as the firm continues to grow.

Another area of improvement uncovered in the study was that basic office operations could be streamlined, increasing productivity and thereby reducing operating expense. Mail delays between the two offices were slowing down many day-to-day business operations. Because of busy schedules, it was often difficult to schedule meetings, as inevitably the last attendee contacted would have a conflict. Although the secretarial staff also had PS/2s and WordPerfect™ for word processing, turnaround time for even a simple memo was getting longer as their workload increased. The project team recommended a computer solution that streamlined office functions and centralized the area demographic information. All PS/2s were to be connected in such a way that they could share information and facilitate business communications.

Figure 7.2 shows the system configuration suitable for Johnson & Thornbush. In this solution, the PS/2 users retain their PS/2s, protecting that investment in hardware, programs, and training. Only now all PS/2s (in Chicago and Ft. Lauderdale) are attached to an AS/400 located in Chicago, allowing them to double as PS/2s and AS/400 workstations. As PS/2s, they can do everything they could before. As AS/400 workstations, the PS/2s allow users to interact with the AS/400, providing some additional capabilities provided by AS/400 programs.

The OfficeVision/400 application program provides the basic office functions needed to streamline operations. The electronic mail feature of OfficeVision allows any user to electronically send documents or quick notes to any other user. This eliminates mail delays and reduces the word-processing workload, because simple notes and messages can be typed and sent by the users themselves. The calendar management function of the OfficeVision application can automatically schedule a desired meeting by electronically checking the calendars of all attendees and finding a time suitable for all. Although OfficeVision has a word-processing function, those with primarily word-processing activities to perform will continue to use the Word-Perfect word-processing program on a PS/2. Since both offices have a heavy word-processing workload, using the intelligence in the PS/2s for this function will provide the highest productivity (lowest response time). This is particularly true in Ft. Lauderdale, since AS/400 response time will be reduced by the relatively slow telephone line communications speeds. Further, since the word-processing tasks are removed from the AS/400, it provides improved response time for electronic mail, calendaring, and demographic activities performed on the AS/400 system.

The PC Support program allows AS/400 disk storage to act as the central repository for the demographic information. In effect, a portion of the AS/400 disk storage appears to be a giant PS/2 disk unit shared by all PS/2s. With PC Support, all PS/2 users can simultaneously share this single copy of the information, ensuring that all are using the same current data for their marketing analysis. This will result in a more accurate market analysis and thus more effective marketing efforts for the firm's clients. With the AS/400 Application Development Tools, SAA Structure Query Language/400, SAA RPG/400, and AS/400 Query, Johnson & Thornbush will develop custom application software over time that will allow the AS/400 to act as a database repository and interact with the PS/2s in a cooperative processing environment.

Through the Token-Ring Network, all of the PS/2s located in Chicago are attached to the AS/400. The Token-Ring Network was selected for its high-speed information transfer rate and because it could utilize the "twisted pair" wiring already installed throughout much of their building. All of the PS/2s in Ft. Lauderdale will be attached to the AS/400 system as remote workstations through a

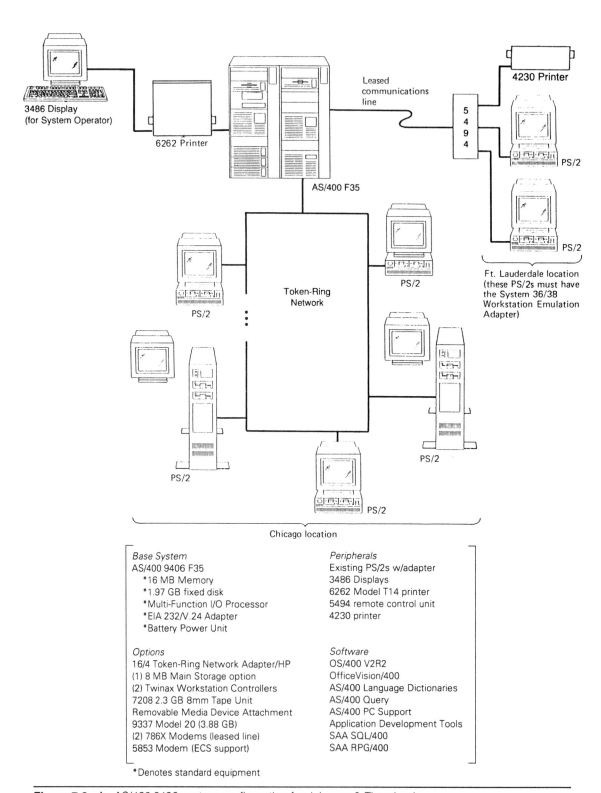

**Figure 7.2.** An AS/400 9406 system configuration for Johnson & Thornbush.

5494 Remote Workstation Controller, appropriate modems, and a leased, voice-grade telephone line. This allows all PS/2s, no matter where they are located, to double as a PS/2 and an intelligent AS/400 workstation. Regardless of whether PS/2 users are in Chicago or Ft. Lauderdale, they will have access to the same functions. However, since the Ft. Lauderdale PS/2 users are attached via a telephone line, their response time will not be as good (fast) as those in Chicago attached over the high-speed Token-Ring Network.

Based on the number of users and the growth being experienced by the business, an AS/400 9406 Model F35 is selected. For now, 24 MB of main storage should meet the need. A 9337 Model 20 with two additional disk units installed will expand the standard 1.97 GB to over 5 GB of disk storage — more than enough for now. The 7208 2.3-GB 8mm Tape Unit provides for efficient backup of the information stored in the AS/400 disk storage. The 16/4 Token-Ring Network Adapter/HP will allow the AS/400 to participate in a 16 Mbps Token-Ring Network. A 16/4 Mbps Token-Ring Network Adapter/A must also be installed in each of the local PS/2s, allowing them to participate in the network. The 6262 printer will provide high-speed printing to all local users.

In Ft. Lauderdale is a 5494 Remote Workstation Controller attached to a communications line to Chicago, where the PS/2s are equipped with the System 36/38 Workstation Adapter/A and attached to the 5494 so they can be used as AS/400 workstations. The smaller 4230 printer, along with the PS/2 printers they already have, will meet printing needs for the Ft. Lauderdale users. While the PS/2s will be attached to the 5494 via twinaxial cable for now, a Token-Ring Network could be later installed at the Ft. Lauderdale location. The PS/2s can then be attached to the 5494 via the Token-Ring Network to provide for more efficiency and flexibility as the Ft. Lauderdale location grows.

## Large Business Environment—Atole Enterprises

The hypothetical large business that will be outfitted with Application Systems is Atole Enterprises. This multinational corporation is a distributor of canned foods and enjoys financial prowess worthy of its Fortune 500 membership. The many benefits afforded by computers are well known at Atole Enterprises. They have been using computers in their day-to-day operations for many years. The U.S. headquarters is in New York City and currently has a large System/390 computer complex. There are 17 distribution centers located from coast to coast. Each distribution center has its own small System/36 and Atole-written application programs to track orders and local inventory, and to transmit information to the System/390 in New York. System/36s were originally selected for their ease of operation, which minimizes the need for technical skills at each distribution center.

A company-wide study sponsored by headquarters came to the following conclusions. Most of the System/36s are fully depreciated and in many cases are not providing enough computing power to meet growing demands. The custom-written application programs written for the System/36s have been around a long time and need major updates to keep the company's competitive edge in customer service. The study therefore recommended that Atole convert all distribution centers from System/36s to AS/400 Model 9404s with improved application programs. The first step is to install an AS/400 system at the U.S. headquarters. The U.S. headquarters programming staff will use the migration tools to quickly move the current distribution-center application programs from the System/36 to that AS/400 system. After the initial migration is complete, the headquarters staff will exploit the programmer productivity features in the AS/400 system to enhance the distribution centers' application programs. It is critical to get the improved application programs ready as soon as possible.

Once this is done, each distribution center will receive an AS/400 computer preloaded with the operating system and updated application programs. The headquarters staff will assist each distribution center in installing, migrating, and performing systems management on the new systems. Figure 7.3 shows the AS/400 Model 9404 configuration that will be used by Atole. The 9404 Model F20 was selected because its performance and capacity best matched the need and because of its upgrade path. The standard F20 configuration will be expanded to 1976 MB of disk storage and 24 MB of main storage to provide enough capacity to meet the needs of the distribution centers for an estimated five years. In the event of a power failure, the Battery Power Unit will provide power to sustain critical components while they ride through short power outages and allow the system to perform an orderly shutdown in case of longer power outages. This will reduce the disruption associated with power failures at the distribution centers. The 5853 Modem will be used for Electronic Customer Support (ECS). In this case, however, Atole chooses to provide the ECS for each distribution center from the headquarters location; that is, headquarters will maintain a help desk and a technical question-and-answer database pertaining to their custom software in addition to the IBM question-and-answer database. They will be the first line of support for the distribution centers.

A second communications line is provided by the EIA 232/V.24 One-Line Adapter and the 7861 Modem. This leased line will be used to communicate with the System/390 at headquarters to consolidate information needed from each distribution center much as before. This will allow for communications at 19,200 bps. The NetView program running on the System/390 will work with the 7861 Modems to manage the communications network. Further, the SAA SystemView System Manager/400 program will be loaded on the central site's AS/400 to allow their S/390 personnel to perform change and problem management for the remote AS/400 systems.

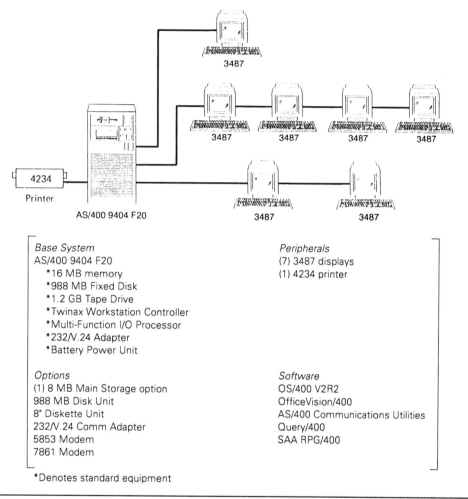

**Figure 7.3.** An AS/400 9404 system configuration suitable for Atole's distribution centers.

Atole will use 3487 color terminals to allow their custom application programs to exploit color to associate and highlight information on the screen. This will result in improved ease of use. Each distribution center will have a 4234 Printer to produce reports and correspondence-quality documents. The standard streaming tape drive provided with every 9404 will be used to back up disk storage.

The AS/400 software needed, in addition to OS/400, includes the Communications Utilities, Query and SAA RPG/400. The Communications Utilities provides some additional communications functions between the AS/400s and the System/390. The Query/400 will allow local distribution center management to development their own custom reports giving them more flexibility. Finally, OfficeVision/400 will facilitate communications between headquarters staff and each distribution center.

## THE BUSINESS DECISIONS

In addition to selecting the hardware and software to solve identified business problems, you must also consider financial questions before you install your computer solution. Two important areas that must be addressed are cost justification and the lease or buy decision. Let us look at these issues.

## Cost Justification

All businesses are the same in one respect: they exist to make a profit. In the final analysis, the only reason for a business to buy a computer is to increase profits. In other words, the computer system must be **cost justified**. There are two parts to the cost justification analysis: costs and benefits. The price you pay to the computer company is easily identified early in the project. What many people fail to consider are the costs of owning a computer system beyond the original price paid. The cost of operating the computer installation after you buy it should also be considered over several years. Some costs that should be considered beyond the price tag include the following:

*Hardware maintenance:* This is usually a monthly or annual fee you pay that basically is an extended warranty for the computer hardware. There are various alternatives, as we saw earlier in the chapter, but the basic deal is that if your computer system breaks down, the service company will come out and effect repairs at no charge. You do not have to put your system on a maintenance contract, but if you do not you will have to pay an hourly fee and parts costs when your system breaks down. Since this parts/labor billing approach can be extremely expensive, most businesses choose to put their system on a maintenance contract.

*Software maintenance:* In some cases, you will have to pay the software supplier a fee to get the ever-present fixes and updates to your programs.

*Technical support:* Some companies charge for technical support. This support provides answers to your questions and resolves any technical problems in either the hardware or software. This kind of support ranges from providing a telephone number to having permanently assigned personnel from the computer company on your premises. Sometimes this support is provided free of charge, and other times it is on a fee basis.

*Facilities:* It is often necessary for you to modify your building to accommodate a computer system. These modifications might include adding additional air conditioning, running cables between workstations and the computer, or modifying the electrical power services available. Fortunately, the costs of such building modifications are relatively low with Application Systems as compared with large computers, which often require water cooling and raised floors.

*Education/training:* The people who will be using the new computer system will need education. The computer operator(s) will need to understand how to manage the day-to-day operations of the computer. The users of the computer system will have to understand the application programs. It may also be necessary to train your own programmer(s) to write custom application programs for your business. Fortunately, Application Systems are easier to operate and use than larger computer systems. However, some education is still necessary. There are many different types of education available, some of which were discussed later in this chapter.

*Communications line costs:* If your computer system is attached to remote workstations or other remote computers, you will incur communications line costs. There are many different communications services available today, and these costs should be considered in your justification.

On the brighter side, the computer is being purchased to solve identified business problems and/or address new business opportunities. You will receive benefits after the computer system is installed (or else why install it). Although it is fairly easy to identify and quantify the costs associated with a computer system, it is often difficult to do the same for the benefits. This does not mean that benefits are any less real than costs; it simply means that they require some more work to uncover. Benefits are also more specific to your business, and so it would be impossible to list them here. But consider some common benefits associated with the application of computer systems to basic business functions.

*Improved business cycle:* The basic cycle of most businesses has the same components. The business buys goods/equipment, takes customer orders for goods or services, makes deliveries to the customer, and bills the customer. The most classic application of computer systems to these areas produces improvements in the basic business cycle resulting in real dollar savings. These savings can result from such basic things as collecting accounts receivable more quickly and taking better advantage of accounts payable discount terms.

*Inventory reduction:* Many carrying costs are associated with a business inventory. These include items such as warehouse space, insurance, taxes, and interest expense.

The proper application of computers can reduce the level of inventory that must be kept on hand, thus reducing carrying costs.

*Improved productivity:* Given the proper tools, anyone in any part of a business can do his or her job more efficiently. This allows a business to get the same amount of work done more quickly or with less people. Excess time can then be redirected to performing other tasks that help meet the business's objectives. Further, as natural attrition reduces the work force, it may not be necessary to hire replacements, allowing for a reduction of the work force over time.

*Improved quality:* By providing more timely or better organized information to personnel, businesses can often improve the quality of the services and/or products they provide. This is particularly true in manufacturing environments, in which computers can be applied to everything from design simulations to statistical quality control.

*Improved customer service:* By allowing a business to respond to customer orders, questions, and special requests, computer systems can improve customer service. These improvements can involve quickly responding to requests for price quotations and accurately quoting/meeting delivery dates.

*Competitive advantage:* The items that have been discussed contribute to reducing costs, improving quality, and improving customer service and therefore all work to improve the competitive posture of the business. The flexibility provided by a computer system can also help improve your competitiveness by allowing you to more quickly respond to changing market demands. Change is inevitable and it represents opportunity for the flexible and doom for the inflexible.

This list of general benefits is in no way comprehensive. Every business can add to the list based on its current position and business objectives. Once benefits have been identified, however, you have still not finished. You should try to quantify the benefits in dollars and cents where possible, to help focus on the areas with the largest payoff first. Quantified benefits also help when comparing computer investments with any other capital projects under consideration. However, quantifying benefits can be difficult and subject to judgment. Unlike the price of a computer, which can be looked up in a catalog, benefits must be calculated according to expected results. For example, if you feel that inventory can be reduced 10 percent by installing an inventory management application program, you would multiply 10 percent of your inventory value times the carrying costs to determine the annual benefit. This is not very difficult. Other areas are more difficult to quantify accurately. For example, if an engineer's productivity is increased by 15 percent, then you might multiply the annual salary and benefit costs by 15 percent, yielding the annual savings. In this case, some would argue that since the engineer is still paid full salary, there is no savings. However, if the time is devoted to developing a product to enter a new market, for example, the actual benefit may be much higher than 15 percent of the engineer's salary. You will have to decide what a benefit is worth to your business. There are other benefits that are typically difficult to quantify and thus are often overlooked when tallying savings. These would include increased sales (resulting from improved customer service) and lower employee turnover (resulting from improved working conditions and pride). The fact that these benefits (and others like them) are difficult to quantify does not make them any less valuable. It does, however, mean that they are often overlooked.

After the costs and benefits have been quantified, you can begin to evaluate the proposed computer project against other capital projects. Two often-used guidelines with which to measure a proposed computer system are

*The payback period*, in which the time to recover the investment from accrued benefits is calculated.

*Net present value*, in which the cash flows are calculated and then discounted based on the cost of money and risk associated with the project.

Although this type of analysis can be valuable, do not overlook other aspects of the capital project such as its strategic value and its effect on customer perceived quality and professionalism. Classic accounting techniques are easy to defend but do not always reveal the entire picture.

## Lease or Buy?

Just when you think you are through analyzing all the software and hardware alternatives, you are faced with a whole new set of questions concerning the acquisition method you will use. Several methods are commonly used to acquire a computer system. The most obvious alternative is to simply pay cash for the computer system — **outright purchase**. This is the least expensive way to acquire a computer system. However, it has a direct and usually substantial impact on the business's cash flow and capital position. The next acquisition alternative is to finance the purchase price over a period of time, just as you would finance a new house. In this case, you simply make a down payment of 10 percent, for example, and take out a loan for the balance. The loan and interest is repaid through monthly payments over a period of from 2 to 5 years typically. Since you must pay back the interest on the loan, this is a more expensive alternative than a cash purchase, but it can reduce cash flow requirements. In either case the title of the computer system passes to the business as do any tax benefits such as depreciation. The purchaser of a computer also has the ability to sell the computer when it is replaced or no longer required, thus recovering the **residual value** of the computer system.

Another acquisition alternative is the **term lease**. In this alternative, the lessor (computer owner) grants use of a computer system to the lessee (the using company), which in turn agrees to make lease payments for some specified period of time or **term**. The term of a lease can be any length, but typically runs from 2 to 5 years. If the lessee decides to terminate the lease before the end of the term, there is usually a termination fee — which can be substantial. Some of the advantages offered by the term lease alternative include the conservation of business capital and lines of credit. This allows the business to use this capital or credit to finance other investments. Two commonly found lease types are a **capital lease** and an **operating lease**. Capital leases are rent-to-own, in which, at the end of the term, you can purchase the computer system for a relatively small fee (e.g., 5 or 10 percent of the original cost). With a capital lease, the lessee is considered the owner and gets the tax benefits of ownership. Capital leases are much like a financed purchase, the major difference being that a capital lease does not require the user to make a down payment as does a financed purchase. Operating leases are real leases in which there is no discounted purchase option at the end of the lease term. The lessor is considered to be the owner and thus retains the tax benefits of ownership. Because of this, the lessee typically makes a lower payment than with the capital lease alternative.

One final acquisition alternative is to rent the computer system month by month. This provides the most flexibility, since this kind of arrangement typically requires only 1 to 3 months' notice to discontinue. Of course, you usually must pay higher rental payments to get this flexibility, and since the payment is usually not fixed, you are subject to increases.

The acquisition of computer software is a whole different story. Typically, you will not have the option to buy software. Most companies **license** software. A software license grants the licensee the right to use the software under the conditions specified in the document supplied by the software company, called the **license agreement**. Typically, these licenses allow the licensee to use the software on a specified computer system for a specified fee. Three common ways to pay for this license agreement are **one-time charge, lease**, or **monthly charge**. With the one-time charge, the licensee pays a set price and retains the right to use the software indefinitely. This can be paid in cash or financed. The leasing alternative is really just another way to finance the one-time charge with no down payment. Finally, the monthly charge is like renting the software month to month indefinitely.

Although I have introduced some basic lease/purchase alternatives in this section, the rules governing these various alternatives are complex and subject to change. The effects on a company's cash flow, income statements, balance sheets, taxes, and so on, can also be strongly affected by these various acquisition alternatives. For this reason, readers should consult the proper professionals to determine the best alternative for their situation.

## EDUCATION

The discussions in the chapter so far should assist you in selecting the appropriate software and hardware to fit your needs. However, no matter what computer hardware and software you select, they will require people to interact with them. To maximize efficiency, these people or users must be educated in the use of the computer system itself as well as its software.

Proper education is critical to the success of any computer automation project. Inadequate education prevents reaping the productivity benefits afforded by moving a task to the computer. The first goal of this education is to make users (and system operators) proficient at using the computer hardware and software they need to do their jobs. Another important goal achievable through education is to make the users' interaction with the computer system an enjoyable experience. If using the computer is enjoyable, users will be more highly motivated. If using the computer represents a frustrating struggle as a result of inadequate education, users will be less productive or perhaps will avoid the computer altogether.

AS/400-specific education is available from Skill Dynamics — IBM's training subsidiary — as well as from other non-IBM companies. The Skill Dynamics educational offerings come in the following forms:

*Classroom courses* are traditional lectures/discussions led by a Skill Dynamics instructor. These forums provide for direct interaction between students and instructors. Hands-on, in-class exercises are often part of a classroom course. Public courses are held regularly at IBM facilities. Alternately, private courses can be arranged and held either at IBM locations or customer locations.

*Personalized Learning Series* courses are basically duplicates of the classroom courses except in a self-study format. The student is provided with transcriptions of the classroom course lectures, in electronic form. The transcribed lectures are loaded on an AS/400 system and read on the user's display screen. Also provided is a booklet containing the foils (illustrations) normally presented in the classroom lectures.

*Discover/Education Series* courses are extensions to the on-line education (Tutorial Support System) provided as standard with every AS/400 system and discussed in Chapter 3. The Discover/Education Series covers additional AS/400-related topics in a format identical to the on-line education provided as standard with AS/400 systems.

*Explore/Education* courses are another style of on-line education that can be loaded on an AS/400 system and viewed on the user's display station. Unlike the other on-line offerings, Explore/Education uses the **hypertext** format. With hypertext, key words appearing in the text are highlighted. If the student wants more information on any highlighted term, he or she selects that term and is immediately presented with more information related to it. When finished reading about the term, the student can jump back to where he or she left off. Hypertext formats allow the student more flexibility of sequence when moving through the course material.

*Education Express* is an AS/400-specific, educational video tape subscription service. When you subscribe to Education Express, you are sent an AS/400 educational video tape each month. You then have the option to keep the tape or return it at no charge within a given time period.

*Learning Centers* are educational facilities that allow students to come in and use the above educational materials (for a fee) without having to buy them. They also sell these educational offerings.

A listing of some specific Skill Dynamics educational offerings for the AS/400 is provided in Appendix C.

In addition to these methods of gaining AS/400 education, there are AS/400 technical conferences conducted every year by IBM, Skill Dynamics, and other companies. Yet another educational forum is provided by **Common** – a large association of IBM users of small and mid-range systems. It is a member-run organization, although IBM provides considerable support. Common has two national conferences each year in the U.S. (April and October), as well as one in Europe each May, run by European Common. There is a large MAPICS Users' Group within Common, and each conference has many sessions on using the various functions in MAPICS, and others on upcoming enhancements. You can contact Common at:

Common
401 North Michigan Avenue
Chicago, Illinois 60611-4267
(312) 644-6610
Fax: (312) 565-4658


## ELECTRONIC CUSTOMER SUPPORT

No matter what computer system a business chooses, the system and its users will require ongoing support. They will have questions that need answering, hardware problems that must be addressed, software updates that must be installed, and so forth. This support can be delivered in many different ways. Personnel from the computer manufacturer, the software company, or the business's own staff are generally involved in supporting the computer system and its users.

With AS/400 systems (as well as with other IBM systems) much of this support can be provided electronically over communications networks. This is called

**Electronic Customer Support (ECS).** Just as electronic mail and on-line business information streamline a business's operation, the delivery of the various types of support needed can also be improved through Electronic Customer Support. There are five basic areas of Electronic Customer Support:

- IBMLink
- RETAIN
- Question and answer database
- File transfer
- Copy screen

The communications hardware and software necessary to participate in Electronic Customer Support are provided with every AS/400 system. Access to Electronic Customer Support is provided through the **IBM Information Network (IIN)**.

The kinds of things provided through IBMLink include electronic announcement letters, product catalogs, education catalogs, publication catalogs, pricing information, product configuration aids, and lists of local dealers. Users can exchange electronic notes with IBM marketing and support personnel. With proper authorization, you can also place orders, access a database of technical questions and answers, author new questions, report service hardware or software problems, and so on, all electronically over IBMLink.

Electronic Customer Support also provides direct access to IBM's **RETAIN** network. Over RETAIN, you can electronically report a hardware problem and send accompanying information helpful in diagnosing the problem. IBM service personnel can then automatically be dispatched — all over the RETAIN network. Similarly, software problems can be reported, and any missing programming fixes (PTFs) that are indicated by the symptoms can often be automatically sent over RETAIN. With the addition of the System Management Utilities extension to OS/400, the user's central AS/400 system can become a repository for PTFs and service any other AS/400 systems over a communications link — thus becoming centralized support for their own organization.

Another element of Electronic Customer Support is the technical question and answer database. Each AS/400 system is shipped with its own electronic copy of the most commonly asked questions and their answers. However, if the question is not contained in this local database, Electronic Customer Support provides access to an IBM database with additional questions and answers. With proper authorization, the user can also author new questions that will be answered (electronically) by IBM support personnel.

The file transfer capability of Electronic Customer Support allows you to exchange information (e.g., a file containing your system's configuration) with IBM marketing and support personnel as necessary. The copy screen facility of Electronic Customer Support allows remote support personnel to see the same image you see on your display for the purpose of education or problem troubleshooting.

With Electronic Customer Support, help is delivered electronically, improving access to technical and product information and streamlining communications between IBM and the users. AS/400 on-line education and IBMLink tutorials are provided along with the on-line user's guide and help text to make the interaction with Electronic Customer Support easier to use.

## ERGONOMICS

No plan would be complete without addressing the human needs that directly affect the day-to-day productivity of computer users – **ergonomics**. Ergonomics is a science dedicated to investigating the designs for effective interaction between devices and human beings. Human beings have many physiological and psychological characteristics that should be considered when designing computers, software, desks, lighting, chairs, and so on. Attention to ergonomics increases effectiveness, work quality, health and safety, and job satisfaction.

Application Systems workstations have been designed with careful attention to ergonomics. Everything from the power switch location to the length of the keyboard cable was scrutinized. Much effort is also expended fine-tuning the ergonomics of most application programs. To get the most out of your Application Systems, you must also provide an ergonomic environment for the users. Organizations such as the American Optometric Association (AOA) and the New York Committee for Occupational Safety and Health (NYCOSH) as well as IBM have probed deeply into the relationship between the computer and the user. Items such as desks, chairs, lighting, noise, and the like are important to productivity. Some of these steps are inexpensive and easily accomplished. Others may be expensive and accomplished gradually over time. Let us explore some specific steps that will help improve the ergonomics in your environment.

### Comfort for the Eyes

The eyes, like any other part of the human body, can get tired as a result of intensive use. This fatigue, called *eyestrain*, is not new to people who work long hours reading material. With the increase in computer use over recent years, however, we have seen an increase in eyestrain. Although eyestrain is only a temporary condition, it can cause users to feel tired and irritated, particularly if they continue to work under the pressures of deadlines.

The eyes function most naturally at distances greater than or equal to arm's length. After all, throughout the majority of history, the eyes were used to pick fruits not read contracts. When the eyes focus on anything closer than arm's reach, be it a computer terminal or newspaper, they are forced to look inward toward the nose. This is extra work for the muscles that move your eye within its socket, resulting in fatigue. To reduce this effect of fatigue, the computer user should take breaks and go to an area in which the tendency is to focus on more distant objects.

Another factor contributing to eye fatigue results from the work done by a muscle in the eye that reforms the eye's lens to maintain sharp focus. Frequent changes in the distance at which objects are viewed (such as a computer display and a paper on your desk) makes the focusing muscles effectively do "push-ups." This also leads to tired eyes. To help prevent these eye "push-ups," it is desirable to put any paper that is frequently referenced during a computer session at the same distance and orientation as the computer screen. A clip-type holder used by secretaries to hold documents as they are typing works well for this.

Poor image quality can cause the eyes to constantly change focus in a futile attempt to correct the image. Application Systems terminals provide a high-quality image helping to minimize eyestrain.

As if this is not enough, there is still another contributor to eye fatigue commonly found in offices, namely, improper lighting. Your eye adjusts to all of the light in the field of vision. Unwanted light reflections called glare can appear in the user's field of vision, causing nonuniform light intensities. If the light intensity varies widely, the iris in your eye will continuously expand and contract to adjust for the light level variance. To reduce the glare in the user's environment, Application Systems displays have an antiglare screen. Similarly, the workstation (desk, table, etc.) surface should have antiglare or nonreflective surfaces. Windows are big culprits as far as causing glare, but almost everyone likes windows. You can reduce the amount of glare caused by windows by positioning your computer display screen at right angles to any window. You can also use curtains or preferably horizontal blinds to direct the light away from the screen. Diffused office lighting will provide fewer "hot spots" and tend to provide the most uniform light and soften harsh shadows. For using computer displays, 30 to 50 foot-candles of ambient light is optimum. The goal is to have the screen brightness three or four times the ambient light. Since typical offices were originally designed to work with paper, not video displays, there is usually more light than this in an office. This may be difficult to change, depending on the type of lighting used in your office. You can try using fewer or lower-intensity bulbs or fluorescent tubes. Another possibility is to install dimmer switches.

## Workstation Comfort

The workstation furniture shared by the computer and the user can also affect productivity. For this reason, attention should be given to the details of the user's workstation, that is, the chair and desk/table to be used.

A properly designed chair can help reduce back problems and make the user more comfortable and more productive. An improperly designed chair can lead to reduced alertness and shorter concentration spans. A user may not even be aware of being uncomfortable, yet may unconsciously but constantly seek a more comfortable position.

What makes a chair a good chair? First, since a chair is typically used by many different people during its life with a company, it is important for it to be adjustable. The height of the seat pan should adjust from around 16 to 22 inches and should allow the feet to rest flat on the floor. Weight should be distributed through the buttocks, not the thighs. The front of the seat pan should roll off smoothly as in the **waterfall** design to provide for proper blood flow in the legs. A 20-mm compression is about firm enough.

Backrests should adjust up or down over a 2-inch range and backward or forward between 80 and 120 degrees for good support. Both the seat pans and the backrests should be upholstered and covered in a material that absorbs perspiration.

If mobility is required, wheels or casters are recommended unless the floor is slippery, making the chair unstable. Hard casters should be used for soft floors and vice versa. A five-legged chair will provide stability and prevent tipping. Seats should swivel if lateral movement is required.

Once seated, the user's relationship with the computer display and keyboard directly affects comfort and thus productivity. The computer display should be positioned properly, with the top of the computer display 10 degrees below eye level and the center of the display at about 20 degrees below eye level and between 14 and 20 inches away. A tilt/swivel stand under the display allows the user to adjust the display angle as desired. The user should avoid bifocal lenses, since they force the head to be tipped back while reading the screen. This can lead to discomfort in the back and shoulders.

The keyboard should also be in a comfortable position. Application Systems' separate keyboard, attached by a flexible cable, allows the user to position the keyboard, as desired. The keyboard height should be such that the elbow is bent at about 90 degrees when typing. Finally, provide sufficient desk space for documents used during the computer session.

## What about Noise?

Noise is not conducive to efficiency. Irregular noise is more distracting than constant noise. Unfortunately, irregular noise is common in the office environment, resulting from nearby conversations, telephones, printers, copy machines, and many other things. If possible, isolate noise sources such as impact printers and copy machines by placing them in isolated areas or separate rooms. Noise can also be reduced by installing doors, carpets, and other sound-insulating materials.

## SECURITY

In many business environments, computer systems are the very backbone of business operations. This makes the information stored on the computers a corporate asset at least as valuable as cash. Like a business's cash, computer information must be protected from loss or theft. Let us look at how this vital information can be protected.

## Loss Prevention

An ever-present hazard when dealing with information (with or without computers) is the possibility that the information will be lost. This loss can occur in many different ways. A computer system's breakdown, such as a disk unit failure, can result in lost information. Further, operator error can cause data to be accidentally corrupted, resulting in lost information. Finally, a disaster (such as a fire or flood) can result in a loss of vital business information. For this reason, **recovery** from the loss of vital business information must be addressed.

One way to deal with the risk of losing vital information is to make backup copies of computer information at regular intervals (e.g., daily). Multiple backup copies should be made on a revolving basis and kept in a place safe from damage or loss. Three copies will allow at least one copy to be kept in safe storage at all times and provide for different levels of backup. In the event of an information loss, the computer system can be restored to the point at which the most recent backup copy was made. Application Systems' operating systems and the various tape devices discussed in Chapter 2 are designed for these kind of **save/restore** operations. Any changes to information after the point of the last backup will have to be re-created after the backup copy is used to restore the system. This may involve manually reentering the transactions since the last backup or exploiting OS/400 features such as Journaling and Checksum (see Chapter 5) or the 9337 RAID models (see Chapter 2).

Any good disaster recovery plan will also consider how the business will operate in the event the current computer system is destroyed. Many companies, including IBM, offer disaster recovery services that essentially provide you with emergency access to a similarly configured computer system located elsewhere. Usually, a test allowance is part of the deal so that you can run disaster recovery drills to insure readiness. The "AS/400 Backup and Recovery Guide" (#SC41-8079), available from IBM, is a good reference when planning your backup strategy.

## Theft Prevention

Theft prevention deals with protecting sensitive information from unauthorized disclosure. These security requirements vary widely from environment to environment. Consider your particular needs early in your planning.

Application Systems provides various levels of security that help deter unauthorized access. Security is provided by the computer system itself along with the associated operating system. Depending on the needs of the environment, one of three levels of security can be activated. The first level is basically no security at all. Anyone can access the system and can do anything they wish. The second level of security requires the user to enter a password before access is granted to the system. After the proper password is entered, the user can perform any task. Finally, the third level of security is user access control, which is just like the second level except that the user can be restricted to various functions as well. A security officer is usually assigned to manage the security of the system.

For sensitive environments, you may wish to consider restricting access to the area in which the Application Systems itself is located. It may also be necessary to restrict access to the area(s) in which workstations are located. These needs should be considered early in a computer automation project.

## SERVICE

Although every effort has been made to make Application Systems as reliable as possible, some computers will fail. If yours does, you must have a way of getting it fixed. All Application Systems come with a 1-year warranty that provides free on-site repairs from IBM's service division 7 days a week, 24 hours per day. Each of the various terminals and printers associated with Application Systems has its own warranty terms and periods ranging from 3 months to 3 years.

After the warranty period, you become responsible for maintenance of the system. IBM and other companies offer service agreements that, for a fee, provide post-warranty on-site service just like that provided during the warranty. There are various maintenance discounts available, depending on the level of system management procedures you are willing to implement in your business.

If your system fails and you do not have any type of service contract, you will have to pay for parts and labor, which can become extremely expensive. For this reason, most people choose to keep their systems on maintenance after warranty.

## MIGRATING FROM SYSTEM/3X TO AS/400

Some businesses may be replacing System/34, System/36, or System/38 computer(s) with an AS/400. AS/400 has been designed to ease the migration of most programs and data from these earlier System/3X computer systems to AS/400. OS/400 functions plus available tools provide a guided and highly automated procedure for these types of migrations. Although programming skills are still required to guide the migration activities, the tools reduce the manual work of analyzing, documenting, saving, and restoring application programs. Programs are migrated to either the AS/400 System/36 Environment or the AS/400 System/38 Environment discussed in Chapter 5. If desired, the programs can be further adapted to take advantage of new AS/400 functions at your own pace after the migration is complete.

Now let us look at some topics related to migrating from S/3X to AS/400:

- Sizing a replacement AS/400
- Migrating S/3X I/O devices to AS/400
- Migrating programs and data from S/36
- Migrating programs and data from S/38
- Migrating programs and data from S/34

## Sizing a Replacement AS/400

Whether AS/400 will be your first computer system or you will be replacing a System/36 or System/38, you will have to choose the appropriate size AS/400. "Size" refers to the processor speed and capacity determined by model, memory size, and amount of disk storage. There are many things to consider when choosing the size AS/400 needed in a given situation. If you are migrating from an S/3X, you can use that system as a starting point for your sizing activity. Here, you know your current memory size, disk storage size, and so on.

If you are migrating programs and data from a System/36 to an AS/400, you will need more disk storage and main storage capacity on the AS/400 system than you needed on the System/36. More disk storage space is needed on the AS/400 for several reasons. First of all, the AS/400's operating system (OS/400) takes up more disk space than that of the System/36 (SSP). Further, the AS/400 automatically generates extra program debug and external data definition information during the migration process not present in the System/36. Finally, the "blanks" in programs are not compressed as they were on the System/36. The net effect of these factors is that load members (object code) will need about 7 times more disk storage (this can be reduced to a factor of 2.5 by removing the extra debug information after migration), source members will require about 3.6 times more disk storage, and data files will require about 1.2 times the space. Mail logs and data dictionaries are approximately the same size on the AS/400 as they are on a System/36.

You will also need more main storage when migrating to the AS/400 from a System/36. This is because the more powerful (and more complex) OS/400 requires more main storage to operate, keeps more information about the current jobs resident in main storage, and uses larger control blocks. The bright side of these facts is that the number of disk storage operations (each of which takes a long time in the context of a computer system) is reduced because more information is in main storage and ready for immediate use.

Those migrating from the System/38 to the AS/400 will also need more disk storage and main storage capacity than with the System/38 for similar reasons. In this case, more disk storage space is necessary mostly because of the increased requirements of OS/400. More main storage is needed because more information about each task again remains resident in memory. More information in main storage has been a traditional advantage of the System/38 because it makes for better system performance. The AS/400 takes further advantage of the same concept.

Whether you are migrating from a System/36 or a System/38, you must also select the correct AS/400 processor model. The performance section of Chapter 1 will give you a rough idea of the relative performance of the various computer systems of interest. To refine your model selection, you must start by examining your current computer system very closely. Tools like the **Systems Management Facility (SMF)** and the **System/38 Performance Measurement Tools** can be used to determine the workload on your current system. The capacity planner portion of the AS/400 Performance Tools (discussed in Chapter 5) can help analyze your current system to determine which AS/400 model is appropriate. An IBM document that will help in using these sizing tools and determining AS/400 disk storage requirements is the "AS/400 Performance and Capacity Planning Newsletter" (GC21-8175). If you are adding additional functions (programs and data) or more users to the new AS/400 system, you must also consider the effect of these new requirements on performance, memory, and disk storage requirements. IBM personnel have tools and resources available to them to help you size the appropriate AS/400 System.

## Migrating System/3X I/O Devices to the AS/400

Most of the twinaxial attached Input/Output devices, such as terminals and printers, are supported on AS/400 systems. One of the design points of AS/400 was to protect current investments in I/O devices. Not all System/3X I/O devices, however, can be supported by AS/400. These include things like some old terminals and disk storage devices. These older devices should therefore stay with the System/3X system being replaced, whether it is sold, redistributed, or otherwise disposed of. Appendix A contains a list of peripheral devices that have been tested for compatibility with AS/400 systems. Those devices found to be compatible as well as those found to be incompatible are listed. Devices not listed may also work; they were simply not included in the testing.

Information stored on System/3X tape or diskettes can be read by a properly configured AS/400 system. However, since AS/400s do not come standard with a diskette drive, it is possible that System/3X users who use diskettes as the backup media (no tape drive) may not be able to exchange information with a particular AS/400. Further, since AS/400 does not support a diskette magazine (a System/3X device that holds a group of diskettes), diskettes must be fed to an AS/400 one at a

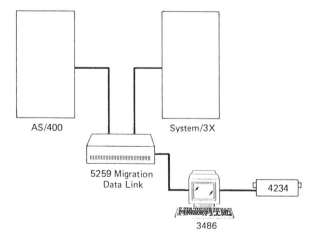

**Figure 7.4.** The 5259 Migration Data Link can be used to transfer information between AS/400 and System/3X computers. It can also be used to provide workstations with access to both systems.

time. Transferring large amounts of information one diskette at a time is time-consuming at best and often impractical. For situations like this, the **5259 Migration Data Link** provides an alternative method to move information between a System/3X and an AS/400. The 5259 allows for the direct attachment of an AS/400 system with a System/3X as shown in Figure 7.4. A twinaxial cable, like that used to attach workstations, attaches the 5259 to the workstation controller of each computer system. With this configuration, information can be transferred at twinaxial cable speeds, resulting in efficient information transfer. By dedicating multiple workstation addresses to the 5259 data transfer function (up to seven), information transfer performance can be further improved. As shown in Figure 7.4, the 5259 can also be used to attach workstations to both computer systems during migration activities. This allows the user of a single terminal to switch from one system to another by simply striking a key. Although printers can also be attached via the 5259, they can be accessed only by one system or the other, not by both.

## Migrating Programs and Data from the S/36

OS/400 and the System/36 to AS/400 Migration Aid work together to migrate programs and data from a System/36 to an AS/400. The basic migration process starts by loading the migration aid on your System/36. You can then begin to analyze data, libraries, files, and programs; that is, you can look for characteristics and functions of the System/36 programs and data that are not supported by AS/400 and thus require conversion. The next step is to save all System/36 items to be migrated on either tape or diskette. Alternately, you could use a communications link to move information from the System/36 to the AS/400. The information is then restored on the target AS/400 system, in which it can be modified as necessary using AS/400 facilities.

Migration is completed by using the migration features of OS/400. These migration aids automatically perform any processing necessary when migrated items are moved to AS/400. Migrated source code is recompiled automatically or under user control. Programs written in BASIC, however, must be modified before recompilation. All programs should be thoroughly tested as the last step in the migration process. Remember that since AS/400 must operate in OS/400 System/36 Environment to run these migrated programs, performance may be reduced over that of an AS/400 native program. However, with proper tuning (modifications) the performance level of System/36 application programs running on an AS/400 in its System/36 Environment can approach the performance of native application programs. Here is a brief checklist of changes you can make that have a significant effect on performance:

- For MRTs, use MRT delay and MRT NEPs.
- Reduce EVOKEs.
- Limit Sign-on/Signoff.
- Use the Defer Write feature (DFRWRT(*YES)) display file attribute.
- Use the suppress input option in Screen Format Generation Routines ($SFGR).
- Avoid 27-by-132 display support.
- Use shared file opens.
- Reduce database file CREATEs and DELETEs.
- Add or increase the DBLOCK parameter for sequential files.
- Increase default batch storage pool size.
- Use logical views instead of sorts.
- Avoid batch-type work in interactive jobs.
- Compile computation-intensive programs with non-S/36 environment computer (e.g., RPG/400).
- Simplify RUF and PROMPTs.
- Don't "stack" operator displays.

In most cases, you can make these changes in a manner that lets you maintain source compatibility with the System/36 (in many cases improving the System/36 performance as well). Emphasis is on simple changes (tuning/tweaking) versus application conversion or redesign. Improvements in current OS/400 releases also help improve System/36 Environment performance. For example, the addition of a **cache library of deleted files** saves processing time when a work file is created by recalling a previously created (but no longer needed) work file rather than creating another from scratch. Since the creation of work files is frequently done in typical System/36 application programs, this cache library of deleted files improves performance for System/36 application programs running in OS/400 System/36 Environment.

Menus provide guidance throughout the migration process. Reports indicating the status of the migration and providing an audit trail can be generated at any point.

The following can be migrated from a System/36 to an AS/400:

- Source members for programs, screen formats, messages, and menus
- Procedures
- Data files and alternative indexes
- Libraries
- Folders

- Data dictionaries
- Security and master configuration information

You can also migrate the following things (e.g., files, folders, directories) used by System/36 SSP and licensed programs:

- Advanced printer function (APF)
- Business Graphics Utilities/36 (BGU/36)
- Data file utility (DFU) programs
- Distributed Data Management (DDM)
- Multiple Session Remote Job Entry (MSRJE)
- PC Support/36
- Personal Services/36
- Query/36

The following things cannot be moved using the migration aid but are not supported by AS/400 systems:

- User-written assembler programs and subroutines
- FORTRAN programs
- Workstation utility (WSU) programs

Finally, there are some things you simply cannot move using the migration aid:

- Load members (object code)
- Communications definitions (except for those created by the workstation support for the master configurations record)
- User-defined configuration records

The AS/400 publication that discusses the details of migrating is called "Migrating from System/36 Planning Guide" (GC21-9623). Other related publications are listed in Appendix B.

## Migrating Programs and Data from the S/38

The migrating of System/38 programs and data is accomplished using the same basic steps as migrating from the System/36. You first load the System/38 Migration Aid on the System/38. You can then analyze and select the objects (data, libraries, files, and programs) to be migrated. The purpose of this step is to look for things that must be changed for them to work properly on an AS/400 system. You can select objects to be migrated by libraries, categories, and other groupings, or you can choose to migrate the entire system. The System/38 objects to be migrated are then transferred to the AS/400 through diskette, tape, or a communications link. Once on the AS/400 system, facilities are available to make the necessary changes to System/38 objects. Personal Services/38 documents and virtual disks are automatically converted to be usable by AS/400. Unlike System/36 programs, System/38 programs can be transported to AS/400 as object code that is automatically adapted (re-encapsulated) to run on AS/400 without recompiling. This is true for programs written in either RPG III, COBOL '74, PL/1, BASIC, or Command Language (CL). Because a few things are supported on System/38 but not on AS/400 (96-column cards and diskette magazines) consideration must be given to programs using those items. As with System/36 migration, menus provide guidance throughout the migration process and reports show the status of migration activities.

Since AS/400's architecture is based on that of the System/38, the migration of programs and data is more direct than when migrating from the System/36. For the same reason, you do not pay a significant performance penalty when running System/38 programs as you do when you run System/36 programs. The following can be migrated from the System/38:

- User profiles
- Most system configuration descriptions
- User libraries, including library QGPL (General Purpose Library)
- Objects in user libraries, except for:
  Printer images
  Documents
  Document lists
  Edit descriptions
  User-defined message queues
  Card files
- Many of the system values

Another migration aid, called the **System/38 Utilities**, runs on the AS/400 and provides support for programs written using the System/38 Data File Utility and Query/38. The Text Management/38 functions of this tool also provide word-processing capabilities to AS/400 users not using OfficeVision/400.

The AS/400 publication that discusses the details of this migration is called "Migrating from System/38 Planning Guide" (GC21-9624). Other related publications are listed in Appendix B.

## Migrating Programs and Data from the S/34

Users of the IBM System/34, a predecessor to the System/36, can also migrate many of their programs to AS/400 systems. As with the System/36, System/34 programs and data are first saved to diskettes and then restored on an AS/400. Optionally, the **System/34 to System/36 Migration Aid (5727-MA1)** can be used to identify missing source members and provide an audit trail during this process. System/34 programs can be modified if necessary, recompiled, and run in OS/400's System/36 Environment. As with the System/36, BASIC subroutines must be converted to source code. The migration of System/34 Data File Utility routines, security, and configuration members is a manual process. A technical newsletter, "System/34 to AS/400 Migration Tips" (GC21-8161), is helpful in such migrations.

# APPENDIX A

# Peripheral Compatibility Guide

To ensure AS/400's compatibility with older peripheral equipment, IBM conducted compatibility testing on selected equipment before announcing the AS/400. This appendix shows the results of this testing. Peripherals not listed in this section are not necessarily incompatible with AS/400 computers. Their absence simply implies that they were not included in the original compatibility test.

## DEVICES SUPPORTED BY AS/400

- 5394 Remote Control Unit
- 5294 Remote Control Unit
- 5251 Model 12
- 3X74 Remote Control Unit
- 5299 Multiconnector and TTPA Adapter
- 3179-2 Display
- 3180-2 Display
- 3196 Display
- 3197 Display
- 5251-011, 999 Display
- 5291 Display
- 5292 Display
- 3812-001, 002 Printer
- 5219-D01, D02 Printer
- 5224-001, 002 Printer
- 5225-001, 002, 003, 004 Printer

- 5256-001, 002, 003 Printer
- 5262-001 Printer
- 6262-T12, T14 Printer
- 4210-001 Printer
- 4224-101, 102, 1C2, 1E2 Printer
- 4234-002 Printer
- 4245-T12, T20 Printer
- 3101-23 ASCII Display
- 3151 ASCII Display
- 3161 ASCII Display
- 3162 ASCII Display
- 3163 ASCII Display
- 3164 ASCII Display
- TeleVideo 910, 925, 955 ASCII Displays
- DEC VT-100, VT-220 ASCII Displays
- Wyse WY30, WY50, WY60 ASCII Displays
- 4201-002 ASCII Printer
- 4202-001 ASCII Printer
- 4207-001 ASCII Printer
- 4208-001 ASCII Printer
- 4224-301 ASCII Printer
- 4224-302 ASCII Printer
- IBM Personal Computer 5150, 5160, 5162, 5170
- IBM Personal System/2 Models 25, 30, 50, 60, 70, 80
- 5208 Link Protocol Converter
- 5209 Link Protocol Converter
- ROLMbridge 5250 Link Protocol Converter

## DEVICES NOT SUPPORTED BY AS/400

- 1255 MICR
- 3203 Printer

- 3262 Printer
- 3370 DASD
- 3410, 3411 Tape Units
- 4245-012, 020 Printer (RPQs are available to convert Models 012 and 020 to Models T12 and T20, which are supported by AS/400)
- 5211 Printer
- 5251-001, 002 Display
- 5251-012 Display/Workstation Controller (when using AS/400 Office and PC Support)
- 5252 Display
- 5424 Multi-Function Card Unit (MFCU)
- 6157 Cartridge Tape Unit
- 6580 Displaywriter (as a printer device)
- 6670 Document Processor
- 8809 Tape Unit
- Diskette Magazine Unit
- Initial 5250 Emulation Adapter for IBM Personal Computers (6072534)
- The 5294 Remote Workstation Controller, 5208 Link Protocol Converter, and the ROLMbridge 5250 are not supported by the IBM AS/400 PC Support program

# APPENDIX B

## Guide to Other AS/400 Publications

Reprinted with permission from the "Application System/400 Publications Guide, Version 2," copyright International Business Machines Corporation 1991.

# Part 2. Which Publications Do I Need?

This section includes descriptions of the types of users and tasks for which the AS/400 system library was designed; then it shows the general tasks included in each library category and which manuals are appropriate for those tasks. The *Library Structure Poster* shows these same groups, but more colorfully; it also shows, for U.S. users, the binder in which the manuals are distributed.

## User Tasks

Following is a description of user tasks addressed in the library and which library category they are usually applicable to.

*Evaluating:* Judging the applicability of a system or program for your use. (*General*)

*Planning:* Making decisions about the options the hardware or programs offer. (*System and application support*)

*Installation:* Preparing the system to do useful work such as installing hardware and programs. (*System and application support*)

*Administering Data Resources:* Managing (designing, defining, allocating, protecting, monitoring) data resources, including databases, data files, data relationships, data declarations, and data definitions. (*System and application support*)

*Administering Network Resources:* Managing (designing, defining, allocating, protecting, monitoring) network resources, including terminals, lines, and control units. (*System and application support*)

*Administering System Resources:* Managing (designing, defining, allocating, protecting, monitoring) system resources, including programs, storage, processor cycles, and input/output paths. (*System and application support*)

*Operating:* Starting and stopping the system, checking and controlling programs, and recording system status. (*System use environment; also sometimes system and application support*)

*Customizing:* Enhancing or extending the system to further benefit the user. (*System and application support*)

*Application Programming:* Designing, coding, compiling, running, debugging, and testing programs. (*Application development*)

*Diagnosing:* Identifying the source of a system problem, describing the problem, reporting a new problem, and correcting the problem. (*Hardware and software service*)

*End Use:* Using the system and its programs to achieve its purpose. (*System use*)

## User Role Descriptions

Following are descriptions of typical AS/400 system users and the library categories in which they would normally find applicable information.

*Administrative Clerk:* Responsible for typing, maintaining business files and lists, adding, updating, and maintaining records, and searching business files for specific records or data. (*System use*)

*Administrative Secretary:* Responsible for answering the telephone, making travel arrangements, making copies, proofing office documents, handling mail, and filing. (*System use*)

*Administrator/Supervisor:* Responsible for managing office equipment and people, supervising training, and scheduling work activities. (*System use*)

*Application Programmer:* Responsible for designing and programming business applications for the end user. (*Application development*)

*Business Professional:* Responsible for communications, management of schedules, and information tracking and screening. (*System use*)

*Correspondence Secretary:* Responsible for typing, editing, changing reports, specifications, forms, and manuals. (*System use*)

*Data Entry Clerk:* Responsible for entering and verifying data into a predetermined format, including entering data. (*System use*)

*Data Processing (DP) Manager:* Responsible for daily system operation, scheduling and monitoring education for operators and users. (*System and application support*)

*Executive:* Responsible for business profitability such as control over processes, people, revenue, materials, assets, and sales. (*System use*)

*Principal/Manager:* Responsible for communications, management, and personnel tracking. (*System use*)

*Service Personnel:* Responsible for servicing the system. (*Hardware and software service*)

*System Operator:* Responsible for operating the console, responding to messages, running backup and recovery procedures, labeling and storing diskettes and tapes, and diagnosing any system malfunction initially (problem analysis). (*System use environment; also sometimes system and application support*)

*System Programmer:* Responsible for managing the system environment, systems architecture design, application flow, file layout, data requirements, audit controls, and backup and recovery procedures. (*System and application support*)

*Technical Professional:* Responsible for project or product design, document creation, specifications, reviews, and analysis. (*System use*)

# Chapter 4. AS/400 Library Structure

## General Publications

```
┌─ Library Information ──────────────────────────────────────────┐
│                                                                │
│  GC41-9678 Publications Guide                                  │
│  GX41-0017 Publications Prices for Release 2                   │
│  SC41-8204 Master Index                                        │
│  S325-6009 Library Structure Poster                           │
│                                                                │
└────────────────────────────────────────────────────────────────┘
```

```
┌─ System Information ───────────────────────────────────────────┐
│                                                                │
│  GC41-9766 System Introduction                                │
│  GC41-9802 System Concepts                                    │
│                                                                │
└────────────────────────────────────────────────────────────────┘
```

## System Use Publications

**Working with the System**

SC41-8211 *New User's Guide*
SC41-8082 *Operator's Guide*
SX41-9573 *Operator's Quick Reference*

**Working with Applications**

**PC Support/400**

SC41-8199 *PC Support/400 User's Guide for DOS*
SC41-8200 *PC Support/400 User's Guide for OS/2*
SC41-2414 *PC Support/400 User's Guide for DOS (PS/55)*
SC41-2415 *PC Support/400 User's Guide for OS/2 (PS/55)*

**Query/400**

SC41-9614 *Query/400 User's Guide*

**SQL/400 Query Manager**

SX41-0010 *SQL/400\* Query Manager Reference Summary*
SC41-0037 *SQL/400\* Query Manager User's Guide*

**OfficeVision/400**

SC41-9615 *Learning about OfficeVision/400\**
SC41-9616 *Using OfficeVision/400\**
SX41-9868 *OfficeVision/400\* Common Tasks*
SC41-9617 *Learning about OfficeVision/400\* Word Processing*
SC41-9618 *Using OfficeVision/400\* Word Processing*
SC41-9879 *Using OfficeVision/400\* Adapted Word Processing Function*

**Business Graphics Utility**

SC09-1408 *BGU User's Guide and Reference*

## Application Development Publications

**Designing Applications**

SC41-9852 *Application Development by Example*
GC09-1377 *Application Development Manager/400 Concepts*
SL23-0191 *OSI Communications Subsystem Programming Concepts and Guide*
SL23-0190 *OSI Communications Subsystem Programming Reference*
SL23-0193 *OSI Communications Subsystem Programming with the Starter Set*
SL23-0192 *OSI Communications Subsystem Abstract Syntax Checker Reference*

**Defining Devices**

SC41-9658 *Data Management Guide*
SC41-0012 *Guide to Programming for Tape and Diskette*
SC41-8194 *Guide to Programming for Printing*
SC41-0011 *Guide to Programming Displays*
SC41-0536 *GDDM Programming Guide*
SC41-0537 *GDDM Programming Reference*

**Defining Data**

SC41-9659 *Database Guide*
SC41-0025 *Distributed Database Guide*
GC41-0070 *Multilingual Application Concepts Using Database*
SC41-9620 *DDS Reference*
SC41-9657 *IDDU User's Guide*
SC41-0090 *Query Management/400 Programmer's Guide and Reference*
SC09-1363 *Sort User's Guide and Reference*
SC41-9600 *DDM Guide*
SC41-9609 *SQL/400\* Programmer's Guide*
SC41-9608 *SQL/400\* Reference*

**Using Communications**

SC41-9590 *ICF Programmer's Guide*
SC41-9864 *Intrasystem Communications Programmer's Guide*
SC41-9592 *Asynchronous Communications Programmer's Guide*
SC41-9593 *BSC Equivalence Link Programmer's Guide*
SC41-9594 *SNA Upline Facility Programmer's Guide*
SC41-8189 *APPC Programmer's Guide*
SC26-4399 *SAA\* CPI Communications Reference*
SC41-9858 *Retail Communications Programmer's Guide*
SC41-8099 *Finance Communications Programmer's Guide*
SC41-9868 *Point-of-Sale Communications Utility/400 Programmer's Guide*
SC41-9867 *CallPath/400\* Programmer's Reference*
SC33-0822 *CICS/400 Application Programming Guide*
SH19-6704 *OSI File Services/400 Programming Guide*

**Using Tools and Utilities**

SC09-1338 *SEU User's Guide and Reference*
SC09-1339 *PDM User's Guide and Reference*
SC09-1361 *APF Guide*
SC09-1340 *SDA User's Guide and Reference*
SC09-1381 *DFU User's Guide and Reference*
SC09-1416 *RLU User's Guide and Reference*
SC09-1170 *CGU User's Guide*
SH18-2416 *AFP Utilities Guide and Reference*
SC09-1375 *Application Development Manager/400 Application Developer's Guide*
SC09-1376 *Application Development Manager/400 Project Administrator's Guide*

---

**Using High-Level Languages**

**RPG**

SX09-1164 *RPG Reference Summary*
SC09-1349 *RPG/400\* Reference*
SC09-1348 *RPG/400\* User's Guide*

**COBOL**

SC09-1380 *COBOL/400\* Reference*
SX09-1209 *COBOL/400\* Reference Summary*
SC09-1383 *COBOL/400\* User's Guide*
SC41-9866 *RM/COBOL-85\*\* for the AS/400\* Reference*
SC41-9865 *RM/COBOL-85\*\* for the AS/400\* User's Guide*
SL23-0201 *OSI Communications Subsystem COBOL Language Examples*

**C Language**

SX09-1217 *C/400\* Reference Summary*
SC09-1347 *C/400\* User's Guide*
SC09-1308 *SAA\* C Reference*
SC09-1294 *Extended Program Model User's Guide and Reference*
SL23-0202 *OSI Communications Subsystem C Language Examples*

**BASIC**

SX09-1050 *BASIC Reference Summary*
SC09-1157 *BASIC User's Guide and Reference*

**PL/I**

SX09-1051 *PL/I Reference Summary*
SC09-1156 *PL/I User's Guide and Reference*
SC09-1294 *Extended Program Model User's Guide and Reference*

**Pascal**

SC09-1210 *Pascal Reference*
SC09-1209 *Pascal User's Guide*
SC09-1294 *Extended Program Model User's Guide and Reference*

**FORTRAN**

SC41-9844 *FORTRAN/400\* Reference*
SC41-9845 *FORTRAN/400\* User's Guide*

---

**Using System Interfaces**

SC41-9758 *Office Services Concepts and Programmer's Guide*
SC41-8223 *System Programmer's Interface Reference*
SC41-8226 *MI Functional Reference*
S544-3699 *PrintManager API Reference*

---

**Using Environments**

**System/36 Environment**

SC09-1418 *SDA User's Guide/Reference for the System/36 Environment*
SX09-1047 *System/36-Compatible COBOL Reference Summary*
SC09-1160 *System/36-Compatible COBOL User's Guide and Reference*
SC09-1162 *System/36-Compatible RPG II User's Guide and Reference*
SC09-1362 *DFU List for the System/36 Environment User's Guide and Reference*

**System/38 Environment**

SX09-1048 *System/38-Compatible COBOL Reference Summary*
SC09-1159 *System/38-Compatible COBOL User's Guide and Reference*
SC09-1217 *DFU/38 User's Guide and Reference*
SC09-1218 *Query/38 User's Guide and Reference*
SC41-9759 *Text Management/38 User's Guide and Reference*

---

## System and Application Support Publications

---
**Planning**

**System**

GA41-0001 *Physical Planning Guide*
GA41-9571 *Physical Planning Guide and Reference*
GA41-0007 *New Products Planning Information for Release 2*
GC41-9877 *National Language Support Planning Guide*

**Applications**

SC41-9626 *Planning For and Setting Up OfficeVision/400**

**Networks**

GC41-9861 *Network Planning Guide*
SC41-9601 *CallPath/400* Planning and Installation Guide*

**Migration**

GC41-0091 *Migrating from System/36 Using the OS/400 Migration Assistant
Function*
GC41-9623 *Migrating from System/36 Planning Guide*
GC41-9624 *Migrating from System/38 Planning Guide*

┌─── **Installing** ─────────────────────────────────────────────────┐

**Hardware**

SA41-9604 *Total System Package Guide*
SA41-0005 *AS/400* 9402 Attaching Workstation and Communications Cables*
SA41-0004 *9404 Attaching Workstation and Communications Cables*
SA41-9957 *9406 Attaching Workstation and Communications Cables*
SC41-8106 *Device Configuration Guide*
SA41-9944 *Twinaxial Workstation Controller Port Tester User's Guide*
SA41-9922 *ASCII Work Station Reference and Example*

**Software**

SX41-9072 *Automatic Installation Guide*
SC41-9878 *Licensed Programs and New Release Installation Guide*
SC41-9993 *Central Site Distribution Guide*

**Applications**

SC41-0006 *PC Support/400 DOS Installation and Administration Guide*
SC41-0007 *PC Support/400 OS/2 Installation and Administration Guide*
SC41-0008 *PC Support/400 DOS Installation and Administration Guide (PS/55)*
SC41-0009 *PC Support/400 OS/2 Installation and Administration Guide (PS/55)*
SC41-9626 *Planning For and Setting Up OfficeVision/400**
SC18-0835 *Installing and Customizing the DOS Direct-Connect Asian Language Feature*

**Networks**

SC41-0001 *OS/400* Communications Configuration Reference*
SL23-0187 *OSI Communications Subsystem/400 Configuration and Administration Guide*
SC41-9601 *CallPath/400* Planning and Installation Guide*
K:SC18-2461 *SNA Hangeul 3270 PC Emulation Installation Guide*
N:SC18-2461 *SNA Japanese 3270 PC Emulation Installation Guide*
SC40-1347 *SNA Traditional Chinese 3270 PC Emulation Installation Guide*

└──────────────────────────────────────────────────────────────────┘

## Administering

### System

SC41-0036 *Basic Backup and Recovery Guide*
SC41-0047 *Basic Security Guide*
SC41-8083 *Security Reference*
SC41-8078 *Work Management Guide*
SC41-8079 *Advanced Backup and Recovery Guide*
SC41-8086 *Q & A Database Coordinator's Guide*
SC41-9993 *Central Site Distribution Guide*
SH23-0529 *CSP/AE User's Guide/Reference*
SC41-8201 *SystemView\* System Manager/400 User's Guide*
SC41-8080 *Cryptographic Support/400 User's Guide*
SC18-2216 *Font Management Aid User's Guide*
SB09-1421 *Advanced Function Printing\* Korean Font Catalog*
SC18-0124 *Advanced Function Printing\* Traditional Chinese Font Catalog*
SC18-0133 *Advanced Function Printing\* Simplified Chinese Font Catalog*
SC18-0137 *Advanced Function Printing\* Thai Font Catalog*
SC18-2332 *Advanced Function Printing\* Japanese Font Catalog*
N:SH18-2179 *IBM 5583 Kanji Print Function User's Guide*
N:SH18-2418 *Advanced Page Printer Writer User's Guide and Reference*
SH18-2419 *Advanced Print Writer User's Guide and Reference*

### Applications

SC41-0006 *PC Support/400 DOS Installation and Administration Guide*
SC41-0007 *PC Support/400 OS/2 Installation and Administration Guide*
SC41-0008 *PC Support/400 DOS Installation and Administration Guide (PS/55)*
SC41-0009 *PC Support/400 OS/2 Installation and Administration Guide (PS/55)*
SC41-9627 *Managing OfficeVision/400\**
SC18-0836 *Using the DOS Direct-Connect Asian Language Feature*

### Networks

SC41-0024 *Communications Management Guide*
SC41-0002 *Remote Work Station Guide*
SC41-9602 *3270 Device Emulation Guide*
SC41-0004 *Local Area Network Guide*
SC41-9588 *Distribution Services Network Guide*
SC41-0005 *X.25 Network Guide*
SC41-8188 *APPN Guide*
SC41-9661 *Alerts and DSNX Guide*
SC41-0003 *ISDN Guide*
SC09-1373 *RJE Guide*
SC41-9875 *TCP/IP Guide*
SL23-0187 *OSI Communications Subsystem/400 Configuration and Administration Guide*
SL23-0189 *OSI Communications Subsystem/400 Operation*
SC33-0821 *CICS/400 Administration and Operations Guide*
SC33-0828 *Communicating with CICS/400*
SC41-0026 *OSI Message Services/400 Guide*
SH19-6703 *OSI File Services/400 User's Guide*

# APPENDIX C

## AS/400 Education

Reprinted with permission from International Business Machines Corporation.

On June 17, 1992, **Skill Dynamics**, a new IBM company for workplace education and training, made its formal debut in the growing education market. Skill Dynamics, based in Thornwood, N.Y., is a consolidation of former IBM Education functions and has locations in all major U.S. cities.

This appendix contains excerpts from *AS/400 Education Planner and Class Schedule*, GR28-2238-06, and is reprinted with the permission of International Business Machines Corporation.

The information in this appendix was current as of February 10, 1993. Skill Dynamics may make additions, changes, and withdrawals at any time without notice. For the most current information about Skill Dynamics courses and services, call **1-800-IBM-TEACh (1-800-426-8322)**.

### Trademarks and Registered Trademarks

The following terms, used in this appendix, are trademarks or registered trademarks of International Business Machines Corporation in the United States or other countries:

AD/Cycle
AFP and Advanced Function Printing
AS/400 and Application System/400
CallPath
COBOL/400
Discover/Education
Explore/Education
ImagePlus
OfficeVision
OS/2 and Operating System/2
OS/400 and Operating System/400
PS/2 and Personal System/2
Personalized Learning Series
RPG/400
Skill Dynamics
SQL/400

WordPerfect is a registered trademark of the WordPerfect Corporation.

## AS/400 Education—Part of Your Total System Solution

The Application System/400 (AS/400) is a tool for effectively addressing the challenges facing you and your workplace. Training is the tool for effectively using this system.

Skill Dynamics, the new IBM company for workplace education and training, offers courses that provide you with training solutions targeted for business professionals who use and support the AS/400 in their daily jobs. These courses give you the maximum return on your training investment. Training improves employees' effectiveness by increasing their productivity and raising their skill levels when using AS/400 tools and applications. You can tailor a training program for an individual or for your entire organization by selecting the courses that suit your needs.

Although Skill Dynamics is new name, we *still* provide the same service you've come to expect from IBM Education. Because we are an IBM company, we still have a direct link with IBM development labs and can offer you the most current technical information. Similarly, because we are still an IBM company, we uphold IBM's long tradition of excellence in workplace education and training. Skill Dynamics delivers courses in a variety of ways. One or more should meet your needs.

**Classroom Courses:** For in-depth discussions between students and instructors and many opportunities for supervised practice of new skills through hands-on and in-class exercises, consider a Skill Dynamics public classroom course.

These courses are regularly scheduled at IBM Education Centers and branch offices throughout the United States. These facilities feature state-of-the-art educational equipment for laboratory exercises.

**Private Classes:** Most Skill Dynamics' classroom courses can also be taught privately, at your business location or at an IBM location. These private classes contain the same material as publicly scheduled classes. Many include hands-on labs.

Private classes are attractively priced to let you train as many as 14 students for a single price. (Maximum class sizes vary by course. Additional students may attend for a nominal fee.) Because you can provide training at or near your own business locatioh, you can reduce class-related travel time and expenses which can more than double the cost of attending a public classroom course.

**Customized Courses:** If one of the classroom courses does not meet your needs, Skill Dynamics can customize a course for you. Skill Dynamics can mix modules from several courses, create additional modules, and tailor examples and exercises to meet the unique needs of your organization.

**Self Study Courses At Your Work Station:** Now you can have Skill Dynamics classroom education quality and depth of course material at your own work station. Skill Dynamics' computer-based training (CBT) offers an alternative to traditional classroom instruction without sacrificing time away from the office and without the cost of travel. Skill Dynamics offers several varieties of CBT for the AS/400—Personalized Learning Series, Discover/Education, Explore/Education, and Education/Express.

**Personalized Learning Series** courses are based on classroom courses and provide many of the benefits of traditional classroom education with the convenience and flexibility of computer-based training. Course materials can be used for initial training, reinforcement, or as an on-the-job quick reference.

Personalized Learning Series courses include an electronic textbook—a transcription of classroom lectures—and a testing section, which you install on a computer. Related visuals are presented in a companion handbook.

Many Personalized Learning Series courses also have hands-on exercises that reinforce skills taught in the course.

**Discover/Education Series** courses teach you how to use your IBM computer system right on your system. This series of computer-based courses provide an interactive, task-oriented, self-paced learning experience. Each course consists of several instructional modules, each focusing on a particular topic or task. Through simulations of software and hands-on exercises, you learn tasks that are regularly performed on the system.

An administration program included with each Discover/Education course lets you tailor the course to meet your needs and maintains information about your progress, the audience path you have chosen, and the modules you have completed.

Discover/Education courses can be purchased or taken at IBM Learning Centers.

**Explore/Education** allows you to become proficient in basic skills in your area of study in a short period of time. The course's hypertext-based design lets you make choices about how to learn, control the extent of details presented, be actively involved in task exercises, and quickly find and review material already taken.

**Education/Express** is a program that periodically delivers a videotaped training course directly to your location on a specific AS/400 subject. Videotapes are already available on AS/400 Query, AS/400 Basic Performance Tuning, AS/400 CL Programming, and AS/400 Database Concepts and Coding. New videotapes on many different subjects are being developed by AS/400 instructors for future releases approximately every four to six weeks.

Once you enroll in Education/Express, you automatically receive the latest videotape. You can view each videotape in the comfort of your own home or office before you decide whether to add the course to your AS/400 education library. Should you decide not to keep the videotape, simply return it to Skill Dynamics within 30 days. Otherwise, do nothing and Skill Dynamics sends you an invoice within 45 days of delivery date.

**AS/400 Technical Conferences:** AS/400 Technical Conferences provide you with a unique, fast-paced educational experience and the opportunity to meet other information processing professionals to share your thoughts and ideas. Highlights include the opportunity to:

- Meet with IBM AS/400 product design and development experts and give your input directly to them
- Listen to the experts describe the latest hardware and software releases
- View demonstrations of many new hardware and software products
- Attend General Sessions and select Elective Sessions that encourage your personal and professional growth
- Earn Institute for Certification of Computer Professionals (ICCP) recertification credits for attending the conference

## AS/400 Curriculum

This section describes the comprehensive set of classroom offerings for the IBM AS/400 System. These classes provide for a variety of AS/400 user skills to help ensure effective installation planning, implementation programming, and efficient day-to-day operations. This section is broken down into the following user skill categories:

- System Operators
- System Administrators and System Analysts
- Programmers
- Personnel with S/36 backgrounds
- Personnel with S/38 backgrounds
- Personnel with previous computer system experience

- Data Processing Managers
- Neural Network Personnel
- Office Applications Users who use
  - OfficeVision/400
  - WordPerfect for the AS/400
- Communications Specialists

Each user skill category contains short descriptions of the AS/400 courses. Each description includes how long the course is, how the course is offered—Public, Private, or Self Study, and what prerequisites you need before you take each course.

## System Operators

### Tutorial System Support   [DE001]

**5 days**    Hands-on Labs
**Self Study, Learning Center**

This **Discover/Education** course teaches you introductory, conceptual, and day-to-day operational skills for the AS/400 system. There are no prerequisites for this course.

### AS/400 System Operator Workshop [S6029]

**3 days**    Hands-on Labs
**Public, Private, Self Study**

This classroom and computer-based **Personalized Learning Series** course enables a new system operator to develop basic to intermediate skills needed for day-to-day operations of an AS/400 system. Specifically, this course explains how to start and end the system, use messages, monitor and control jobs, output, and devices, and resolve system problems. You practice these skills in hands-on lab exercises. Before attending this course, you should take Tutorial System Support [DE001].

### AS/400 Advanced System Operators Workshop   [S6041]

**3 days**    Hands-on Labs
**Public, Private, Self Study**

This classroom and computer-based **Personalized Learning Series** course teaches the features of the AS/400 system that help you operate the system more effectively. Specifically, it teaches tips and techniques that can be used in the daily operation of the AS/400 System. This course is designed for the person who has a basic knowledge of AS/400 operations. Before attending this course, you should take AS/400 System Operator Workshop [S6029].

### AS/400 Operations Support   [DE021]

**4.5 days**    Hands-on Labs
**Self Study**

This **Explore/Education** course teaches you tasks that you would need to do in a day-to-day operation of an AS/400 system. This course is a hypertext-based training package that allows you to learn any one or more of a 120 specific tasks during times available to you. You do not have to take all of the course at one time or in a specified sequence. Before taking this course, you should take Tutorial System Support   [DE001].

## System Administrators and System Analysts

### AS/400 Facilities and Implementation [DE018]

**3 days**    Hands-on Labs
**Self Study, Learning Center**

This computer-based **Discover/Education** course teaches you systems implementation. Before taking this course, you should take Tutorial System Support  [DE001].

### AS/400 Fundamentals and Implementation Topics  [PS101]

**1 to 4 days**
**Self Study**

This computer-based **Discover/Education** course provides you with the prerequisite material you need to prepare for advanced AS/400 classroom courses or their Personalized Learning Series counterparts **before** you install your AS/400 system. The length of the course depends upon the number of advanced AS/400 courses you are preparing to take. Before taking this course, you should have a general knowledge of computer fundamentals.

### PC Support/400 Implementation for DOS [S6018]

**3 days**    Hands-on Labs
**Public, Private**

This course teaches you how to install and implement PC Support/400. Specifically, you install PC Support on twinax and token-ring networks and implement and use the functions of PC Support, such as the transfer function, virtual printers and shared folders. Before attending this course, you should be familiar with the Personal Computer disk operating system (DOS).

### Advanced PC Support/400 Workshop [S6047]

**5 days**    Hands-on Labs
**Public**

This workshop provides you with an in-depth understanding of PC Support/400. The workshop addresses DOS memory management, PC Support/400 coexistence with Novell and IBM Local Area Network (LAN) servers, PC Support/400 and Windows 3.0, PC Support Central Administration, PC Support/400 remote connectivity, and PC Support/400 with DOS 5.0 and OS/2 Version 2. Before taking this course, you should attend PC Support/400 Implementation for DOS  [S6018].

### AS/400 System Administration and Control [S6019]

**4.5 days**    Hands-on Labs
**Public, Private, Self Study**

This classroom and computer-based **Personalized Learning Series** course explains how to plan for, implement, and manage the security and back-up and recovery functions of the AS/400 system. This course also provides an introduction to problem determination and PTF application. You learn how to perform tasks such as creating security profiles and user environments and implementing recovery.

Before attending this course, you should take Discover/Education AS/400 Facilities and Implementation  [DE018] or Discover/Education AS/400 Fundamentals and Implementation Topics [PS101].

## AS/400 Security Concepts and Implementation [S6050]

**2 days**   Hands-on Labs
**Public, Private**

This classroom course explains how to plan for, implement, and manage the security functions of the AS/400 system. This course also examines AS/400 security journaling and auditing facilities. You learn how to perform tasks such as creating security profiles, restricting access to system resources, securing sensitive data, and creating user environments. You practice these skills in in hands-on labs. Before attending this course, you should take Discover/Education AS/400 Facilities and Implementation [DE018].

## AS/400 Recovery and Availability Management [S6051]

**2 days**   Hands-on Labs
**Public, Private**

This classroom course explains how to plan for, implement, and manage the back-up and recovery functions of the AS/400 system. You also learn how to perform tasks such as implementing recovery functions. You practice these skills in hands-on labs. Before attending this course, you should take Discover/Education AS/400 Facilities and Implementation [DE018].

## AS/400 Availability and Recovery Workshop [S6039]

**4.5 days**   Hands-on Labs
**Public**

This course teaches you how to perform availability and recovery functions on the AS/400. Before attending this course, you should take AS/400 System Administration and Control [S6019] or AS/400 Recovery and Availability Management [S6051] or have equivalent knowledge.

## Operating System/400 Structure, Tailoring and Basic Tuning [S6023]

**2 days**   Hands-on Labs
**Public, Private, Self Study**

This classroom and computer-based **Personalized Learning Series** course explains how to balance workload on the AS/400 system to maintain optimum system performance. Specifically, this course explains how to manage workloads, measure system performance and tune the Operating System/400 (OS/400) to meet processing requirements. Hands-on exercises give you an opportunity to use the system functions that are available for controlling workload and tuning system performance.

Before attending this course, you should take AS/400 Facilities and Implementation [DE018].

## AS/400 Performance Analysis and Capacity Planning [S6027]

**3 days**   Hands-on Labs
**Public, Private**

This classroom course explains how to use the IBM AS/400 performance monitor and some of the AS/400 Performance Tools features. Hands-on labs include a complete case study and give you the opportunity to analyze data from a real system with significant performance problems. Before attending this course, you should take Operating System/400 Structure, Tailoring and Basic Tuning [S6023].

## AS/400 Performance Workshop [S6040]

**4.5 days**   Hands-on Labs
**Public**

This course teaches you how to implement performance and capacity planning on a complex AS/400 system. Before attending this course, you should take AS/400 Performance Analysis and Capacity Planning [S6027].

## Programmers

### AS/400 Concepts and Programming Facilities Workshop  [S6049]

**4 days**      Hands-on Labs
**Public, Private**

This classroom course provides an in-depth look at the unique concepts of the AS/400 for systems analysts, systems programmers, and application programmers. It also covers how to use the many programming facilities of the AS/400 system, including: Programming Development Manager (PDM), Source Entry Utility (SEU), Screen Design Aid (SDA), and Data File Utility (DFU), and Query/400. Before attending this course, you should take Tutorial System Support  [DE001].

### AS/400 Application Design and Development Tools  [DE019]

**3 days**      Hands-on Labs
**Self Study, Learning Center**

This computer-based **Discover/Education** course continues the education of the data processing professional begun in the AS/400 Facilities and Implementation course. Before taking this course, you should take AS/400 Facilities and Implementation  [DE018].

### AS/400 Relational Data Base Design and Coding  [PS146]

**2 days**      Hands-on Labs
**Self Study**

This computer-based **Personalized Learning Series** course shows you how to design and create a database for the AS/400 system as well as how to use the database in application programs. The course also explains how to create physical and logical files, and joining logical files. As a course exercise, you design a database and use it in sample application programs. Before taking this course, you should take Discover/Education AS/400 Facilities and Implementation  [DE018].

### AS/400 Relational Database Design and Coding  [S6052]

**4 days**      Hands-on Labs
**Public, Private**

This classroom course shows you how to design, create and maintain a database for the AS/400 system. Emphasis is on database performance and considerations for application program design. This course also explains how to create physical files, logical files, and how to join logical files. You design, create and use a database in sample application programs in classroom exercises and reinforce what you learn in lab exercises. Before attending this course, you should take AS/400 Concepts and Programming Facilities Workshop [S6049] or take Discover/Education AS/400 Application Design and Development Tools [DE019].

### AS/400 Control Language Programming Workshop  [S6020]

**4 days**      Hands-on Labs
**Public, Private, Self Study**

This classroom and computer-based **Personalized Learning Series** course explains how to write Control Language (CL) programs that are easy to use, efficient, and require little or no involvement by system operators. It also explains how to write user menus and commands and how to modify commands provided by IBM. Before attending this course, you should take AS/400 Concepts and Programming Facilities Workshop  [S6049] or take Discover/Education AS/400 Application Design and Development Tools  [DE019].

## RPG Programming  [DE005]

**10 days**    Hands-on Labs
**Self Study, Learning Center**

This computer-based **Discover/Education** course teaches you how to code, test, and run RPG programs in batch and interactive environments for the following RPG compilers:

- 5728-RG1 for the AS/400 system
- 5714-RG1 for the System/38
- 5727-RG1 or 5727-RG6 for the System/36

Before taking this course, you should take Discover/Education AS/400 Application Design and Development Tools  [DE019] or have equivalent job experience.

## AS/400 Interactive Program Design [S6014]

**4 days**    Hands-on Labs
**Public, Private, Self Study**

This classroom and computer-based **Personalized Learning Series** course introduces you to features of the AS/400 system that are key to designing effective and efficient interactive programs. This course explains how to structure programs, design screens, and use system resources. Before attending this course, you should take Discover/Education RPG Programming  [DE005].

## AD/Cycle CODE/400 Workshop  [U3591]

**3 days**    Hands-on Labs
**Public, Private**

This course teaches you how to use CODE/400's cooperative processing facilities in the development, testing, and debugging of RPG programs in the AS/400 environment. Instruction is also provided in use of optional CODE/400 feature, Data Description Specification Utility (DSU). Before taking this course, you should be familiar with the AS/400 and RPG programming fundamentals.

## RPG/400 Interactive Programming Workshop  [PS111]

**4 days**    Hands-on Labs
**Self-Study**

This computer-based **Personalized Learning Series** course explains how to write RPG/400 programs that run on the AS/400 system. Specifically, this course explains how to write programs that take advantage of the unique capabilities of this system, concentrating on those facilities that can improve your productivity while producing code. This course shows how to use techniques such as structured programming, subfiles, subprograms, error recovery, data structures and data areas. Before taking this course, you should attend AS/400 Interactive Program Design  [S6014].

## RPG/400 Interactive Programming Workshop  [S6043]

**5 days**    Hands-on Labs
**Public, Private**

This classroom course explains how to write RPG/400 programs that run on the AS/400 system. Specifically, this course explains how to write programs that take advantage of the unique capabilities of this system, concentrating on those facilities that can improve your productivity while producing code. This course shows how to use techniques such as structured programming, subfiles, subprograms, error recovery, data structures and data areas. Before attending this course, you should take AS/400 Interactive Program Design  [S6014].

## COBOL/400 Interactive Programming Workshop   [S6016]

**5 days**      Hands-on Labs
**Public, Private, Self Study**

This classroom and computer-based **Personalized Learning Series** course shows you how to code, compile, run and test COBOL/400 programs. This course emphasizes IBM extensions to ANSI 1985 COBOL that support database and interactive processing. In hands-on labs, you practice writing and running these programs. Before attending this course, you should take AS/400 Interactive Program Design   [S6014].

## AS/400 Cooperative Processing Workshop [S6037]

**5 days**      Hands-on Labs
**Public**

This course teaches you how to develop cooperative processing applications between a Programmable Work Station (PWS) and the AS/400. Before attending this course, you should have experience programming on both the AS/400 and programmable work stations.

## SQL Workshop   [U4045]

**2 days**      Hands-on Labs
**Public, Private, Self Study**

This classroom and computer-based **Personalized Learning Series** course teaches you how to use the Structured Query Language (SQL). It includes instruction on the common SQL that can be run in the relational database management system in the Systems Application Architecture (SAA) environments: MVS DB2, VM SQL/DS, OS/400, and OS/2 Extended Edition.

## Structured Query Language/400 Programming Workshop   [S6026]

**2 days**      Hands-on Labs
**Public, Private, Self Study**

This classroom and computer-based **Personalized Learning Series** course explains how to write application programs that use Structured Query Language (SQL) databases. Specifically, this course explains how to create SQL databases and imbed SQL statements into programs written in C/400, COBOL/400, PL/1 and RPG/400. Before attending this course, you should take SQL Workshop   [U4045].

## Performance Tuning for SQL/400 Applications   [S6044]

**3 days**      Hands-on Labs
**Public**

This workshop teaches you how to get the best performance out of your applications using SQL/400. Hands-on labs give you the opportunity to use the tools available to examine the performance of applications. You learn tips on how to improve application performance, which is critical in developing SQL/400 applications that perform well. Before attending this course, you should take Structured Query Language/400 Programming Workshop   [S6026].

### Managing AS/400 Application Development [S6053]

**1 day**
**Public, Private**

As more corporate executives recognize the importance of application development (AD) in increasing their organization's overall competitiveness, more AD tools are available. This classroom course introduces the application development tools available on the AS/400 and shows how a strategic approach to AD improves the productivity of AD professionals. This course also teaches you how to choose and successfully implement a methodology. Hands-on labs reinforce the lectures. Before attending this course, you should know the objectives and strategy of your enterprise's application development department.

### Benefits of AS/400 Data Driven Design [S6054]

**2 days**      Classroom Exercises
**Public, Private**

If you are redesigning databases every time there is a new application, you are wasting time, money, and talent. This classroom course can bring a stop to the waste. This course teaches a methodology for planning and designing databases that can be shared by current and future applications. Hands-on labs reinforce the lectures. There are no prerequisites for this course.

### AD/Cycle for the AS/400    [S6055]

**2 days**      Classroom Exercises
**Public, Private**

This classroom course explores the solutions found in AD/Cycle for the AS/400. This course teaches

you what AD/Cycle means in the AS/400 environment, what CASE tools and other life cycle tools are available for the AS/400 developer, and how you can use these tools with your current applications. Other topics include IBM products and services and International Alliance Partners products and services and how they fit in the AD/Cycle framework. Hands-on labs reinforce the lectures. Before attending this course, you should take AS/400 Relational Database Design and Coding   [S6052] and RPG/400 Interactive Programming Workshop   [S6043] or COBOL/400 Interactive Programming Workshop   [S6016].

### IBM SAA ImagePlus WAF/400 Implementation   [K2711]

**4 days**      Hands-on Labs
**Public**

This course teaches you how to configure, install and customize an IBM SAA ImagePlus WAF/400 environment on an AS/400 system. Before taking this course, you should be familiar with AS/400, PC Support and communications in the IBM Token-Ring environment.

### ImagePlus WAF/400 2.3 New Features Update   [K2712]

**2 days**

**Public, Private**

This course introduces you to the new features and functions available with ImagePlus WAF/400 Version 2.3. The basic design and implementation topics taught in this course enable you to plan for and evaluate the new release of WAF/400 Version 2.3. Before attending this course, you should attend IBM SAA ImagePlus WAF/400 Implementation   [K2711] or have equivalent experience and knowledge.

## ImagePlus WAF/400 APIs and Exits [K2713]

**2.5 days**    Hands-on Labs
**Public, Private**

This course teaches you the capabilities of and how to use AS/400 ImagePlus APIs. Other topics include how to tailor WAF/400 using user exits. Hands-on labs reinforce the lectures and give you experience integrating image APIs into sample business applications. Before taking this course, you should attend IBM SAA ImagePlus WAF/400 Implementation [K2711] or have equivalent experience.

## AS/400 Printing: Basic to Advanced Function [K2510]

**3.5 days**    Hands-on Labs
**Public, Private**

This course teaches you the fundamentals of printing, how to take advantage of existing print capabilities, and how to plan for and implement Advanced Function Printing (AFP) on the AS/400 System. Before attending this course, you should take AS/400 Concepts and Programming Facilities Workshop [S6049] or have equivalent experience.

## Personnel with S/36 Background

## AS/400 System Using the System/36 Environment [S6002]

**4 days**    Hands-on Labs in Classroom Course
**Public, Private, Self Study**

This classroom and computer-based **Personalized Learning Series** course explains how to replace a System/36 with an AS/400 system. Specifically, this course introduces you to AS/400 architecture and facilities and compares them with the architecture and facilities of System/36. This course also explains how to run System/36 applications on the AS/400 system and how to use the security features of the AS/400 system. Before attending this course, you should take Tutorial System Support [DE001].

## Advanced Function Printing: AS/400 AFP Workshop [K2402]

**2 days**    Hands-on Labs
**Public, Private**

This course teaches you how to use the Advanced Function Printing Utilities/400 and the Advanced Function Printing capabilities available with Operating System/400 (OS/400). Before attending this course, you should take AS/400 Concepts and Programming Facilities Workshop [S6049]. Familiarity with RPG or COBOL programming is also a plus, but not a requirement.

## AS/400 Advantage for System/36 Programmers [S6034]

**4.5 days**    Hands-on Labs
**Public**

This course teaches you how to use the tools and facilities of the AS/400 to develop programs and convert System/36 applications to AS/400 native mode. Before attending this course, you should take Tutorial System Support [DE001].

## Personnel with S/38 Background

### AS/400 System for the Experienced System/38 Implementer [S6003]

**4 days** Hands-on Labs in Classroom Course
**Public, Private, Self Study**

This classroom and computer-based **Personalized Learning Series** course focuses on the differences between the AS/400 system and the System/38. Specifically, this course focuses on differences in security procedures, commands, system utilities and related application programs. This course also explains how to configure, install and operate the AS/400 system, how to use the migration utility to transfer objects from the System/38 to the AS/400 system, and how to use the System/38 environment of the AS/400 system. Before attending this course, you should be an experienced S/38 system analyst, programmer, or data processing manager.

## Personnel with Previous Computer System Experience

### AS/400 Implementation: System Module [S6057]

**4.5 days** Hands-on Labs
**Public, Private**

This classroom course introduces the OS/400 operating system to managers, programmers, and analysts with previous computer system experience. You learn about system architecture, how work is managed, what the options are for backup and recovery, how security is handled, and how to use various techniques to tune the system. Hands-on labs reinforce the lectures. Before attending this course, you should take Tutorial System Support [DE001].

### AS/400 Implementation: Application Module [S6056]

**5 days** Hands-on Labs
**Public, Private**

This classroom course teaches application design and coding techniques for the AS/400 to application programmers and analysts with previous computer system experience. This course also explains how to use the AS/400 application tools. Hands-on labs reinforce the lectures and provide an opportunity to use the application tools. Before attending this course, you should take AS/400 Implementation: System Module [S6057].

## Data Processing Managers

### Manage/400 for the AS/400 System [DE020]

**3 days** Hands-on Labs
**Self Study**

This **Discover/Education** course concentrates on the management of a data processing installation, rather than presenting a series of technical topics. It explains the various skills required to manage a data processing department, as well as how to act as an interface to the user departments. There are no prerequisites for this course.

# Neural Network Personnel

## Neural Network Utility Workshop  [S6045]

**4 days**
**Public**

This course teaches how to use the IBM Neural Network Utility (NNU). *Neural Networks* are an innovative approach to information processing based loosely on how the mind processes information using previous knowledge. Unlike a traditional data processing application, a neural network application is not programmed. It is trained to identify and classify complex data relationships using historical data. Once trained, the network application uses the identified data relationships to make predictions about new data.

Example application areas for neural networks include risk assessment (credit scoring), fraud detection, portfolio management, "fuzzy" database query, psychological profiling, character recognition, market segmentation, trend analysis, detail filtering, resource allocation, scheduling, and truck routing.

There are no prerequisites for this course, however, AS/400 and/or PS/2 experience is recommended.

# Office Applications Users

## OfficeVision/400 Support   [DE003]

**1 day**
**Self Study, Learning Center**

This computer-based **Discover/Education** course teaches you how to use OfficeVision/400 and Query/400. Before taking this course, you should take Tutorial System Support  [DE001] or have equivalent knowledge.

## OfficeVision/400 Support - Additional Topics [DE007]

**1 day**
**Self Study, Learning Center**

This computer-based **Discover/Education** course teaches you how to use query, mail and messages functions, document library services, and additional document processing functions. This course continues the training begun in OfficeVision/400 Support  [DE003], which is a prerequisite.

## OfficeVision/400 End User Training

In addition to the publicly-scheduled OV/400 classroom courses, Skill Dynamics also offers basic OfficeVision/400 end user training. This curriculum is designed to address the specialized needs of organizations with a growing number of office application end users. These courses can be taught at your location or at an IBM facility.

You tailor your organization's OfficeVision/400 end user training by selecting training modules that meet your specific training needs. Your IBM representative can provide you with information on modules available and can help you develop your customized training.

Training modules may be selected in any combination and range from a half hour to 2 1/2 hours in length. Most modules average about 1 1/2 hours, including lab time. Modules may be combined to create courses as short as one-half day in length. A course day consists of six hours.

After you select the modules and calculate the duration of the course, a course code is assigned from the following list.

| Duration | Course Code | Duration | Course Code |
|----------|-------------|----------|-------------|
| 0.5 day  | B3880       | 3.0 days | B3883       |
| 1.0 day  | B3881       | 3.5 days | B3887       |
| 1.5 days | B3884       | 4.0 days | B3888       |
| 2.0 days | B3882       | 4.5 days | B3889       |
| 2.5 days | B3885       | 5.0 days | B3890       |

### Advanced OfficeVision/400 for End Users [B3866]

**3.5 days**    Hands-on Labs
**Public, Private**

This course introduces the OfficeVision/400 Text Editor. End users learn how to take advantage of OV/400 functions. Topics include how to manipulate files, work with query definitions, work with the data dictionary, and perform problem determination exercises. Before attending this course, you should take OfficeVision/400 Support [DE003] and OfficeVision/400 Support - Additional Topics [DE007]. Attending OfficeVision/400 for System Implementers [B3845] would be helpful as well.

### OfficeVision/400 for System Implementers [B3845]

**4.5 days**    Hands-on Labs
**Public, Private, Self Study**

This classroom and computer-based **Personalized Learning Series** course teaches system administrators how to plan for, implement, and administer OfficeVision/400 (OV/400) systems. Topics include a discussion of the OV/400 functions, planning and managing document storage, and handling security, calendars, mail, and print queues. It does not cove, AS/400 system implementation topics. Before taking this course, you should read the following IBM publications:

- *AS/400 System Introduction* (GC41-9766)
- *AS/400 SAA OfficeVision/400: Planning for and Setting Up OfficeVision/400* (SC41-9626)

### OfficeVision/400 API Workshop [E4648]

**3 days**    Hands-on Labs
**Public, Private**

This course teaches experienced AS/400 support personnel how to use Application Programming Interfaces (APIs) to integrate OV/400 with business applications. Other topics include OV/400 backup and recovery. Extensive hands-on labs reinforce the lectures. Before taking this course, you should have job related experience in the areas of AS/400 work management, security, backup, and system maintenance. Office skills or programming skills are not required. However, if you have programming experience, more challenging lab exercises are furnished.

### Basic WordPerfect for the AS/400 [B3933]

**1 day**    Hands-on Labs
**Public, Private**

This course introduces the WordPerfect for the AS/400 Editor to end users. This course teaches you how to create and revise documents, use the linguistic aids, format documents, generate page numbers, create outlines, build macros, and use line draw. There are no prerequisites for this course.

### Implementation of WordPerfect for the AS/400 [E4521]

**1 day**    Hands-on Labs
**Public, Private**

This course teaches administrators how to plan for, implement, and administer WordPerfect for the AS/400. Topics include Planning for and steps to install, preparation for printing, system setup and customization for use in the WordPerfect for the AS/400 environment.

Before taking this course, you should be familiar with the AS/400. You should also review the following IBM publications:

- *Introduction: AS/400* (GC41-9766)
- *OfficeVision/400: Planning Guide* (SC41-9626)

## Communications Specialists

### AS/400 Introduction to Data Communications [DE004]

**1 day** Hands-on Labs
**Self Study, Learning Center**

This systems delivered **Discover/Education** course introduces communications concepts and describes AS/400 communications equipment and software. Before taking this course, you should take Tutorial System Support [DE001] or have equivalent experience.

### AS/400 Communication Introduction [G3770]

**1 day**
**Public, Private**

This course gives an overview of workstation, host, and peer communication facilities on an AS/400 system. Both hardware and software communication capabilities are discussed. Before attending this course, you should take Discover/Education AS/400 Introduction to Data Communications [DE004].

### AS/400 to S/390 Communications [G3772]

**3 days** Classroom Exercises
**Public, Private**

This course teaches you how to use and implement an AS/400 system for data communications in an SNA S/390 network. Before attending this course, you should take AS/400 Communication Introduction [G3770], or have equivalent knowledge.

### AS/400 Peer Communications [G3771]

**3 days**
**Public, Private**

This course teaches you how to use and implement an AS/400 system for data communications in an SNA peer network. Before attending this course, you should take AS/400 Communication Introduction [G3770], or have equivalent knowledge.

### AS/400 Distributed Systems Management Workshop [S6048]

**3.5 days** Hands-on Labs
**Public**

This workshop teaches you how to implement, use, and customize several key AS/400 distributed systems management tools. To reinforce the lectures, emphasis is placed on hands-on usage of the tools from both a central focal point and remote user standpoint. Mainframe S/370 and S/390 products will not be covered in this workshop. Before attending this course, you should have some hands-on AS/400 experience and be familiar with the available AS/400 distributed systems management tools.

### AS/400 Communication Programming Workshop Using CPI-C [G3811]

**3 days** Hands-on Labs

**Public, Private**

This course teaches you how to write programs using the Common Programming Interface for Communications (CPI-C) on AS/400 systems which communicate with programs on other systems. CPI-C allows programs to be written in a Systems Application Architecture (SAA) language (such as RPG/400 or COBOL/400) using the same set of calls regardless of operating system platform. Before taking this course, you should know how to program in either RPG/400 or COBOL/400.

### AS/400 Communications Problem Determination Workshop [S6030 ]

**3 days** Hands-on Labs
**Public**

This course teaches you how to diagnose errors in system hardware, system software, and application software using methods for detecting, isolating, and finding the cause of problems in AS/400 communications. Before attending this course, you should take AS/400 Peer Communications [G3771].

### AS/400 Networking [PS110]

**4.5 days**
**Self Study**

This computer-based **Personalized Learning Series** course teaches you how to use an IBM AS/400 system for data communications in a network with IBM System/36s, System/38s, and System/370s or other AS/400 systems. This course enables you to work with other system personnel in establishing communications between an AS/400 and other mid-range and large IBM systems, but does not qualify you to work on the other IBM systems.

### Fundamentals of Voice Communication [32510]

**10 — 14 hours**        Hands-on Labs
**Learning Center**

This SRA self-study course is available through the Learning Centers using course code Z2510 for enrollment. It provides an introduction to the technology, operation, and structure of voice communication systems. It provides the basic concepts of the technology and language of the voice communication portion of the telecommunication world. Before taking this course, you should take Fundamentals of Data Communication Systems (32507), or have equivalent knowledge.

### Planning for CallPath Services Architecture [G3747]

**2 days**        Classroom Exercises
**Public, Private**

This course teaches you planning information for CSA-based host systems designed to enhance telephony applications that include inbound and outbound teleservicing, message desk, and personal phone services. Before attending this course, you should take Fundamentals of Voice Communication [32510].

### CallPath/400 Implementation Workshop [S6033]

**3 days**        Classroom Exercises
**Public**

This course teaches you how to install and implement CallPath/400 and write application programs that use CallPath Services Architecture and CallPath/400 program calls and message support. Before attending this course, you should take Planning for CallPath Services Architecture [G3747] and Discover/Education AS/400 Introduction to Data Communications [DE004].

## How to Receive Additional Information About AS/400 Education

### Call 1-800-IBM-TEACh to:

- Request current schedules and locations for AS/400 classroom courses
- Enroll in AS/400 classroom courses
- Request a copy of the *AS/400 Education Planner and Class Schedule* (GR28-2238) or *Your Guide to AS/400 Courses* (GR20-5047)
- Request a copy of the *Skill Dynamics Catalog of Education* (G320-1244), which contains complete descriptions of all of the courses offered by Skill Dynamics

### Call 1-800-456-1426 to:

- Get more information about AS/400 self study courses to take at your work station
- Order Education/Express video tapes

### Call 1-800-IBM-CALL to:

- Order AS/400 self study courses to take at your work station

### Call 1-800-677-5789 to:

- Request a brochure for an AS/400 Technical Conference
- Enroll in an AS/400 Technical Conference

# Index

# WE NEED YOUR HELP!

Your comments (good or bad) and suggestions are very important in shaping future revisions of this book. Please jot down your thoughts here, detach this page, and fax or mail it to:

Katherine Schowalter
Associate Publisher
John Wiley and Sons
605 Third Avenue
New York, NY 10158
Fax (212) 850-6088

Comments:

_____

_____

_____

_____

_____

_____

_____

_____

_____

_____

_____

_____

_____

_____

_____

_____

_____

_____

_____